100 Australian Birds

Georgia Angus

EXPLORE
AUSTRALIA

Taungurung names were provided by the Taungurung Land and Waters Council, in Broadford, Victoria. The Taungurung people are the Traditional Owners of a large area of central Victoria. Their Country encompasses the area between the upper reaches of the Goulburn River and its tributaries north of the Great Dividing Range. The western boundary extends from Kyneton, along the Campaspe River to Rochester in the north-west, eastward to Mt Buffalo and beyond Mt Buller, and from Benalla in the north down to the top of the Great Dividing Range. Their boundaries with neighbouring First Nations groups are respected in accordance with traditional lore and practice.

Gumbaynggirr names were provided by Senior Language Worker Dallas Walker and Brother Steve Morelli, in association with the Muurrbay Aboriginal Language and Culture Co-operative in Nambucca Heads, New South Wales. The Gumbaynggirr nation is located on the Mid North Coast of New South Wales. Its southern edge is the Nambucca River, its western edge lies in the Great Dividing Range, and its northern edge is the Clarence River.

Wiradjuri names were provided by the Wiradjuri Condoblin Corporation Language Program and sourced from the Wiradjuri Dictionary app, which is based on the work of Dr Stan Grant and Dr John Rudder. Wiradjuri Country is encircled by the rivers Wambuul (Macquarie), Galari (Lachlan) and Marrambidya (Murrumbidgee), and the Great Dividing Range in the east.

Published in 2021 by Hardie Grant Travel, a division of Hardie Grant Publishing

Hardie Grant Travel (Melbourne)
Building 1, 658 Church Street
Richmond, Victoria 3121

Hardie Grant Travel (Sydney)
Level 7, 45 Jones Street
Ultimo, NSW 2007

www.hardiegrant.com/au/travel

Explore Australia is an imprint of Hardie Grant Travel

Assistance with research: The publisher would like to thank Ebird.com and Atlas of Living Australia for assistance with data and information.

A catalogue record for this
book is available from the
National Library of Australia

Hardie Grant acknowledges the Traditional Owners of the country on which we work, the Wurundjeri people of the Kulin nation and the Gadigal people of the Eora nation, and recognises their continuing connection to the land, waters and culture. We pay our respects to their Elders past, present and emerging.

100 Australian Birds
ISBN 9781741177220

10 9 8 7 6 5 4 3 2 1

Publisher
Melissa Kayser

Project editor
Megan Cuthbert

Editor
Marg Bowman and
Rosanna Dutson

Cartographer
Emily Maffei

Design
Ngaio Parr

Typesetting
Megan Ellis

Index
Max McMaster

Colour reproduction by Splitting Image Colour Studio
Printed and bound in China by LEO Paper Products LTD.

FSC
www.fsc.org
MIX
Paper from
responsible sources
FSC® C020056

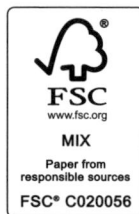

The paper this book is printed on is certified against the Forest Stewardship Council® Standards and other sources. FSC® promotes environmentally responsible, socially beneficial and economically viable management of the world's forests.

100 Australian Birds

Contents

Foreword

Birdwatching offers an easy way into the natural world. But it really helps if you know what you're looking at, which is why *100 Australian Birds* is such a fabulous book. It's an easy-to-use beginner's field guide – a jumping-off point for those wanting to enrich their experience of the world around them.

While I'm only a recreational and rather casual birdwatcher, birds are of profound emotional importance to me. My youngest son, Coleby, bears the Eora name for the white-bellied sea-eagle. The Eora are the First Nations people of the Sydney area, and many important Eora leaders have borne that name, not least being the Coleby of First Fleet times, who played a vital role in protecting his people from European aggression.

Like such leaders, sea-eagles are strong and knowing. They pair for life, and in the mating season will test potential mates by locking talons and spiralling downwards in a spectacular display. I once saw a pair locked together with such intensity that they didn't separate as they fell, instead plunging into an estuary far from the shore. I got into my tinnie and, armed with a yard broom, went out to them. They were drowning, but still fighting, when I arrived. I placed the broom-head under the female. It took all my strength to lift her out of the water. She gazed at me fiercely, then launched off. The male was panicked and unwilling to perch on the broom. He had a savage gash in his breast, and after I scooped him into the tinnie he took hours to recover. I still watch the sea-eagles of that estuary and wonder whether that relationship, with its rocky, intense start, survived.

Watching birds can put you in touch with the world. Whether it's the shearwaters and grey plovers that migrate from Siberia to southern Australia each year, or the channel-billed cuckoos that fly south from New Guinea to New South Wales, you learn something of distant realms as you watch them. And birds can let you travel in time. The rock warbler, which is found only in the sandstone country surrounding Sydney, is the only Australian member of its genus. But it has two relatives in New Guinea, which tells me that there must have been a time, millions of years ago, when ancestral rock warblers extended from the Sydney region right along the east coast. For me, watching rock warblers is like watching a living fossil – a unique survivor of ages of adversity.

But as I watch these fearless little birds, hopping confidently and noisily around my feet, I'm linked also to a more recent past. Rock warblers build their suspended, pendulous nests in rock shelters in the Sydney sandstone. The Eora must have lived intimately with them, as they too inhabited rock shelters. The chirruping, bright little birds, so confident around people, make me suspect that they had a special relationship with the Eora. Many other Indigenous peoples have special relationships with small birds such as the willie wagtail, which they never harm. Perhaps the Eora saw the rock warbler as a bringer of good fortune, or an alarm system against intruders. Whatever the case, I feel that these tiny birds link me to the Eora. They have found a special place in my heart.

The rock warbler is vanishing from many areas where it once abounded, and it is not the only Australian bird in decline. Studies show that Australia's threatened bird populations have declined by nearly 60% over the last 30 years. Such knowledge is hard-won, and much of it comes from the observations of amateur birdwatchers who conduct regular counts of birds. Birdwatching can be citizen science at its best, allowing ordinary people to contribute in invaluable ways to the preservation of the nation's biodiversity. If you're interested in protecting Australia's unique natural heritage, 100 Australian Birds can empower you. It can also open the door to a lifelong source of emotional and intellectual enrichment.

Professor Tim Flannery

Professor Tim Flannery is one of the world's leading scientists, explorers and conservationists. He has held positions in renowned institutions across Australia and internationally, including Director of the South Australian Museum, Visiting Chair in Australian Studies at Harvard University and Distinguished Research Fellow at the Australian Museum. He was named Australian of the Year in 2007. He has published more than thirty books, including the award-winning Here on Earth *(2010),* The Weather Makers *(2005),* Atmosphere of Hope *(2015) and* Weird, Wild, Amazing! *(2020). He is a frequent presenter on ABC Radio, NPR and the BBC, and has also written and presented several series on the Documentary Channel.*

Introduction

When did I start birdwatching? Well, easy. It was the same day that a pair of binoculars saved my life.

The drama! Who knew being a bird-nerd could lead to such adrenaline-pumping adventure? There were cliffs. There were rugged hiking trails. There was the potential – albeit a distant one – of death. While there wasn't an Indiana Jones-esque cliff fall involving a backpack strap and a scramble above a snake-filled gorge – it was still a turning point that marks the beginning of my birdwatching journey.

I got lost.

Not in a wishy-washy poetic sense. Literally. One minute, I was walking on the plateau of Kanangra Walls in New South Wales with a big smile on my face. My degree was finished. I had a bag full of trail mix, water and thermos of coffee. I had maps, printed from the internet. I had my cheap binoculars, a last-minute purchase. The sun was shining, the bush was lush, and my thumbs were tucked into the straps of my pack. I was out, walking, soaking it all in.

The next minute, I had no idea which way I was facing.

Was that the cliff I had walked in along? Or was it *that* one? I was facing another gorge, but I didn't remember taking enough turns to end up back where I'd started. I peered at my maps and couldn't make sense of them. On paper, there was one thick line marking the trail, but when I turned to walk back the way I had come, I was faced with several trails, each equally trodden, all heading different directions into the bush.

Well. This is a pickle.

I sat cross-legged on the cliff and stared into the gorge. I willed my innate, monkey instincts to kick in and tell me which way to go (they did not).

I had no idea what to do. I investigated the trails a little way but recognised none of the scenery.

Pickling in self-pity, I decided to pour myself a cup of coffee.

As I was pulling out my thermos I spotted the cheap binoculars, stuffed deep in my bag. On a whim, I pulled them out and scanned the cliff edges. A flash of white caught my eye. *Phew!* The signpost for the lookout I had passed hours before. It was tiny, kilometres distant, and in the opposite direction than I had expected (*gulp*). But it was there. I knew the way home.

I made my way back to the car with my tail between my legs and a big bruise to my bushwalking ego. I had no idea about *anything*. I didn't know how to navigate by the stars (note: I still don't), I didn't know how to read a topographic

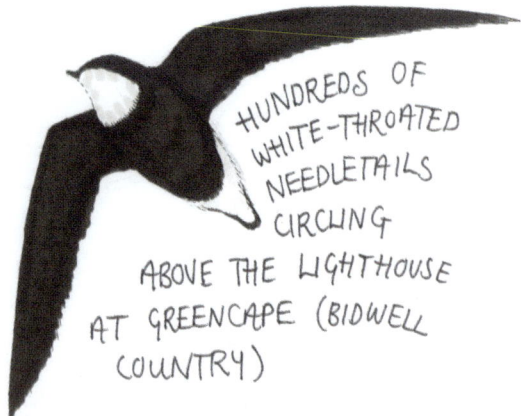

HUNDREDS OF WHITE-THROATED NEEDLETAILS CIRCLING ABOVE THE LIGHTHOUSE AT GREENCAPE (BIDWELL COUNTRY)

WEDGE-TAILED EAGLES CIRCLING OVER THE WARRUMBUNGLES (SPIRITUAL PLACE OF THE GAMILAROI, WIRADJURI & WEILWAN PEOPLES)

map (also don't really know how to do that), I didn't know how to survive in the bush – I didn't even know what birds I had seen on the path I'd been walking along. I knew that I at least needed to start paying more attention to my surroundings. My immediate aim wasn't necessarily about navigation, but about the Australian environment in general. I had lived here all my life and I didn't know anything about it – not really.

So, yeah – binoculars saved my life, kinda-sorta. Maybe we can twist that statement a little further and say, *birdwatching*, by requiring me to have binoculars, saved my life? No, you're right, that's a bit much. But without doubt – birdwatching has *improved* my quality of life. It taught me how to look and listen. After that day on Kanangra Walls, I kept my binoculars around my neck when walking – not stuffed in my backpack. The rest of the trip began to take shape in light of that ego check. I succumbed to a childlike feeling of ignorance. I knew nothing! What bird is that? What tree is that? I don't know! That was quite liberating to accept – under the obligation that I was willing to start learning.

I started by watching the birds.

On the road, I got hold of a second-hand field guide: *The Slater Field Guide to Australian Birds* (2nd edition, 2009, to be precise). In the guide,

there were many words I didn't understand (what on earth were 'coverts'? 'cryptic colours'? and, by gum, 'superciliaries'?), but I persisted. I started to identify the birds: I learned their names, where they 'hung out' and what they liked to eat. I felt like Sam Neill in Jurassic Park, racing around the bush – every new species I identified felt like a revelation.

Whenever I spoke about different things I'd seen on my trip, people always had a story to share about their own experiences with wildlife. Most often people spoke to me about birds. Some were stories about the family of Australian magpies living in their backyard or the spotted doves they fed on their driveway. But often people didn't know the exact birds they were describing. They'd seen a flock of tiny red birds and they wanted to know what they were. Or they'd seen a mysterious yellow bird that loved looking at its own reflection in the kitchen window. People were already interested in learning, just as I was – they'd seen these funny creatures doing things in their local area and they wanted to know more about them.

Like me, something has led you to want to know more about the birds in your environment. Maybe there are birds in your backyard that you don't recognise. Maybe there are birds you *do*

28/02
☐ AUSTRALIAN MAGPIE
☐ NOISY MINER
☐ RAVEN
☐ BROWN
    THORNBILL
☐ ROBIN?
☐ SULPHUR-CRESTED
    COCKATOO

GUIDE TO AUSTRALIAN BIRDS

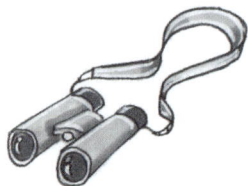

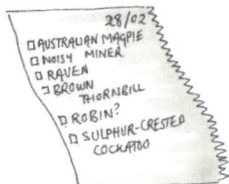

FLAME ROBIN POSING ON BRANCHES IN DEAD HORSE GAP (JAITMATANG/ NGARIGO COUNTRY)

recognise – but you'd like to know more about them. Maybe there used to be birds in your suburb, in your local park, but now there aren't any, and you're not sure why.

Perhaps you feel like I did that day on Kanangra Walls – out of my depth, but desperate to know more. I didn't understand why some birds were in some places, and why they weren't in others. They can fly, right? Why aren't there birds everywhere, all the time? Why can't I walk out the front of my house and look at a palm cockatoo? Why aren't there toucans in the Australian bush?

When I arrived back home, I continued with my birdwatching. Just because I wasn't in the gullies of the Blue Mountains didn't mean I couldn't learn more about the environment. Even in the city there were plenty of birds to be found. My partner and I pulled out the *Slater* field guide and used it to identify the species that we saw on my street in East Brunswick. We spent a lot of time flipping back and forth, trying to remember which types of bird were in what section of the book, wondering what on earth 'scapulars' meant. And … it was fun. We were feather detectives, on a mission to discover the identity of the mysterious bird who lurked on roof gutters, the streaky birds that screeched from our neighbour's hedge.

As we identified species, we started to understand some of their behaviours. The white-plumed honeyeaters eat nectar and they were common along the flowering gum trees on side streets. *Aha!* Trees with flowers = lots of nectar = birds arrive to feed (= good atmosphere on street). Crested pigeons were always on grassy verges or on people's driveways. We

discovered that they will often eat seed put out by residents – another aha moment. We were like Sherlock and Watson, using the smallest details – wing patterning, subtle behaviours – to figure out what we were seeing and how they related to the suburbs where we found them.

After the Kanangra Walls incident, and after learning more about birds around my suburb, I was hungry to keep building my knowledge. I visited some local field naturalists meetings and started trying to photograph some of the species I spotted. I discovered open data websites, and began to get more involved in citizen science, logging lists online with eBird. I changed the focus of my studies at university to science and biology and began to speak with experienced birdwatchers and ecologists. (Many of these people helped me to clarify and supplement the information included in this volume.) The birdwatching community – in person and online – proved invaluable in teaching me the best ways to start looking for and learning about birds.

As I delved into other field guides and conversations, I found that birdwatching – rather than 'taking over' and defining my daily walks, holidays or camping trips – became the means by which I found greater meaning in the outdoors. I was using birdwatching as a gateway for getting outside, soaking up the environment and exchanging knowledge with other people.

This book gives you the opportunity to do the same, introducing you to some of the most common birds in Australia. The bird entries include names, illustrations, identification information, and behavioural anecdotes from my own observations and those of other birdwatchers. By using this book as a reference in your travels – be it between cities, towns, or suburbs, or simply a walk from home to the corner store – it will help you appreciate and understand what used to be just a backdrop in your life.

As you start to watch birds, you will begin to notice other things about the environment they inhabit. Each type of bird has a distinctive character, and hangs out in different areas. These animals interact with other animals and plants – even rocks, soil and water – in diverse ways. By using your skills as a birdwatcher, you'll find you start watching other things too. You start to notice the ways things are connected. The way a bird eats fruit for energy, unconsciously spreading the seeds and allowing more plants to grow. The way a hollow forms after a tree branch falls, allowing a bird to nest there and raise their chicks. If you spend time looking at one small part of the environment, you will start to see how an individual creature is connected to the rest of the ecosystem. This is the beauty of birdwatching. It isn't just staring at birds. It's a way of using your observation skills to explore your surroundings with curiosity.

This is the first step in bringing the 'wild' into your everyday life, in being engaged, observant, and noticing the feedback loops between us and the land we live on. Realising that local life is rich – and appreciating the ways that we interface directly with the rest of nature – is empowering. Being aware of the species with which you share your space can help you give space back to them. Maybe you can create that space by planting spiky hakeas so that native birds have places to hide, or by growing other

KNOWLEDGE ABOUT YOUR SURROUNDS →

TIME SPENT OUTSIDE → NOTICING

NOTICING YOUR ENVIRONMENT

SPENDING TIME OUTSIDE

~ BIRDWATCHING ~

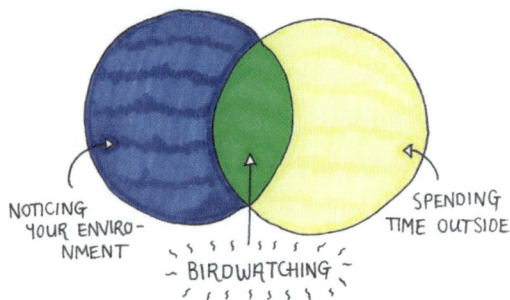

plants that birds can feed on. Maybe it's about picking up rubbish from the waterway near your house, or simply visiting the local reserve or park, and *noticing* – seeing who is there, who you hear, and what it tells you about where those animals are carving a niche for survival. These small daily acts provide you with a sense of enrichment that can carry through the rest of your day. They allow you to slow down, take a breath, and be in the moment.

The information in this volume is a compilation of my own experiences as a (relatively new) birdwatcher and the valued wisdom of several highly experienced birdwatchers. The entries brim with information, but there is always more to be learned about an individual species – I leave that for you to explore in the field, and to share with your community. There are no hard and fast rules on how to practise birdwatching. Do it the way that works best for you, as long as you find it serves your curiosity about your surrounds. Many birdwatchers now use applications and online registers for their birdwatching finds. Go as far as you'd like with this – you may find that your interests are satisfied by the overture this book provides. But it may also create a bigger itch that needs scratching, sending you off in the direction of more extensive field guides that drill down into the scientific details.

In the following pages you will find a guide for how to use this book: you can take it to the park, take it camping, keep it in your car, or leave it by the kitchen window. Whether you cover it in notes and fold over a hundred dog-ears, or keep it pristine, it is for you to use as a framework upon which you can build your knowledge and understanding.

So, how do we actually do this thing, 'birdwatching'? Well, it starts with looking, and with listening.

How to use this book
Some practical information for birdwatchers

Welcome, fledglings, to my birdwatching tutorial. This is a course I sorely missed at the beginning of my 'birding' journey, and I want to help ease you into the world of obscure terminology and identification methods. Start by flicking through some pages, and you'll see the layout of this book. Birds are ordered according to their appearance, and by the kinds of areas in which you are likely to spot them. For example, many of the birds that paddle and wade in fresh water are arranged close to ducks. Honeyeaters and fruit eaters that hang in similar areas of bushland are also close to one another. If you open a section of the book, you will be looking at a group of birds that both look similar and will be found in the same kind of area.

In each entry, a distribution map is included, which shows the parts of the country where a species is usually seen. Some tropical birds, like the comb-crested jacana (*see* page 97), rarely venture further south than Sydney, while other birds stick to inland arid areas, like the malleefowl (*see* page 133). If you're within the 'zone' shown on the map for a particular species, then you have a good chance of seeing the bird if you head to the areas indicated in the entry. If you're outside the zone on the map, clearly you may have to wait until you are able to visit that area of the country.

The most obvious things we are likely to observe about a bird are its shape, size and colour. For shape and size, I have added a guide in the following pages showing the major bird groups in context, so you can directly compare the sizes and shapes of birds without flicking between pages.

When you do start comparing species entries directly, though, it's important to know what information means what.

ROSE ROBIN I SPOTTED ON MT FEATHERTOP (JAITMATANG /WAVEROO COUNTRY)

How to read a species entry

① **Common English name** (there are many):
e.g. Superb lyrebird

② **First People's name and pronunciation guide**
(an example or multiple examples): e.g. Jaawan
[jah-won] (Gumbaynggirr) which includes the
pronunciation guide in square brackets and
identifies the Indigenous language in brackets
(the generous suppliers of First Nations
translations are listed in the Acknowledgements)

③ **Scientific name:** e.g. *Menura novaehollandiae*

Note: The taxonomic names I have provided for
each species have been written in accordance
with the IOC World Bird List (version 10.1). Some
older guides may provide variations on these
names, and, inevitably in years to come, newer,
more accurate taxonomic classifications for bird
species will arise.

④ **Map:** The map will display a shaded area,
which indicates where the featured species may
be spotted. (And so the species is unlikely to be
seen in the unshaded areas.) For this example,
the map indicates the superb lyrebird is only
found in areas of south-eastern Australia.

⑤ The entry will begin with some anecdotal
information about the bird's behaviour, which is
a conglomeration of personal experience and
the experience of some wiser birdwatching
allies (*see* Acknowledgements, page 216, for a
list of these generous bird-loving souls). This
information will inform you more broadly about
the particular bird you're looking at, and will
explain a little bit of its character or behaviour.

WHAT TO LISTEN FOR

A description of the bird's song or call. If you
come across a page that doesn't have a 'What
to listen for' entry, the species rarely calls, or is
rarely heard. In this instance, you will need to
relying on actually seeing the bird to identify it.

WHAT TO LOOK FOR

A description of the bird's appearance (this
also describes the differences in **gender** and
immature birds, where they apply).

WHERE TO START LOOKING

Some suggested areas to explore in your quest
to see this species. As mentioned above, you
will need to ensure you are looking for this bird
within the range shown on the map.

WHAT THEY EAT

A list of some of the favourite snacks this bird
likes to eat. This information can be really helpful
when you're out looking for a particular bird.
If you know your sought-after bird loves to
eat certain fruits or likes to swoop for insects
from farm fences, this can narrow down your
search area.

SIMILAR BIRDS

A list of some birds that look similar to this
species. Often – but not always – these
similar-looking birds will share some of the
same habitats, so it is important to observe
subtle differences between two (or more)
kinds of look-alike birds. Where possible, I've
included illustrations of look-alike birds for
easy comparison.

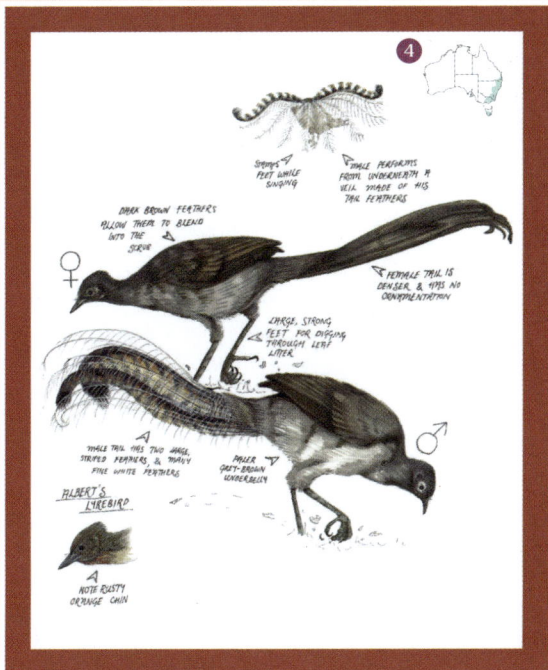

Superb lyrebird

Jaawan [jah-won] (Gumbaynggirr); **dyagula** [dya-gu-la] (Wiradjuri); **buln buln** [buln buln] (Taungurung)
Menura novaehollandiae

Despite their overlong tails, superb lyrebirds are surprisingly adept at staying hidden among rainforest shrubbery. Like the superb fairywren (*see page 67*), superb lyrebirds are polygynous – meaning one male courts several females. Once, when walking in Melbourne's Dandenong Ranges, I was able to hear a series of different bird calls all coming from the same spot amongst the bracken. I crept over towards the noise and peered through the shrubbery to see a male lyrebird, alone in a small circular clearing he had made – his 'stage'. As I watched, he lifted his tail up and over his body like a bride's veil, then proceeded to sing in the voices of many other birds – the laughing kookaburra (*see page 161*), golden whistler (*see page 65*), eastern whipbird (*see page 141*) and yellow-tailed black-cockatoo (*see page 179*). This performance, to my joy, was accompanied by the stamping of his large feet. He was dancing and singing in his own self-made theatre. As he danced, his long, veil-like tail shimmered, topping off this mesmerising display.

Male lyrebirds will spend much of their time performing this mimicry and dance as 'practice', singing year round, regardless of the breeding season. The female birds are more secretive than the males, finding secluded areas to build their nests, where they will eventually lay (most often) a single egg per season.

WHAT TO LISTEN FOR	The superb lyrebird is most widely known for its impeccable mimicry of other bird songs. If you're lucky enough to see a lyrebird during its courtship display, you'll also hear a repeated metallic sound, kind of like the bouncing of a metal spring, which the male birds make as they dance.
WHAT TO LOOK FOR	The superb lyrebird is a large ground-dwelling bird with a long, ornate tail. Their bodies are a dark chestnut brown, with a paler, grey-brown underbelly. Males have long, delicate tails, comprised of two broad, striped feathers that frame several white, filamentous feathers. Though this fancy plumage makes fast movements through dense bushland more difficult, these tails prove essential in their courtship displays (see above). While the males have a flashy tail, females have a long, denser tail of brown feathers. The feet of both the male and female lyrebird seem disproportionately large for the bird's size, but these hefty claws make them very efficient at digging and sorting through leaf litter and soil for food.
WHERE TO START LOOKING	Try going to areas of wet bushland (places where it rains regularly). Superb lyrebirds are most often heard singing in rainforest or heavily wooded areas, especially in gullies. These ecosystems tend to have a good layer of leaf and wood debris on the forest floor, which the superb lyrebird relies on for adequate food. As the male lyrebirds like to find a nice high perch from which to sing (so that their performances will carry a good distance), slopes alongside deep gullies are good spots to keep an eye (and ear) out. Places like the Dandenong Ranges in Victoria, denser bush along the east coast, New South Wales' Blue Mountains, and in the forests of the Australian Alps are well worth trying. Otherwise, head to shadier sections of forest in the closest hilly reserve to you – and keep an ear out for rustling, and the bird calls of five or more different species coming from the one place.
WHAT THEY EAT	Lyrebirds pick through leaf debris for insects, grubs and even small yabbies and scorpions.
SIMILAR BIRDS	Albert's lyrebird (pictured opposite), a rare species found in an isolated patch of coastline where the Queensland and New South Wales borders meet.

Superb lyrebird 139

STAMPS FEET WHILE SINGING

MALE PERFORMS FROM UNDERNEATH A VEIL SHADE OF HIS TAIL FEATHERS

DARK BROWN FEATHERS ALLOW THEM TO BLEND INTO THE SCRUB

♀ FEMALE TAIL IS DENSER & HAS NO ORNAMENTATION

LARGE, STRONG FEET FOR DIGGING THROUGH LEAF LITTER

MALE TAIL HAS TWO LARGE, STRIPED FEATHERS & MANY FINE WHITE FEATHERS

PALER GREY-BROWN UNDERBELLY ♂

ALBERT'S LYREBIRD

NOTE RUSTY ORANGE CHIN

♀♂ INDICATES FEMALE OR MALE BIRD, RESPECTIVELY

"IMMATURE" IS A YOUNGER BIRD OF THE SAME SPECIES

ARROWS INDICATE A USEFUL IDENTIFYING FEATURE

ALBERT'S LYREBIRD ENTRIES WILL ALSO INCLUDE SOME SIMILAR SPECIES FOR COMPARISON

SOME BIRD GROUPS & THEIR APPROXIMATE SIZES

TREECREEPER

NOISY MINER

SWALLOW

SHRIKETHRUSH

CUCKOOSHRIKE

WATTLEBIRD & FRIAR-BIRD

ORIOLE & FIGBIRD

BLACK COCKATOO

LORIKEETS

WHISTLERS

PARDALOTES

MISTLETOE BIRD

SEA EAGLE & WEDGE-TAILED EAGLE

BOWERBIRD

BUTCHERBIRD

SCRUBWREN

KITE & HARRIER

KESTREL

FANTAIL

SILVEREYE

THORNBILLS

THE CUCKOOS

MAGPIE-LARK

MAGPIE

ROSELLA

KING PARROT

ROBINS

NEW-HOLLAND HONEYEATER

BEE-EATER

CHOUGH, RAVEN & CURRAWONG

FINCHES

SPINEBILL

RED RUMPED PARROT

DARTER & CORMORANT

THE KINGFISHERS

MAGPIE GOOSE

DOLLARBIRD

WAGTAIL

CHAT

LEWIN'S HONEYEATER

BLACK SWAN

AUSTRALASIAN SWAMPHEN

SUPERB FAIRY-WREN

MUSK DUCK

SOUTHERN BOOBOOK

DUSKY MOORHEN

CHESTNUT TEAL & PACIFIC BLACK DUCK

WOOD DUCK

GALAH CORELLA SULPHUR-CRESTED COCKATOO

PIED OYSTERCATCHER

TAWNY FROGMOUTH

GRASSBIRD & REED WARBLER

CASPIAN TERN

AUSTRALASIAN GREBE

PACIFIC GULL

PELICAN

RED-CAPPED PLOVER

SILVER GULL

NANKEEN NIGHT-HERON

MASKED LAPWING

EURASIAN COOT

CRESTED PIGEON

BRONZEWING

COMB-CRESTED JACANA

AUSTRALIAN BRUSHTURKEY

WHITE-HEADED PIGEON

SUPERB LYREBIRD

EMU

BROLGA

EASTERN WHIP-BIRD

APPROX. 150 cm

GREAT EGRET

WHITE-FACED HERON

YELLOW-BILLED SPOONBILL

WHITE & STRAW-NECKED IBIS

BUSH-STONE CURLEW

MALLEE FOWL

BROWN QUAIL

xvi   100 Australian Birds

The birds in this book

There are several bird 'types' which make up the 100 species I have chosen to include in this book. Each bird type or group is pictured opposite, with relative sizes shown to help you get your eye in!

These birds, as you can see, are diverse and are adapted for many different walks (and flights) of life. They are just as varied in colour and pattern, so read on for some guidance on the role feathers play in how we pick who's who in the world of birds.

We need to talk about plumage

Birds vary *a lot* (think about it – something as big as an emu (*see* page 131) and as weeny as a brown thornbill (*see* page 51) are placed under the same umbrella, 'Birds'). Considering all this diversity, one of the most useful identification tools for birdwatchers is feathers (or 'plumage').

The colour and pattern of feathers on a bird is often what we notice first. In looking at a bird, we are usually observing the way their feathers make them appear, and that's one of the aspects that help us figure out what species they are. However, feathers can vary *within* a species in three main ways, and this can make identifying a bird quite tricky.

The first major difference in feathers is *seasonal plumage* (or *breeding* and *non-breeding* plumage.) This occurs in a species that grows a particular kind of feather-outfit for the time of year when they're trying to find a hot date, and hopefully raise some chicks (aka the *breeding season*). This *breeding plumage* is usually bold and bright, which may catch the attention of a mate. These vivid feathers will alternate with a less striking – and perhaps more camouflaged – set of feathers in *non-breeding seasons*.

Note: There are some interesting objections to this rule of '*breeding*' and '*non-breeding*', and not all species go through a seasonal cycle. However, this is a good general starting point for those species that do.

AUSTRALASIAN GREBE IN BREEDING PLUMAGE

AUSTRALASIAN GREBE IN NON-BREEDING PLUMAGE

(AUSTRALASIAN GREBE, *TACHYBAPTUS NOVAEHOLLANDIAE*)

The second major variation in appearance is due to age. Just as you may have experimented with different haircuts over your adolescence, most birds will have multiple 'moults' before they grow their adult feathers. This is why many of the entries in the book include pictures of 'immature' birds. These young birds sometimes have different coloured feathers, different *amounts* of feathers, even different coloured beaks, eyes and feet from their adult counterparts. These immature birds often look so different from the adults that they may trip you up in the field, and make you believe you are seeing a different species.

Note: The term 'immature' is used in this book to describe any bird that has not developed 'mature' adult feathers. This means that 'immature' representations are only one of a few stages of moult a bird may go through before reaching an adult set of plumage. I have chosen to include the stage of immature feathers I have most often seen, but you may find others on your explorations.

MALE GOLDEN WHISTLER

FEMALE GOLDEN WHISTLER

(GOLDEN WHISTLER, *PACHYCEPHALA PECTORALIS*)

IMMATURE RED-BROWED FINCH

ADULT RED-BROWED FINCH

(RED-BROWED FINCH, *NEOCHMIA TEMPORALIS*)

The third major difference in feathers is due to something called *dimorphism*. This is a word meaning 'two forms', usually male and female. *Dimorphism* in birdwatching ordinarily describes a bird where the female looks different to the male. This may be a difference in size or shape, but most often it's alternative plumage colour and pattern.

Feathers serve several important roles in the lives of birds – including warmth, looking fancy (aka sexual selection), camouflage and, not to mention, flight – but they also have a fascinating structure that deserves your appreciation (*see* 'The structure of feathers', opposite).

Now that we understand some of the fantastic diversity of the ways birds can look, we can start to learn how to observe these differences.

THE STRUCTURE OF FEATHERS

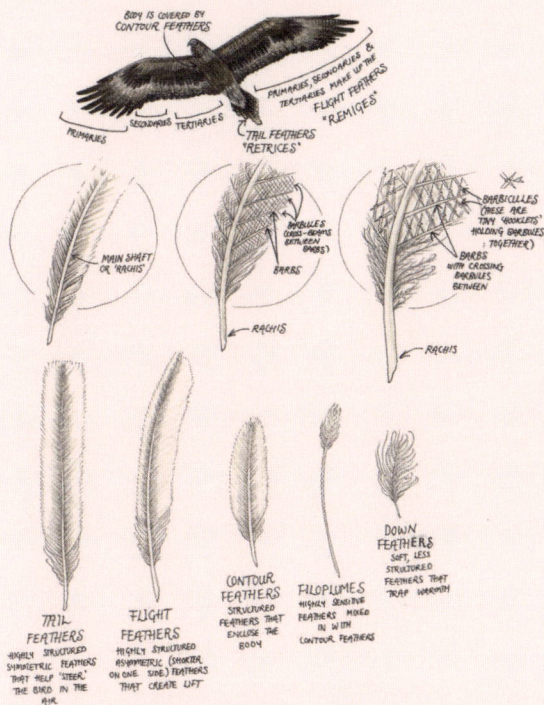

BODY IS COVERED BY CONTOUR FEATHERS

PRIMARIES, SECONDARIES & TERTIARIES MAKE UP THE FLIGHT FEATHERS "REMIGES"

PRIMARIES

SECONDARIES TERTIARIES

TAIL FEATHERS "RETRICES"

MAIN SHAFT OR 'RACHIS'

BARBS

BARBICELLES (THESE ARE TINY 'HOOKLETS' HOLDING BARBULES TOGETHER)

BARBS WITH CROSSING BARBULES BETWEEN

BARBULES (CROSS-COMBS BETWEEN BARBS)

RACHIS

RACHIS

TAIL FEATHERS
HIGHLY STRUCTURED SYMMETRIC FEATHERS THAT HELP 'STEER' THE BIRD IN THE AIR

FLIGHT FEATHERS
HIGHLY STRUCTURED ASYMMETRIC (SHORTER ON ONE SIDE) FEATHERS THAT CREATE LIFT

CONTOUR FEATHERS
STRUCTURED FEATHERS THAT ENCLOSE THE BODY

FILOPLUMES
HIGHLY SENSITIVE FEATHERS MIXED IN WITH CONTOUR FEATHERS

DOWN FEATHERS
SOFT, LESS STRUCTURED FEATHERS THAT TRAP WARMTH

Tips for birdwatching beginners

When you find yourself out and about – be it in the park, camping, making your way home through the suburbs, at the river, beach, or on a road trip – keep your eyes open. Birds are going to be there – it's just a matter of noticing them. Though not necessary, a pair of binoculars (even a small pocket-sized pair) will make your birdwatching experience much more enjoyable. Think of all the tiny beaks, eyes and tails you'll be able to see through these lenses!

When I spot a bird I am unfamiliar with, I try to stand quietly and observe the bird for as long as I can. (I try not to go straight to the guide! The bird will be gone again before I know it, so instead I try to soak it in before looking in the book.)

I make note of size and shape, and then hone in on any notable details that may distinguish the bird. Is there a fancy pattern on the feathers? A coloured strip on the wing? A weird tail? A large beak? I repeat these observations in my mind as I watch the bird, trying to take in some of its details before, inevitably, I lose sight of it. If the bird has been singing, I try and remember the 'quality' or 'tone' of the song, as this may also help with identification.

Usually I will then peruse a field guide, going by habitat, shape and general colour to look in a relevant section. I then scan the birds that seem most relevant by appearance and make a little list of birds that are comparable (there may be a surprising amount of similar-looking birds, even when you think the bird you've seen was particularly distinctive!). Using the details noted while watching the actual bird, I whittle down towards a particular species the bird may be. I look at details about geographic location (am I in the recorded range for that species? i.e. does the species map show that the bird is usually in my area?) and habitat (does that bird frequent open, grassy areas?). Does the species entry describe some peculiar habits that distinguish it? (For example, the black-faced cuckooshrike often 'shuffles' its wings at perch. Did the bird I saw do anything distinctive like that?) Does the silhouette of the bird in flight have a particular shape? Does it sing while at perch, and what does its voice sound like?

With these details gathered and taken into account, ideally I will find an accurate description of the same bird in my guide. How great is that? We've identified a bird species!

If you have a list, you can write down the species you have spotted (some people keep life lists, annual lists and even daily lists), or if you're using an online database – like eBird – you can add it to a checklist there. You'll be amazed by how quickly you can build a list of identified species.

A few quick pointers

Patience, padawan. Often a bird will hop in and out of sight while you try and ID it. If you can't get a good look at a bird, try and hold steady for a minute or two, and it will likely shift into a better position. Chasing a bird or rapidly crunching closer to a tree will often scare the bird off or stress it out unnecessarily. Move slowly and quietly.

Keep voices low. Birds watch and listen too. They're likely to know you're there – so don't scare them any more than you already have.

Listen! As I've mentioned, birdsong can prove a vital method for identifying bird species. For some bird groups, the call alone is the most certain way to distinguish one species of bird from another, as is the case with the grey currawong versus the pied currawong (*see* page 11), or between the Australian raven (*see* page 7) and the several other species of raven found in Australia. As I spend more time listening to birds, I'm finding it's easier to become familiar with the 'tone' of a bird's song than trying to learn the specific melody or noise they make, as their songs can vary so much.

Put the sun at your back. Just as we discover when trying to take sunset selfies, when a shape has the sun behind it, it will be cast in a silhouette. Even the most brightly coloured birds (like the rainbow bee-eater, *see* page 153) will look grey or black when backlit. If you're able, move around so the sunlight is lighting up the bird, rather than shining from behind it.

Scan the flock. Oftentimes what looks like a huge flock of musk ducks (*see* page 81) on a lake will actually hide several other waterbird species. Scan them to see if any bonus birds become visible among the masses. Think of it like Minesweeper, only much more rewarding. Scan the banks too! Many birds hide among reeds and grass, especially shy wading birds.

Head out in the morning or evening.	The bookends of the day are often the times when birds are lower in trees (so more visible), and are more actively feeding. During the middle of the day – often the hottest part of the day – many birds will stick to thick, shady canopies where they are much harder to spot.
Look at the forecast.	Heading out in windy weather will make things very difficult. Most birds hunker down in wild weather, and wind noise also makes birdsong difficult to hear.
A note on identifying birds of prey (e.g. eagles, kites and harriers – *see* pages 181–189).	I find predatory birds are *frustratingly* difficult to identify. The most likely time to see these birds is when they're in flight. To observe them, you usually have to crane your neck at a painful angle, and the birds are usually backlit against the blue or clouded sky, making colour and pattern hard to see. The silhouettes of cruising hunting birds are usually similar to one another, scale is hard to perceive at those heights, and making an identification may come down to small details like the fanning of tail feathers or the eye colour. But we birdwatchers live for the struggle, so grit your teeth and spin the focus knob on your binoculars. It's time to see a white-bellied sea-eagle (*see* page 187). Trust me, it's worth it. To help you get started, I've put a comparative guide to tails of hunting birds in the appendix (*see* page 208).
Take part in citizen science!	Citizen science usually means logging your observations through platforms like eBird (aka the better version of Pokémon Go). This is as simple as listing the birds you've seen on your walk. By doing this, you can assist eBird, Birdata, Atlas of Living Australia and other platforms to see which species are seen where, how often they are seen, where these birds may migrate to, and at what times of the year this occurs. The data from citizen science databases goes on to assist in conservation and management projects – even if your 'field' is the local creek or golf course. In fact, data from these seemingly 'unlikely' places are particularly valuable – many species carve out surprising homes in our otherwise urban landscapes.

A cautionary note: birding ethically

There have been many ethically questionable actions practised by early birdwatching groups, including bird killing and egg stealing. Though in modern birdwatching these damaging practices have largely ceased, there is still some call to be cautious while observing animals. By being careful you will ensure you avoid endangering or damaging the little critters you're trying so hard to appreciate.

- Pay attention to the behaviour of birds. If a bird (or birds) you are observing is becoming agitated and swooping, you are likely causing them stress (this may be because they have a nest close by and they are afraid for their eggs or chicks). Parents will often defend nests to the point of damaging themselves – please retreat from an area if birds are behaving defensively.
- Speaking of nests – don't go poking them or even approaching them too closely. Be aware when walking that some species (such as masked lapwings, *see* page 119) nest on the ground in long grass.
- If you hear birds in undergrowth, it is sometimes tempting to intentionally scare or 'flush' them into the open. ('Flush' is a term that means scaring a bird, whether intentionally or unintentionally, which usually makes them flee.) While this may allow you to get a glimpse of them, the stress and energy costs of such a threat is damaging to birds.
- Looking for owls (*see* page 191) and other night-birds (*see* page 193) may include heading out after dark with headlamps or torches to 'spotlight' birds in the canopy. I recommend using a red filter on your light, as this dramatically lessens the disturbance to nocturnal wildlife. In addition, try to avoid 'frying' birds by leaving them in the spotlight for any lengthy period of time. Often directing a spotlight onto an adjacent branch will allow enough light to 'spill over' and partially illuminate the species you're trying to get a look at. By the same token, flash photography – day or night – is a no-no.
- Avoid disturbing habitat areas by sticking to better worn trails, and, of course, leave no litter behind (or pick some litter up and help keep the bush clear!).
- There are many negative impacts humans can have on birds, unless caution, patience and reasonable judgement are exercised. Consider the potential stress placed upon an individual bird if you were to pursue them relentlessly. Their hearts are tiny! Don't make them beat any faster than they already have to.

Where birds live (and where to see them)

While the words 'I'm going birdwatching' often conjure images of bush bashing through a remote jungle, there are many local areas that require little physical or financial commitment to visit. Start local! Get familiar with the birds you see often in your area. Different parks and waterways close to you are usually accessible by public transport, are wheelchair accessible *and* rich in bird species.

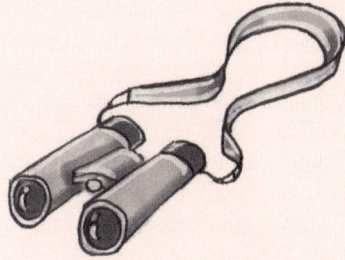

LOCAL LAKES, RIVERS, CREEKS, STREAMS & DAMS

SEASHORES (BOAT RAMPS) & JETTIES USUALLY HAVE SOME BIRD ACTION

PARKS, GOLF COURSES SPORTS GROUNDS/OVALS, BOTANIC GARDENS & WELL-PLANTED/GREEN SUBURBS

FARMLAND & IRRIGATED PASTURE

NATIONAL & STATE PARKS & CAMPGROUND

ANY REMNANT PATCHES OF OLDER NATIVE TREES

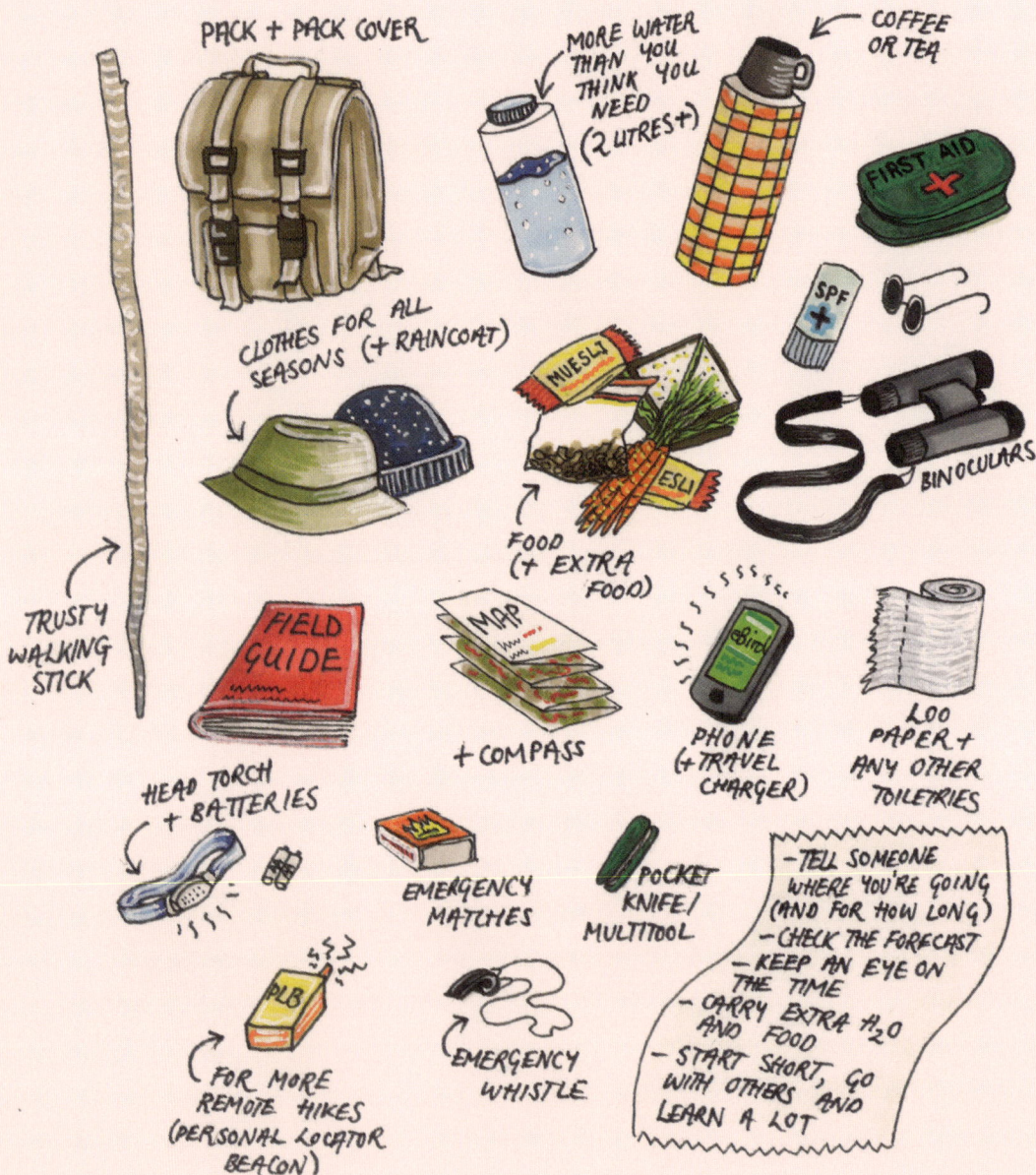

GOING BUSH

PACK + PACK COVER

MORE WATER THAN YOU THINK YOU NEED (2 LITRES+)

COFFEE OR TEA

FIRST AID

CLOTHES FOR ALL SEASONS (+ RAINCOAT)

MUESLI

SPF

BINOCULARS

FOOD (+ EXTRA FOOD)

TRUSTY WALKING STICK

FIELD GUIDE

MAP

+ COMPASS

PHONE (+ TRAVEL CHARGER)

LOO PAPER + ANY OTHER TOILETRIES

HEAD TORCH + BATTERIES

EMERGENCY MATCHES

POCKET KNIFE / MULTITOOL

- TELL SOMEONE WHERE YOU'RE GOING (AND FOR HOW LONG)
- CHECK THE FORECAST
- KEEP AN EYE ON THE TIME
- CARRY EXTRA H_2O AND FOOD
- START SHORT, GO WITH OTHERS AND LEARN A LOT

PLB

FOR MORE REMOTE HIKES (PERSONAL LOCATOR BEACON)

EMERGENCY WHISTLE

A note on 'going bush'

As you may have gathered from the introduction, it's easy to get in over your head *very* quickly in the bush. I recommend you circumvent disaster by doing a small amount of preparation. Of course, some birdwatching sessions you won't need to prep for – e.g. heading to the corner shop or going out on a bike ride (helmets are good). However, if you go out for longer sessions in more remote areas, it's good to 'insure yourself' to avoid stress, and to help you enjoy the moment as you are out on your bird walk.

Everyone practises birdwatching differently, and I encourage you to embrace your own way of learning about your environment. Some ideas on how to spend your time noticing are shown below in the pie charts.

You can modify and plan your outings to suit your needs. Many people enjoy finding a quiet spot to sit in a reserve or picnic ground as fulfilling as going on a long walk.

A guide, not gospel

This book is your portal into looking at birds, and learning about your environment. In each illustration, I have tried to portray the birds with accurate character and colour, but your impression of these animals may vary from what I have provided here. Given this, I hope the book brings you closer to identifying more birds without it necessarily being the sole source of your information. I have provided a further reading list at the conclusion of this book, and I encourage you to investigate some of the more exhaustive field guides to assist you in observing birds. There are around 800 species that can be seen in Australia's mainland and islands. The 100 strange and beautiful birds I have chosen to include in this book are the species you are most likely to see in suburban and accessible bushland areas. The book also includes a few notable endangered species (e.g. the malleefowl, *see* page 133). I hope these rarer birds will whet your appetite to go further abroad on your adventures, to places where you can appreciate even more of Australia's biodiversity.

Finally, I hope you revel in your own skills – observe how quickly your senses can attune to your surroundings. On your first day, you might not recognise a particular bird, and find it frustrating. Soon you'll be recognising species left and right – a magpie family on your verandah, a noisy miner *peeping* in a eucalypt, a magpie-lark couple giving an alarm call, a pied currawong in your garden, and a raven laughing from a branch. You'll be soaking it all up like a sponge in no time!

Go forth, dear reader, and watch the birds.

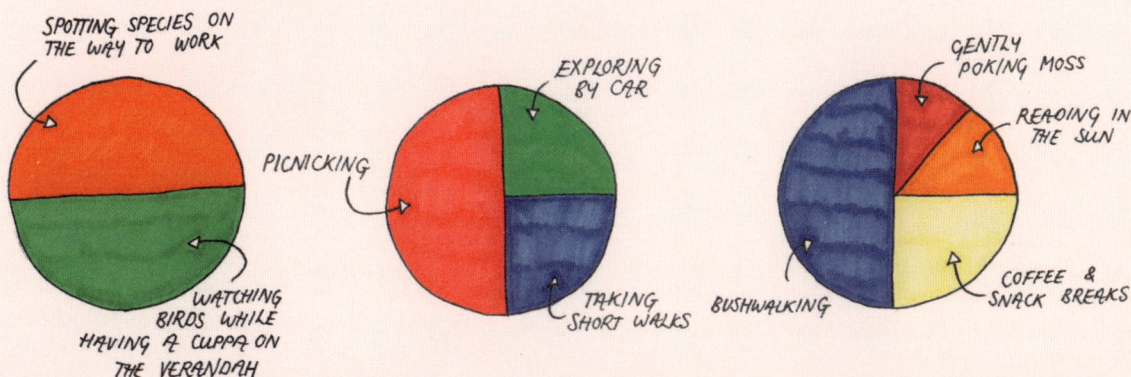

SPOTTING SPECIES ON THE WAY TO WORK

PICNICKING

WATCHING BIRDS WHILE HAVING A CUPPA ON THE VERANDAH

EXPLORING BY CAR

TAKING SHORT WALKS

GENTLY POKING MOSS

READING IN THE SUN

COFFEE & SNACK BREAKS

BUSHWALKING

IN FLIGHT

(IN FEMALES) WHITE FEATHERS MOTTLED

MALES HAVE GLEAMING WHITE BACKS

WHITE UNDER TAIL

FAINTLY HOOKED BEAK TIP

♀

♂

BLACK UNDERBELLY

Australian magpie

Ngaambul [ngahm-bool] (Gumbaynggirr);
garru [ga-rru], **garrubang** [ga-rru-ba-ng],
wibigang [wi-bi-ga-ng], **dyirigang** [dyi-ri-ga-ng]
(Wiradjuri); **barwang** [bar-wang] (Taungurung)
Gymnorhina tibicen

The Australian magpie is a particularly intelligent and wily bird. They are sociable, playful and aggressive. You have likely had an encounter (or two) with magpies during springtime, when they readily swoop passing threats. This is most often a male magpie using intimidation tactics to try and protect the nest. You may also have seen magpies playfighting on the ground – they will sometimes lie on their backs with legs waving in the air, wrestling with other magpies. They are almost always seen in 'family units' with parents and a number of juveniles, and a particular magpie family will occupy a territory for a lifetime, if they can adequately defend it. The magpies you spot in your backyard will very likely be the same birds you've been seeing there for years. Sometimes older birds will attack one of their adolescent young, which is likely a tactic to encourage it to 'leave the nest' (perhaps the bird equivalent of getting kicked out of home after you've finished school). If you watch a magpie closely as it stalks over a grassy patch, you can see it step, pause and turn its ear towards the ground a little. Their hearing is so sharp, they can sometimes hear earthworms and grubs moving in the soil beneath them.

As these wily birds hunt for grubs and insects, they are almost always hopping or running over the ground like buff football players. Sometimes they will perch on a tree branch or powerline to sing out over their territory, or to swoop on unsuspecting birds. No matter where they are, the Australian magpie gives the overall impression of a highly diligent groundskeeper – one that absolutely does not tolerate loitering on the grass.

WHAT TO LISTEN FOR	A trickling, warbling song is the most familiar call of the Australian magpie, usually heard in the early morning or at twilight. Often juveniles 'whinge' for food, a high *meep-meep-meep*. The Australian magpie can also mimic – they sometimes sing the songs of other bird species, or, in more recent times, imitate fire sirens and other human-made noises. I've also heard magpies performing a 'moonlit serenade' in the middle of the night, which is quite surreal!
WHAT TO LOOK FOR	The Australian magpie is a medium-sized black and white bird, and is a familiar resident in many Australian gardens. It has a white panel on the back of the neck, on each of its 'shoulders', and around the base of the tail. (Note that there is much variation across the continent in the arrangement of white and black on magpies, so some may appear to have more or less, depending on where you live.) Magpie beaks are large and grey with a black tip, and a slight downwards hook to the point of the beak. Females and males look similar, though where the male has almost 'pristine' white feathers, the white patches on females are greyer and more mottled.
IMMATURE BIRDS	Young magpies are much like the females, only greyer and even more mottled overall.
WHERE TO START LOOKING	Magpies are seen in many places, excluding dense bushland or rainforest, as they prefer open patches of ground where they can dig for grubs. Lawns, gardens, backyards, ovals, nature strips – the magpie seems to thrive anywhere humans dwell.
WHAT THEY EAT	Worms, insects and opportunistic scraps.
SIMILAR BIRDS	Magpie-lark (or 'mudlark', *see* page 3), pied currawong (*see* page 11), pied butcherbird (pictured on page 4), grey butcherbird (*see* page 5).

♂

SEPARATE BROW
& NECK
PATCH

WHITE-WINGED
TRILLER
(♂)

WHITE
CHIN

MALE
FACE &
BELLY
IS
BLACK

WHITE
PANELS
IN BLACK
WINGS

NO SEPARATE
BROW

♀

FEMALE HAS A
WHITE 'MASK' AROUND
BEAK

WHITE BELLY

WHITE-TIPPED
TAIL

Magpie-lark

Jijigurrin [ji-ji-goo-rrin] (Gumbaynggirr);
burrindin [bu-rri-n-di-n], **guliridy** [gu-li-ri-dy]
(Wiradjuri); **dit dit** [ditdit] (Taungurung)
Grallina cyanoleuca

The magpie-lark, a common sight in most areas of Australia, is the bird with a thousand names: peewee, mudlark, Murray magpie, pugwall, piping shrike and peewit. These birds mate for life, defending a permanent territory fiercely. As a result, they are some of the dreaded 'springtime swoopers', along with the Australian magpie and masked lapwing (*see* page 119), you may have run away from in the early warm months of the year. Also like the Australian magpie, these birds like to stalk over grassy lawns in search of insects. However, magpie-larks are less assertive than the magpie, instead hurriedly bobbing their heads as they walk, as if in a rush, and readily fleeing if they sense any threat. They build dense nests of grass, twigs and mud in the fork of a branch.

WHAT TO LISTEN FOR	A two-note piping *dye-eep-dye-eep!* alarm call, quite piercing. This call earns the magpie-lark the alternate name 'peewee'. The song is actually the male and female birds singing back and forth to one another, in opposing ('antiphonal') song, *dye-eep -doo -dye-eep -doo.*
WHAT TO LOOK FOR	The magpie-lark is a narrow-bodied, black and white bird and is commonly seen grabbing insects on open ground. The head and wings are predominantly black, with a white panel on each wing. The tail is black with a white tip. Males have two patches of white on either cheek, above and below the black eye, which is ringed with white. Females have an additional white patch which encircles the beak and runs down onto the chest. The females also have a slightly enlarged cheek patch, so they have no separate 'eyebrow'.
IMMATURE BIRDS	Young magpie-larks do not develop a white eye-ring until adulthood.
WHERE TO START LOOKING	Like the Australian magpie, the magpie-lark is one of the beneficiaries of land clearing. These birds are a common sight in areas where humans have cleared land for agricultural or suburban uses. I most often see magpie-larks out on farmland, in suburbs, at parks or ovals, in urban gardens, on roadsides, and on the edges of dams. Any area of well-watered grassland is a pretty good bet for seeing these birds.
WHAT THEY EAT	Insects and grubs.
SIMILAR BIRDS	White-winged triller (pictured opposite), Australian magpie (*see* page 1), pied currawong (*see* page 11), pied butcherbird (pictured on page 4), common blackbird (common in similar areas, *see* Introduced species in the appendix, page 208).

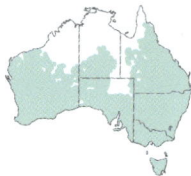

PIED BUTCHERBIRD

IMMATURE

BROWN CAP

MOTTLED COLLAR & CHIN

DARK BROWN-GREY WINGS

NOTE: WHOLE HEAD IS BLACK WITH A 'BIB' ON CHEST

BLACK CAP

ADULT

HOOKED BEAK

DARK GREY-BLACK WINGS & TAIL

PALE WHITE CHIN & COLLAR

LIGHT GREY BELLY

Grey butcherbird

Wulaaran [woolahrun] (Gumbaynggirr)
Cracticus torquattus

Like the magpie, grey butcherbirds can become quite tame with extended human contact, and are relatively common in Australian backyards and parklands. At a glance, they look very much like a 'mini-magpie', and it might take you a second inspection to recognise this as a different species. Usually singing as the sun comes up, and through the morning, the grey butcherbird loves to perch on overhead branches to lord over its territory. Their voice is quite particular, and, as vocal birds, their calling is usually the best tip-off that they're in the area. These birds tend to dwell in trees much more than magpies do, perhaps because they commonly hunt larger prey and need to 'pounce' from above. Most often I see grey butcherbirds singing on the upper branches of trees, with their feathers fluffed up to stay warm. As they sing, they lift their beak high and straighten out their bodies, as if they are full of song and only need to unbend their neck for the melody to spill out.

WHAT TO LISTEN FOR	A noise like someone rubbing glass with a wet cloth, *waa-woo-woowoowoo* and *dwupp-upp-dwoo, dwupp dwupp*. The tone of their song is a warbling, muted whistle, which you are most likely to hear in the morning after first light.
WHAT TO LOOK FOR	Reminiscent of a small Australian magpie, the grey butcherbird is a black, white and grey bird often perched on branches or powerlines. The belly and chin is white, and the head is capped with black. The wings and tail are black with white tips, and the back is grey. The beak is proportionately larger to the body than that of the magpie, and there is also a more obvious hook to the beak. Female grey butcherbirds are subtly more brown than the males, which are black, but I find them tricky to tell apart in the field!
IMMATURE BIRDS	Young grey butcherbirds are an overall dilute brown, with darker sections that mimic what will develop into the patches of the adult.
WHERE TO START LOOKING	Grey butcherbirds are common in many of the greener suburbs, local parks and gardens across the country. You may have more luck seeing them in areas with fairly established eucalyptus tree stands nearby, as they often perch in trees during the morning.
WHAT THEY EAT	Butcherbirds are so named for their tendency to 'butcher' their prey – be it tiny mammals, small birds or reptiles. Sometimes they will hoard ('cache') food by storing it in a tree crevice, or, gruesomely, by stringing it on barbed wire.
SIMILAR BIRDS	Australian magpie (*see* page 1), black butcherbird (northern coastlines in thicker forests), pied butcherbird (pictured opposite; I see these birds more often in drier, inland areas), pied currawong (*see* page 11).

BROWN EYE

IMMATURE

FEATHERS ARE LESS GLOSSY

WHITE EYE

ADULT

LAYERS OF 'GULLET' FEATHERS

HEALTHY ADULT FEATHERS ARE GLOSSY

Australian raven

Waagan [wahgun] (Gumbaynggirr); **waagan**
[waa-ga-n], **wandyu** [wa-n-dyu] (Wiradjuri);
Waang [Waang ('aa' as in 'c<u>ar</u>t')] (Taungurung)
Corvus coronoides

As they are often the companion to villainous characters in film – or perhaps the embodiment of horror themselves, as in Hitchcock's *The Birds* (1963) – ravens have scored a bum rap. As a part of the corvids (the *Corvidae* group, which also contains European choughs and European magpies), they are eerily smart birds whose schemes warrant some appreciation. They have an excellent memory, which makes their constant feature as harbingers of doom in Gothic literature all the more disconcerting, and makes me wary of insulting them – they'll remember what I said. Due to their size and wiles, they are very dominant and will bully other species in a given area. Being large glossy black birds, ravens are hard to miss. They often saunter over the ground with robotic-like confidence, twisting their heads to take in their surrounds. Their white eye-ring makes their analytical way of looking around a bit unsettling, as they seem largely unintimidated by humans. Usually you will see these birds lurking in a small group, calling from atop lightposts or trees, or stalking over the ground, looking for scraps.

WHAT TO LISTEN FOR	The Australian raven performs a rasping laugh, *mwah-ha-haaaaargh*. Take a pack-a-day supervillain, cross them with Tom Waits, and slow their chuckle down to half speed. And there you have the call of the Australian raven.
WHAT TO LOOK FOR	Often referred to as a 'crow', the Australian raven is a large dark, glossy bird. They are entirely black, except for a stern-looking white eye-ring. The beak is strong and relatively sharp at its tip. The feathers are quite long and are often 'fluffed' at the throat, forming a gullet.
IMMATURE BIRDS	Young Australian ravens are smaller, less glossy, and the eye is brown instead of white.
WHERE TO START LOOKING	As opportunistic feeders (namely, they eat a wide variety of things, meat and vegetable matter included), the Australian raven does well in most eastern and south-western areas of Australia. They will cope in the city as well as rural areas. Keep your eyes peeled as you go to and from work and you're likely to spot a raven in roadside trees or at the local park.
WHAT THEY EAT	Australian ravens are generalist eaters in the truest sense, mostly due to human proximity. In less urbanised areas, Australian ravens eat mostly insects and small lizards, and graze on seeds and fruit. They will also thieve eggs or young chicks from the nests of other birds. However, when exposed to scraps and feeding at picnic grounds, they are taught to expect food and will often hassle any picnickers who aren't readily feeding them. They are discerning and will observe what people are eating, and try their darned hardest to get whatever it is they're missing out on, tearing through plastic, cracking open containers, and dragging things off tables or out of bags. I would not recommend feeding ravens at campsites – just as Pandora couldn't put the lid back on the box of chaos, so you, too, will never stop a raven from creeping up on your food supplies once your back is turned.
SIMILAR BIRDS	Pied currawong (*see* page 11), male eastern ('common') koel (*see* page 195), male satin bowerbird (*see* page 149). Just to complicate things, there are actually three different species of raven in Australia, and two species of crow: the Australian raven as described, the forest raven, little raven, little crow and Torresian crow. The most reliable method for distinguishing these similar birds is to compare their calls, a tricky feat in itself.

WING
DISPLAY

OFTEN
PERFORMING
'WHISTLE'
CALL

IMMATURE

ADULT
(red eye)

SLENDER,
CURVED
BEAK

WHITE WING
PATCH MAY BE
VISIBLE

White-winged chough

Gundyung [gu-n-dyu-ng] (Wiradjuri)
Corcorax melanoramphos

Sometimes called the jaybird, the white-winged chough (pronounced 'chuff') is a rewarding bird to identify. Because they look very much like a pied currawong or an Australian raven, they are often overlooked, but if you pay attention, you should be able to notice the slight differences in their appearance. They are colonial, so are almost always seen in a rasping, exuberant crew. They often hop into and hang out in trees as a 'family', or group on the edges of agricultural land where there are shrubs and leaf debris for them to pick through.

These birds are also renowned for their 'kidnapping' (chick-napping?). Remember those white wing spots we mentioned earlier? Choughs will often flash these wing patches, and it's likely they are actually used to help communicate within a family, kind of like a bird version of Morse code. However, some choughs have used this wing-patch communication for more sordid ends. I've come across several anecdotes about adult choughs using these 'wing signals' to coax a young chough of *another* family to come and join their family instead. Perhaps this is achieved by confusing the youngster with mixed wing signals, or by promising the youngster extra tasty grubs – how precisely this occurs remains a bit of a mystery. With this coercion completed, the 'chick-napped' bird is co-opted into feeding and raising the youngsters in the new family. Dirty tactics! I imagine this is close to what it feels like to be inducted into a cult, albeit a very feathery and noisy one.

WHAT TO LISTEN FOR	White-winged choughs give a repeated, mournful, descending whistle, followed by an explosion of raspy-throated alarm calls, *weeeeeew, weeeeeew, weeeew … scraghh! scraagh!* These birds live in family groups, so the sound of the collective calling can often be cacophonous. I remember the two-part call of the white-winged chough by thinking of fireworks. The whistle of the firework shooting into the air, then the abrupt crackling or detonation.
WHAT TO LOOK FOR	White-winged choughs are large black birds, much like a raven or currawong, only with a smaller and more curved beak. They have red eyes and a large patch of white on each wing. When seen on the ground (which is often), they will appear to be entirely black, though you may be able to spy a sliver of white at the edge of the folded wing. However, when they are in flight or displaying their wings to one another, you will be able to see these large white spots.
IMMATURE BIRDS	Young white-winged choughs are more brownish overall, have brown eyes, and have no white patch on the wing.
WHAT THEY EAT	Insects and grubs, with some general grazing of seeds.
WHERE TO START LOOKING	I associate choughs with drier, more inland bush, but their range is fairly well spread along the eastern coast, partially extending into the alpine regions. I've seen them in drier suburban areas where enough trees and shrubs are left to provide them cover, and in open bushland (that is, bush with less ground-covering plants; these birds like to peck through leaf litter on the forest floor while feeding and gossiping, so they avoid more dense forests).
SIMILAR BIRDS	Australian raven (*see* page 7, and all other raven species), pied currawong (*see* page 11), apostlebird. You might notice the boisterous, familial behaviour of the apostlebird is similar to that of the white-winged chough (these birds also live in colonies).

LARGE STRONG BEAK

IMMATURE
(less yellow eye)

GREY CURRAWONG
(many variations to plumage make this species hard to distinguish from the pied currawong)

LIGHTER PLUMAGE

VIVID WHITE BARS ON TAIL

WHITE PATCH UNDER TAIL

ADULT
(yellow eye, dark plumage)

Pied currawong

Dawaalam [doh-wah-lum] (Gumbaynggirr);
djiin djiin [djiin djiin ('dj' as in 'danger', 'ii' as
in 'sleep')] (Taungurung)
Strepera graculina

The pied currawong is a familiar sight in suburban areas, but I seem to see them most densely in open bushlands on the slopes of mountains, where they are easily confused with their relative, the grey currawong. Despite their love of mountains, pied currawongs are impressively successful in both urban and bushland areas, whereas many other species of birds are restricted to only one or the other. At campgrounds, currawongs will become comfortable enough with campers to ask, beady eyed, for some of the potato salad. Like the Australian raven (*see* page 7), pied currawongs are renowned for taking eggs or young chicks out of nests when the parents are distracted. These are indeed calculating birds, and sneaky when they want to be. One particularly cheeky currawong visited our well-netted fig tree every day, seemingly to check if the figs were ripe enough. Just when one seemed juicy enough to pick – *bam*, the currawong had snapped it up through the net and had gone on its merry way before we could say fig jam. Suffice it to say – currawongs are perceptive birds that are excellent at judging risk, and are opportunistic to boot. After the terrible bushfire season at the beginning of 2020, we found we had a large influx of pied currawongs arrive in our suburb after they'd been driven out of the Victorian High Country.

Note: Illustrated opposite is also an image of the grey currawong, which is a bird largely restricted to the southernmost regions of Australia, including Tasmania. These birds have quite a different call from the pied currawong, closer to the screech of a bird of prey. However, telling them apart from the pied currawong can prove tricky, as both species have a lot of variation in the colour of their feathers – hearing their call is the best way to identify them.

WHAT TO LISTEN FOR	The call of the pied currawong will be familiar to most of us along the eastern coast. They sing a throaty, cyclical *deww-whee-whup*, or *qwaa-waa, qwadada, quirrup!* Sometimes currawongs make the same noise a cartoon character makes when they slip on a banana peel, *whoop!*, my personal favourite.
WHAT TO LOOK FOR	The pied currawong is a large, predominantly black bird. The tail has a white tip, and a white band where the tail meets the body. It also has two white bands over the middle joint of the wing. The eye is yellow. Females may have plumage that edges more towards grey-brown than black. Females are also slightly smaller than males.
IMMATURE BIRDS	Young pied currawongs are more dilute in colour overall, with a dark eye.
WHERE TO START LOOKING	Pied currawongs are widespread and common. Often parks, picnic areas, campgrounds, gardens with fruit-bearing plants or sportsgrounds are a good place to start looking.
WHAT THEY EAT	Opportunistic feeders, pied currawongs have a diverse diet, taking insects, fruit, scraps, lizards and, like ravens, sometimes (gruesomely) other smaller species of birds and their eggs.
SIMILAR BIRDS	Australian magpie (*see* page 1), Australian raven (*see* page 7, and other species of raven), white-winged chough (*see* page 9).

IMMATURE

BLACK BAND ACROSS EYE

MOTTLED CHIN (BEFORE MASK DEVELOPS)

WHITE-BELLIED CUCKOOSHRIKE (dark morph)

ADULT

BLACK MASK OVER FACE & CHIN

PALER UNDERBELLY

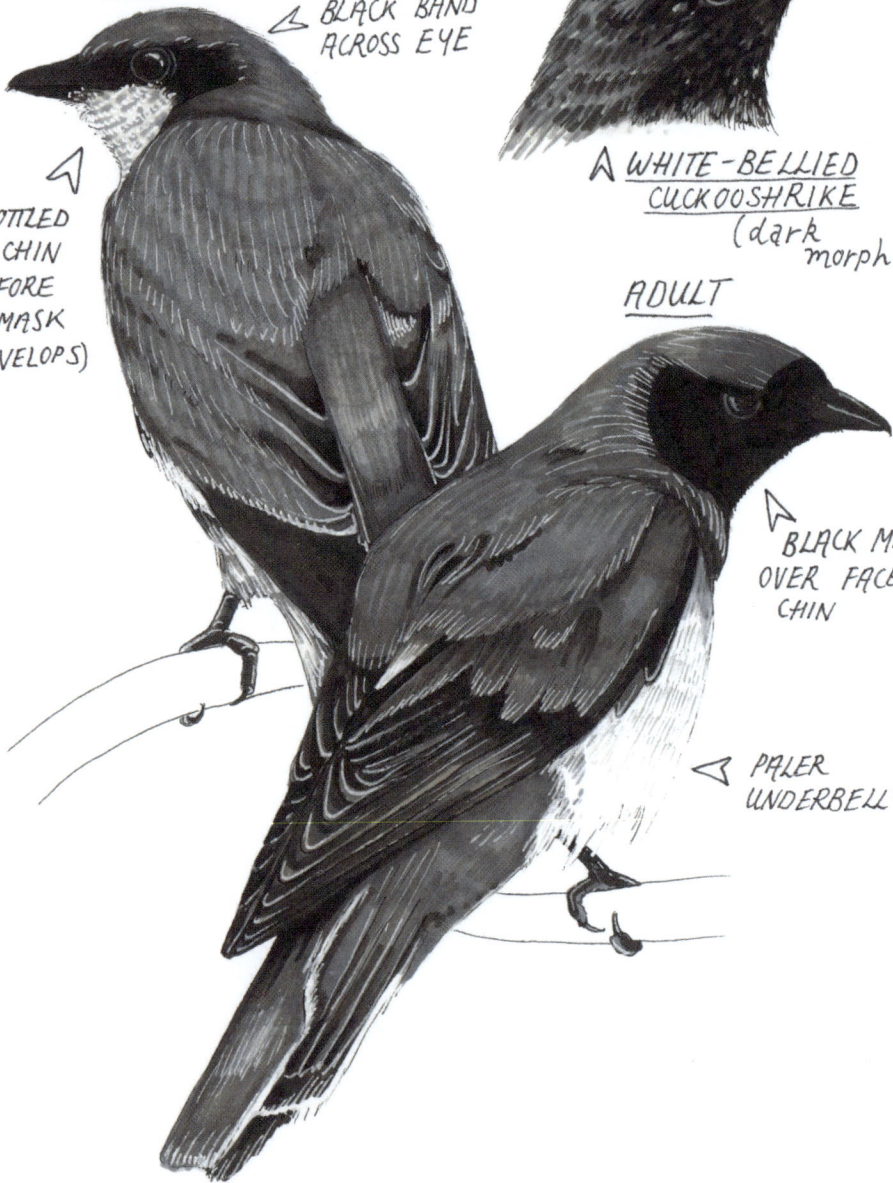

Black-faced cuckooshrike

Djilbi djilbi [djil-bi djil-bi ('dj' as in 'da<u>ng</u>er')]
(Taungurung)
Coracina novaehollandiae

I most often see black-faced cuckooshrikes flying near roads, between the higher branches of gums that still border a lot of Australian highways.. They're distinctive as they are fairly large, and the black face mask is usually visible even when they're flying. When they land at perch, they will often alternately lift each of their wings, left and right, as if 'settling in', earning them the colloquial name 'shufflewing'. Like other insect-eating birds, they like to perch on dead or exposed branches where they can easily spot and swoop down on insects. Their nests are usually a shallow, cup-shaped structure of twigs and spiderwebs, high in the fork of a eucalyptus tree.

WHAT TO LISTEN FOR	Robotic, springy call from the throat, *druwnn-drunn-drun*.
WHAT TO LOOK FOR	The black-faced cuckooshrike is a large grey bird with a black mask. They are mostly grey, with a circular area of black feathers covering their face and beak. The upper section of their chest is grey, while their underbellies are much paler, becoming almost white towards their feet.
IMMATURE BIRDS	Young black-faced cuckooshrikes have a narrow black band across their eyes which will eventually develop into a fully fledged mask. Before the adult feathers develop, they have a paler, more mottled chin.
WHAT THEY EAT	Insects and occasionally fruits.
WHERE TO START LOOKING	Though they venture some way into urban areas, I most often see black-faced cuckooshrikes in dry, open bushland, often perched in taller eucalypts growing along the edges of roads, or flying between windbreaks on farmland.
SIMILAR BIRDS	Cicadabird (a smaller bird, darker overall, with a similar body shape), pied currawong (*see* page 11), grey currawong (pictured on page 10) and white-bellied cuckooshrike (pictured opposite). The white-bellied cuckooshrike is the most likely to trip you up, especially as there are a few different 'morphs' of this similar-looking bird. Pictured opposite is the 'dark morph', which resembles the adult black-faced cuckooshrike. There is also a 'light morph', which very closely resembles the *immature* black-faced cuckooshrike. To help you identify it, in all forms of the white-bellied cuckooshrike, the black areas of feathers are less cleanly defined than in the black-faced cuckooshrike.

IMMATURE
(note rusty
patch over eye)

TILTS HEAD TO
GET A BETTER LOOK

'RUST'
PATCH ▷

STREAKED
CHEST

FEMALES
HAVE A DULLER
CHEEK PATCH
& PALE STRIP
ALONG SIDES
OF THE BEAK

MALES
HAVE A
MORE
VIVID
WHITE CHEEK
PATCH &
DARK BEAK

Grey shrike-thrush

Yurung [yu-ru-ng] (Wiradjuri); **baledmum** [ba-led-mum] (Taungurung)
Colluricincla harmonica

My parents call this bird the Australian songthrush or Australian thrush, so you may encounter others who still use these names. As the grey shrike-thrush often moves by hopping between branches rather than flying longer distances, the initial impression one might gain of these birds is that they are shy. But despite being stealthy birds, they are actually quite inquisitive, hopping along trails to observe you, or staying just ahead by flying from tree to tree. Their beady dark eye seems very analytical as they follow your progress down a trail. I think of them as the pied pipers of the bush, singing from afar, coaxing you along as you walk. This impression is helped by their incredible song, which carries a long way through the bush. I have heard stories of them flying into rural homes to perch on the furniture (though this inquisitiveness is more likely to be common among bold juvenile birds, or birds that have been fed regularly and are desensitised to human contact).

WHAT TO LISTEN FOR	I think the song of the grey shrike-thrush has to be one of the most beautiful bird calls I've heard. Their song is similar to that of the golden whistler (*see* page 65) and rufous whistler (*see* page 63), though the cadence is different. Their voice is deeper and more guttural, verging on electronic, but still resonant and bell-like in its clarity. It gives a call that makes me think of a sneeze: two 'build-up' calls before a more throaty yet beautiful whip-like run of whistles. *Aaaah-aaah … woo-whip-whoo-wing!* It's a song that you'll grow familiar with quickly if you start listening out for it in the bush.
WHAT TO LOOK FOR	The grey shrike-thrush has an appearance so unassuming it belies its spectacular song. They are a similar size to a magpie-lark, and are largely grey with pale underbellies. They have dark, scrutinising eyes in profile and a pale patch between the eye and the beak. There is also a patch of rust colour over the shoulders of the birds. Males and females look largely the same, which seems to sometimes go hand in hand with birds who have beautiful songs. (Sometimes it's not about how you look, but how well you can perform a complex set of whistles.) If you get a really good look at a pair of grey shrike-thrushes, you may notice <u>females</u> have a duller 'white patch' than the males, and have white sides to their beak.
IMMATURE BIRDS	Young grey shrike-thrushes have a patch of rust colour over their eye and some dark streaks on their chest.
WHERE TO START LOOKING	Try looking for them in open bushland, less dense rainforest and well-treed outer suburbs. Grey shrike-thrushes are successful in most regions, though they are well-camouflaged in most Australian habitats, so you need to be very diligent to spot one. They sometimes venture into gardens that are adjacent to bush reserves or parkland, but they usually stick to native, established vegetation in less urban areas. Windbreaks on farmland are also a good place to look out for them.
WHAT THEY EAT	Insects, frogs, lizards and other small critters.
SIMILAR BIRDS	Crested bellbird (dry, inland areas of Australia), little shrike-thrush (north and north-east coastlines), female golden whistler (*see* page 65) and rufous whistler (*see* page 63) – these whistlers are also plain, grey perching birds, and I often confuse them with the grey shrike-thrush.

WAGS TAIL
SIDE TO SIDE

WHITE
EYEBROWS

BLACK WINGS,
BACK &
HEAD

WHITE
UNDERBELLY

NESTS
ARE WOVEN OUT OF
TWIGS, FUR, GRASS,
SPIDERWEBS & MUD

Willie wagtail

Ganyjarr-ganyjarr [gun-jar-gun-jar]
(Gumbaynggirr); **djirri djirri** [djirr-i djirr-i
('dj' as in 'da<u>ng</u>er')] (Taungurung)
Rhipidura leucophrys

The willie wagtail is so named because, when perched, it regularly 'wags' its tail from one side to the other. These birds will fly in short, looping turns to catch insects, returning to perch and wag side-to-side again, as if feeling satisfied at having caught such an excellent meal. I often see willie wagtails alone or with a single partner grazing from fencelines or on the ground alongside jacky winters, grey fantails (*see* page 19), yellow-rumped thornbills (*see* page 41) or house sparrows (*see* Introduced species in the appendix, page 208). Despite hanging out with other species with equanimity, the willie wagtail defends its nesting area fiercely, especially against larger birds such as the Australian magpie (*see* page 1) or the Australian raven (*see* page 7). The nests of willie wagtails are crucible-shaped, densely woven with fine twigs and threaded with spiderwebs.

WHAT TO LISTEN FOR	The willie wagtail has a piercing, trickling song, *deww-dewwit dew*. It gives a hoarse, scratchy alarm call when its territory is intruded.
WHAT TO LOOK FOR	Willie wagtails are small black and white birds with long tails and are usually seen on fencelines or feeding on the ground. Adult birds have a glossy black back, upper breast and tail. The belly is a crisp white. Above the eye there is a distinctive white eyebrow, and, if you look closely, you may be able to spot whiskers at the base of the beak.
IMMATURE BIRDS	Young willie wagtails look similar to adults – look for a rusty-brown tinge to wingtips and throughout black feathers (these will darken with age as the adult plumage develops).
WHERE TO START LOOKING	Willie wagtails are widespread, and can most often be found at 'edges' (edges of bushland reserves, agricultural regions, parklands, shrubs on nature strips – strips of habitat where there are both places to hide and open areas for feeding in close proximity). The place I see them most often is along gravel roads and fencelines on the edges of farmland, though you may have luck at your local park or creek.
WHAT THEY EAT	Insects.
SIMILAR BIRDS	Magpie-lark (*see* page 3), grey fantail (*see* page 19), white-winged triller (pictured on page 2).

RUFOUS
FANTAIL
(note red
brow)

OFTEN FANS
TAIL AT
PERCH

WHITE
EYEBROWS

HOLDS WINGS
SLIGHTLY AWAY
FROM BODY AT
PERCH

TAIL
LOOKS NARROW
WHEN FOLDED

VIVID
WHITE CHIN
STRAP

Grey fantail

Rhipidura albiscapa

Grey fantails are always in motion, flitting in looping circles from their perch, into the air and back again, or switching their position along a branch. They're acrobatic in their pursuit of insects – if you watch them long enough, you will be able to see them spinning rapid u-turns in midair while chasing a snack. They have a peculiar, twirling way of flying, almost moth-like (an effect that is magnified by their elongated tail). They're often identifiable by their posture on branches – their wings, when folded against their sides, hang down below their body, making them look like they're ready to swan dive off their branch. Otherwise, the 'fanning' tail is a giveaway.

Lovely as they are, I consider grey fantails to be the bane of my birdwatching ventures. On many an occasion, a grey fantail, caught at a strange angle in an unusual light, has somehow looked like an unfamiliar beauty of the tropics rather than the widespread and common bird it truly is. However, these energetic birds are always worth observing, especially when they are skilfully pursuing insects in the forest canopy.

WHAT TO LISTEN FOR	A series of glassy, twinkling squeaks, rising in pitch, *yip-yippity-yipyup-yup!*
WHAT TO LOOK FOR	Grey fantails are small grey birds that are often seen looping through the air, or fanning their tail feathers when at perch. They have grey backs, with a white-tipped tail. Their bellies are pale and they have white 'brows' on their forehead. You may be able to spot small whiskers over their beaks and a distinctive white strap under their chin.
IMMATURE BIRDS	Young grey fantails look much like adults, but are greyer overall with more dilute colouring and have 'fluffier' feathers on their bellies.
WHERE TO START LOOKING	Try looking in dense suburban hedges or shrubs, trees and bushes planted along farmland or park edges, along fencelines, in tree canopies and circling from branches over creeks and streams. Grey fantails are equally happy in denser areas of bushland but will remain in the higher sections of trees, where they can still swoop in on small gnats and bugs.
WHAT THEY EAT	Insects.
SIMILAR BIRDS	Willie wagtail (*see* page 17), rufous fantail (pictured opposite), Arafura fantail (north-west coast of Australia), superb fairywren (*see* page 67).

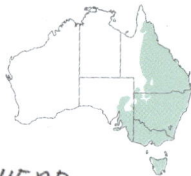

ADULT

BELL MINER

BLACK MARKINGS OVER FACE & NECK

ADULT HEAD FROM SIDE

PALE GREY UNDERBELLY

IMMATURE

LESS DEFINED MARKINGS ON FACE & NECK

OLIVE PATCH ON WING

Noisy miner

Manorina melanocephala

Noisy miners are common, shrewd and highly aggressive birds. I was once chased by a noisy miner along the edge of Princes Park in Melbourne (for about thirty metres, I ran like Usain Bolt – they are scary birds!). As noisy miners live in small colonies, several of these birds can 'gang up' and readily chase off other species from an area. (As I write this at my desk, I can hear two noisy miners chasing a magpie-lark on my front lawn. They are relentless.) These noisy bullies thrive in 'edges', where habitats bump against one another or cross over (e.g. the edges of parkland, stands of trees along the edges of highways and paddocks, or the remnant native trees in your backyard). As a result, noisy miners have proven to be incredibly successful in many suburban gardens, thwarting the progress of birds that would otherwise thrive in urban parks and nature reserves.

These birds love to feed on nectar when trees are in flower, but often feed on lerp as well. Lerp is the sugary cap made by the larvae of certain psyllid insects, and it is usually seen forming on the branches and leaves of native trees. These sweet structures serve as a little 'house' in which the psyllid larvae grow whilst happily feeding on tree sap. These sugar 'houses', if eaten, make for a tasty, high-energy snack for some of Australia's native birdlife. The sugary lerp is an excellent alternative source of energy to nectar, particularly when few species of plants are in flower. To read more about the ways Australian birds use (and abuse) lerp, see the 'Did you know' box on page 23.

While these forceful and brutish birds are extremely successful in areas along the edges of parks and in suburban gardens, noisy miners seem less able to dominate sections of denser bushland, making national parks, state parks and nature reserves all the more important for sustaining a diversity of bird species in Australia.

WHAT TO LISTEN FOR

Noisy miners live up to their name. The adult birds give a piercing call of the same note, *trip-trip-trip*, repeated many times. Young birds demand food with a continued *chip-chip-chip-chip*, or yipping. I can't help but feel their call sounds almost petulant, especially having learned how overbearing these birds are.

WHAT TO LOOK FOR

The noisy miner is a medium-sized grey bird. The head is capped in black, which extends down onto each cheek. The black eye has a distinctive yellow patch behind it, and the beak and legs are also yellow. The wings are a darker grey than the chest and belly, with an olive-yellow section of wing sometimes visible at perch. (One thing to remember when identifying the noisy miner: no other bird I know flies with such stony-faced precision. They open their wings and zoom towards their target unflinchingly, seemingly without a single flap of the wings. They are like little torpedoes, zooming over suburban gardens.)

IMMATURE BIRDS

Young noisy miners are mottled grey, with a faintly yellow eye and beak.

WHAT THEY EAT

Like honeyeaters, noisy miners thrive on flower nectar and fruits, although they are generalists and survive well in a large range of urban habitats. They sometimes feed directly on manna (sugary sap) that 'leaks' from eucalypts. As I mention on page 23, they also love to feed on lerp-infested trees, especially if other food sources are limited.

NOISY
MINER

BELL
MINER

YELLOW-
THROATED
MINER

BLACK-EARED
MINER
(ENDANGERED)

WHERE TO START LOOKING	Noisy miners are common in suburban gardens and parks – any areas with flowering native plants. Keep an ear out for their intense, yipping calls when you're in green suburbs, in the park or passing stands of eucalyptus trees in the countryside, especially if those trees are in flower.
SIMILAR BIRDS	Bell miner (pictured opposite; the bell miner is restricted to the south-eastern coastline; in Melbourne, you can hear bell miners calling around the zoo in Royal Park – their song is decidedly more lovely than the noisy miner, though their aggressive behaviour is similar), yellow-throated miner (pictured opposite; common in drier, inland regions, these birds have less black on their heads), black-eared miner (pictured opposite; this species is confined to a tiny area of mallee at the upper corner of Victoria and South Australia; it is highly endangered).
DID YOU KNOW?	While some birds dominate a territory and strip it of its resources, other birds are much more wily, learning how to play the 'long game' when it comes to food. A close relative of the noisy miner called the bell miner – sometimes colloquially called a 'bellbird' (see picture opposite) – are known for their damaging role as lerp 'farmers'. These birds dominate a territory and exclude birds that would otherwise eat lerp, taking control of this important food resource.
	As described on page 21, lerp is the sugary 'house' that contains growing psyllid larvae on a tree branch or leaf. Most birds will eat both the lerp and the larvae within, slowing the growth of these psyllid colonies over trees. Alas, not the bell miner: it eats the lerp with delicate precision, taking only the sugary cap and leaving the larvae intact underneath. The intact larvae live on to exude another sugary coating, providing ongoing food for the bell miners. The psyllid larvae are gradually able to mature into adult insects, breed, and rapidly colonise the tree, all the while being defended by their 'farming' bell miner supervisors. As these psyllid populations boom, trees die off from the sheer number of psyllid larvae feeding on the tree. In turn, the bell miners to greedily lap up the sugary lerp produced by these cultivated populations, causing significant damage to areas of forest where this feedback loop occurs.

IMMATURE

LESS DEFINED PATCHES ON YOUNG BIRDS

WHITE-CHEEKED HONEYEATER
(note dark eye)

LARGER CHEEK PATCH

WHITE EYE

ADULT

SMALL WHITE CHEEK PATCH

VERY STREAKED CHEST

YELLOW WING PATCH

New Holland honeyeater

Phylidonyris novaehollandiae

New Holland honeyeaters are aggressive little birds who 'hold their own' in areas where flowers are blossoming. They cling acrobatically to bottlebrushes, banksias and grevilleas to drink nectar from the flowers, often in a chirping group. I've seen trees bustling with twenty or more of these honeyeaters, crowding out the flowering plants so thoroughly that the foliage seems to seethe with them. No wonder other small birds can't get in for a sip of nectar! New Hollands will do their best to chase off any other birds from their desired feeding spot, so I often see them scaring away the tiny eastern spinebills from the patch of kangaroo paws in my parents' garden.

WHAT TO LISTEN FOR	Single, brief, whipping *cheep* or *doop-doop*, often repeated monotonously and insistently while feeding. They also perform a rasping 'bark', similar to that of the red wattlebird (*see* page 27), only higher in pitch.
WHAT TO LOOK FOR	The New Holland honeyeater is a black and white bird, around twenty centimetres in length, usually seen feeding in blossoming trees. The belly and chest is white, with black vertical streaks. The black head is framed with a cheek patch, ear patch and a cap of white, giving the overall impression of the bird being mottled black and white, like a little Cruella De Vil of the birding world. The eye has a white ring, and the back is black. There is a yellow panel on the outside of each wing, and a strip of yellow down the tail. The beak is curved, making it easier to feed on nectar from long flowers.
IMMATURE BIRDS	Young New Holland honeyeaters are browner overall, and have a greyish eye instead of white.
WHERE TO START LOOKING	Try keeping an eye out for small black and white birds in heathland, flowering bushland, eucalyptus forests and fruit plantations – any areas with thick, dense flowering shrubs. These birds love areas where flowering trees are abundant, so coastal heathlands and flowering eucalyptus stands are just their kind of paradise.
WHAT THEY EAT	Nectar, and the occasional insect.
SIMILAR BIRDS	White-cheeked honeyeater (pictured opposite; these birds have a larger white cheek patch and a black eye where the New Holland has a small cheek patch and a white eye), white-eared honeyeater (pictured on page 34).

WESTERN
WATTLE-
BIRD

YELLOW
(TASMANIAN)
WATTLEBIRD

BLUE-
FACED
HONEYEATER

IMMATURE

SHARP,
CURVED BEAK
(USEFUL FOR
DRINKING
NECTAR!)

ADULT

NO RED
WATTLE
(WHEN
YOUNG)

RED
WATTLES

YELLOW
BELLY

LESS
YELLOW ON
BELLY

WHITE-TIPPED
TAIL

WHITE PANEL
OVER FACE

ADULT

RED
WATTLES

LAYERED
BROWN-GREY
FEATHERS

Red wattlebird

Dhalarug [dha-la-rug] (Wiradjuri); **yanggak** [yang-gak ('ng' as in 'si_ng_')] (Taungurung)
Anthochaera caranculata

Red wattlebirds are common, aggressive honeyeaters that chase smaller birds out of their territory so they can claim the local nectar-producing trees as their own. In a flowering garden, the red wattlebirds will inevitably move in and swoop on other smaller birds until the territory is firmly claimed and the smaller birds are forced to feed elsewhere. They are so fiercely territorial that they almost inevitably become the rulers of the 'nectar-economy'. I can't help but view red wattlebirds as the bushland equivalent of a 'fast food chain', forcing the smaller 'traders' (smaller birds) to go elsewhere. The territorial ambitions of the red wattlebird will occasionally bring it to blows with bigger birds like the Australian magpie or the laughing kookaburra, which results in a noisy, feathery clash of the titans. Sometimes I spot them in large flocks, moving between trees as they make their way through neighbouring suburbs.

WHAT TO LISTEN FOR	Red wattlebirds make a barking *charck!* They usually squawk their smoky-cough call in the wee hours of the morning. Imagine the bird version of Lil Jon in Usher's track *Yeah!* (2004): *Yeeeahhh!* Another sound to listen for is their rattling alarm call, which sounds like someone shaking a box of matches. You can often hear the sharp 'clack' of their beaks as they chase insects, smaller birds or one another.
WHAT TO LOOK FOR	Red wattlebirds are big, bossy honeyeaters, about the length of the Australian magpie (*see* page 1) but much more 'slender'. They have a red flap on each cheek, which are the 'wattles' from which their name comes. There is also a white patch on each cheek, framed by darker brown feathers. The body is brown-grey, with a paler underbelly that is patterned with white streaks. There is also a small patch of yellow feathers between the legs. The tail of the red wattlebird is long and brown-grey with a white tip.
IMMATURE BIRDS	The young red wattlebirds are smaller and a slightly darker grey, with either a tiny or non-existent red 'wattle' and a less yellow underbelly.
WHERE TO START LOOKING	The red wattlebird lives in most coastal bushland habitats, but in particular wins out over other birds in the suburbs, dominating the scene in urbanised areas with well-planted gardens. If you know of a nearby area with plenty of grevilleas, bottlebrushes, kangaroo paws or similar flowering natives, you're likely to see a wattlebird there.
WHAT DO THEY EAT	Like all honeyeaters, red wattlebirds love to drink nectar from flowers, but they are opportunistic feeders too, eating fruit and insects to supplement their diets.
SIMILAR BIRDS	Female Australasian figbird (*see* page 31), olive-backed oriole (*see* page 33), noisy friarbird (*see* page 29), little wattlebird (south-eastern and eastern coastlines). Two other forms of wattlebird are also pictured opposite. The first is the western wattlebird, found only in south-west Western Australia; it is smaller than the red wattlebird and has no visible flaps on its cheeks. The second is the yellow wattlebird, which is found in Tasmania; it is larger than the red wattlebird and, as the name suggests, has yellow cheek flaps ('wattles'). Also pictured opposite is the blue-faced honeyeater, a comparably-sized bird that hangs out in similar environments to the red wattlebird (along the eastern and northern coast of Australia). The Gumbaynggirr name for the blue-faced honeyeater is **Gawang** [go-wung].

'NOTCH'   CAPPED HEAD

ADULT

LITTLE
FRIARBIRD

A smaller
slightly
browner
birds

LONGER
FEATHERS
ON NECK

IMMATURE

FACE ONLY
PARTIALLY
MASKED

YELLOWISH
IN SOME AREAS
(no white neck
feathers)

Noisy friarbird

Galguna [gul-goo-nah] (Gumbaynggirr); **galguraa** [ga-l-gu-raa], **babala** [ba-ba-la] (Wiradjuri)

Philemon corniculatus

The noisy friarbird is also known as a 'leatherhead', a testament to the Batman-esque mask that covers their head and beak. They're similar to red wattlebirds – and Batman – in their aggression and precociousness regarding territory, though I find these similar birds rarely cross territories with one another. From below, the uniquely sharp beak and pale breast of the noisy friarbird can be very hard to distinguish from that of the red wattlebird, so take a few extra moments to be sure of which bird you're seeing! I mostly see friarbirds feeding in high sections of the canopy, but they are very mobile and will head anywhere in pursuit of food. The combination of leathery head, fluffy collar and piercing eyes makes me think of the noisy friarbird as a kind of Argus Filch character – a bit dishevelled, grumpy and over-defensive of the nearby flowering trees. When not feeding, the noisy friarbird often remains at perch on a high branch, constantly scanning its surrounds, and making its frog-ish, guttural call.

WHAT TO LISTEN FOR	A call that is kind of like a guttural record scratch, a froggy squawking that goes back and forth, *waagagga-wuhh, waagagga-wuhh*. Imagine a DJ who loves to scrub and has had too many coffees before hitting the deck. Now hybridise that with the clucking of a domestic chicken. There, you have it! The call of the noisy friarbird.
WHAT TO LOOK FOR	The noisy friarbird is a medium-sized black-headed bird that could – at first glance – be mistaken for a red wattlebird. These birds are largely grey-brown, with a pale underbelly. The legs are black, and the head is masked in a waxy-looking black 'cap', encompassing the head and the sharp, dagger-like beak. Their entire heads are bald – hence the name 'friar' (friars sometimes remove the upper portion of their hair as a symbol of religious devotion). The base of the underbelly, where it meets the tail, is nearly white, and the base of the neck is fluffy white, like the collar on a fur coat.
IMMATURE BIRDS	Young noisy friarbirds have a brown eye (where adults have a red iris), and are a tawnier colour overall, with a less developed black 'cap'.
WHERE TO START LOOKING	The noisy friarbird, like the red wattlebird, loves to frequent areas with a good density of flowering plants. They are less common than red wattlebirds, and more often seen in 'bushier' urban areas, as well as picnic grounds, parks, campgrounds and thicker gardens in the suburbs.
WHAT DO THEY EAT	As another member of the honeyeater group, noisy friarbirds love nectar and fruits, supplementing with insects and lerp (*see* noisy miner, page 21, if you want to learn more about lerp).
SIMILAR BIRDS	Little friarbird (pictured opposite; eastern and northern Australia), helmeted friarbird (northern coastlines), silver-crowned friarbird (northern Australia), red wattlebird (*see* page 27).

♂

RED AROUND
EYE

BLACK
CAP

PALER
UNDERBELLY

YELLOW
UNDERBELLY

PALER
FEATHERS ON
UNDERSIDE OF
TAIL

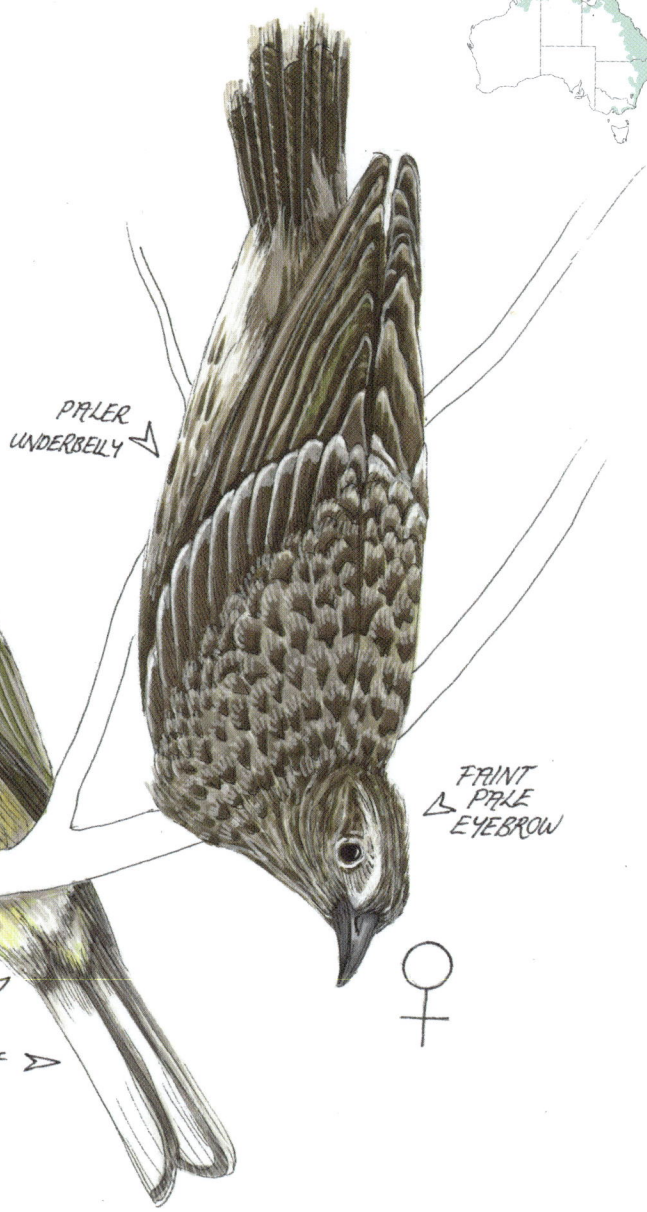

FAINT
PALE
EYEBROW

♀

Australasian figbird

Sphecotheres vieilloti

Australasian figbirds usually sit in the upper canopy of bushland feeding or singing. Several times I have been woken by figbirds in the wee hours of the morning, and happily watched from the window as a pair hopped around in our ornamental fig tree. (Nothing like a good birdwatching session in your pyjamas!) The male figbird was mostly impersonating the Australian magpie (*see* page 1; a species that is both common and very vocal), though I imagine they imitate a large range of birds. The male birds often find a nice high perch from which to sing out their impressions of other species, which can sound almost like someone tuning between radio stations (albeit radio stations that play exclusively Australian bird songs). Australasian figbirds tend to cruise in mating pairs or in small flocks, migrating southwards over the warmer months, following the fruiting seasons of trees. As the weather cools, they retreat north again, wherever the call of figs takes them.

WHAT TO LISTEN FOR	The Australasian figbird is an excellent mimic, so discerning their own call among the flurry of other birds they imitate can be tricky. However, they often intersperse impersonations with a double pulse of a metallic, raspy *chew-dupp, a-choo-dupp*, or a single sharp *dyipp!*
WHAT TO LOOK FOR	The Australasian figbird is similar in size and shape to the red wattlebird (*see* page 27), but is a dimorphic species, so the male and female birds look quite different. <u>Males</u> have a yellow-green underbelly and wings, with black outer wing edges. The head is cloaked in black, and the eye is surrounded by a ring of red. The lowest part of the belly and the underside of the tail is white. <u>Females</u> have a dark eye, and beautiful vertical brown-olive streaks against the cream underbelly (patterning very reminiscent of the red wattlebird, *see* page 27). The back body and head is olive-brown.
IMMATURE BIRDS	Young Australasian figbirds are very similar in appearance to the adult females.
WHERE TO START LOOKING	These birds hang out on the edges of areas with plenty of fruiting trees. This may include well-tended gardens, rainforest, the edges of denser bushland, parks and river edges. If you know of an area in a bush reserve or along a waterway near you, or any area with fruiting trees, try heading there.
WHAT THEY EAT	Mostly fruit, especially figs!
SIMILAR BIRDS	Olive-backed oriole (*see* page 33), red wattlebird (*see* page 27), noisy friarbird (*see* page 29).

ADULT

GREEN
CATBIRD ▷

ORANGE
BEAK &
EYE

STREAKY
PALE
BELLY ▷

OLIVE-GREEN
BACK

IMMATURE

BROWN
BACK

BROWN
BEAK
& EYE

LIGHTER
STREAKS
ON BELLY

Olive-backed oriole

Oriolus sagittatus

The olive-backed oriole is a common but quiet bird that is usually seen feeding in forest canopies. These birds tend to linger on the higher branches of trees in bushland, calling from a relatively hidden spot, usually alone or in a pair. Despite these birds usually being shy, I have encountered one olive-backed oriole that stuck very close to me as I moved along a trail in Taungurung Country on Mt Buffalo. This bold oriole flew to nearby branches, looking at me and twisting its head inquisitively at the sound of the camera shutter. (Though, on reflection, this particular bird may have grown familiar with regular campers heading through that area of bushland.)

These birds are widespread along the northern and eastern coastlines; however, it took me a while to associate their peculiar *orr-rhee-ohl* call with the actual bird making the noise! Once you've made the association between the oriole's song and the bird itself, I'm sure you'll have the patience to stick around under one of their trees long enough to spot one as it hops elusively through the upper canopy.

WHAT TO LISTEN FOR	The call of the olive-backed oriole reminds me of a currawong call – the same throaty, descending 'trickle', making a warbling three notes, *ohh-rhee-ohl*. The tone of the call is reminiscent of water being poured into a glass.
WHAT TO LOOK FOR	Olive-backed orioles are medium-sized green and cream–coloured birds that, like the Australasian figbird (*see* page 31) and noisy friarbird (*see* page 29), may initially be mistaken for a red wattlebird (*see* page 27). They have a red eye and orange beak, which contrasts strongly with their rich green backs. Their bellies are creamy white, with dark streaks that intensify at the front of the neck. Their wings are dark, as are their tail feathers.
IMMATURE BIRDS	Young olive-backed orioles have more dilute patterning overall and are more brown than green.
WHAT THEY EAT	Fruit and insects.
WHERE TO START LOOKING	Bushland, rainforest, denser gardens in outer suburbs, trees on golf courses, at lake edges and other similarly 'vegetated' areas. Like the Australasian figbird (*see* page 31), these birds love to feed on fruit, so try looking for them in areas where you know trees are bearing berries or other small fruits.
SIMILAR BIRDS	Green (or 'yellow') oriole (has a green underbelly and is restricted to the northernmost sections of Australia), Australasian figbird (*see* page 31), female satin bowerbird (*see* page 149), green catbird (pictured opposite and on page 150; found in the midsection of the eastern coast).

WHITE-EARED
HONEYEATER

YELLOW-FACED
HONEYEATER

YELLOW BAR
BENEATH EYE

YELLOW
CHEEK
PATCH

ADULT

OLIVE-
BROWN
BACK &
TAIL

IMMATURE

LESS VIVID
CHEEK
PATCH
AND NO
BAR BENEATH
EYE

GREY
UNDERBELLY

Lewin's honeyeater

Meliphaga lewinii

Lewin's honeyeaters are common along the east coast, where they forage and nest in denser areas of undisturbed bushland. I have only seen Lewin's honeyeaters foraging alone, but I have heard of bushwalkers seeing them in large groups, descending on fruiting trees to feed as flocks. When breeding, they build a bowl-like nest of twigs and vegetation that is 'messy' beneath but has a densely woven interior, which they carefully line with spiderwebs, downy feathers and other forest debris to make a cosy spot for brooding eggs.

The name 'Lewin's' is a reference to the British artist John Lewin, who illustrated many nature publications relating to Australia in the early 1800s. In his own illustration of the bird that would later carry his name, he labelled it a 'yellow-eared honeysucker', a less dainty name, but perhaps one more appropriate for these sugar-feasting birds.

WHAT TO LISTEN FOR	The Lewin's honeyeater gives a 'machine gun' call – a long, rapid-fire *dewwwwrrrrrrrrrr!*, like an extended rolled 'r', or a cat's purr.
WHAT TO LOOK FOR	The Lewin's honeyeater is a medium to large honeyeater with an olive-brown back and a distinctive yellow crescent moon on its cheek. This patch of yellow is accompanied by a horizontal streak of yellow under the eye. The rest of the face is dark brown, nearly black, while the wing feathers and tail are closer to brown-olive in colour.
IMMATURE BIRDS	Young Lewin's honeyeaters are greyer, with a higher 'fluff factor'. The 'dash' beneath the eye is nearly invisible and they have a less developed yellow crescent on the cheek.
WHERE TO START LOOKING	Bushland, areas with flowering or fruiting trees, especially coastal bushland and heath. They prefer denser forests and areas that have had recent rain or with water access.
WHAT THEY EAT	Primarily fruit and nectar, and some insects.
SIMILAR BIRDS	Graceful honeyeater (restricted to far northern Queensland), yellow-spotted honeyeater (restricted to far northern Queensland), white-eared honeyeater (pictured opposite; southern and eastern coastlines of Australia), yellow-faced honeyeater (pictured opposite; eastern Australia).

WESTERN SPINEBILL
(RESTRICTED TO WA) ♂

GREY BACK

ORANGE CHIN (WRAPS AROUND WHOLE NECK)

IMMATURE

ENTIRELY YELLOW CHIN & BELLY

♂

RED EYE

GREYER CROWN & LESS DEFINED CHIN PATCH ♀

LONG BEAK

DARK CHIN PATCH

WHITE COLLAR

DARK BACK & TAIL

TAWNY UNDERSIDE

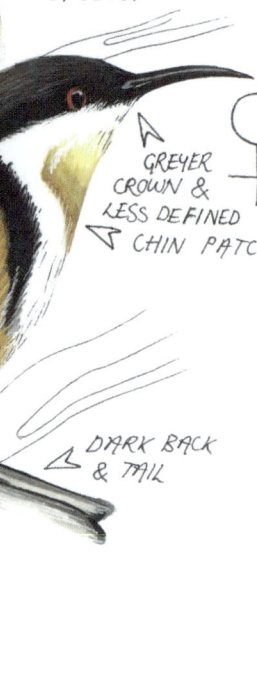

Eastern spinebill

Acanthorhynchus tenuirostris

Eastern spinebills are agile, fast-flitting honeyeaters. They will pop out of cover to drink nectar from bell-shaped flowers, especially correas, kangaroo paws and grevilleas. They delicately siphon the nectar out using their long beaks, lapping up sugary syrup from the flowers. Between these drinks, they zip back into cover. These birds are very wary, as they're often chased away by larger honeyeaters, such as the New Holland honeyeater (*see* page 25), and the red wattlebird (*see* page 27). The spinebills are never in the open for very long, so you'll need to be quick with your binoculars to spot these beauties.

If you're lucky and manage to get a close look at a spinebill as they feed, sometimes you can spot a 'milk moustache' of pollen at the base of the beak. This pollen is deposited there as the bird reaches its beak into flowers to feed. As the spinebill feeds, it inevitably brushes against the anthers (the tip of the 'antennae-like' parts of a flower, where the pollen sits). By carrying this deposited pollen between flowers as they feed, these birds actually transfer pollen between plants, fertilising them as they move from one plant to another, and enabling them to reproduce, in the same manner as bees. This beneficial process of 'blind' pollination is performed by many other nectar-drinking birds in Australia. To the benefit of many plants, there are lots of pollen-covered beaks out there!

WHAT TO LISTEN FOR	A rapid, 'panicked' whistle, *wii–wii–wii–wii*, reminiscent of the call of the white-throated treecreeper (*see* page 205). Almost as often as I hear the spinebill singing, I hear the distinctive 'purr' of their rapidly flapping wings as they fly between plants.
WHAT TO LOOK FOR	Eastern spinebills are tiny, ochre-coloured honeyeaters, their most notable feature being their needle-like beak, long and curved, which allows them to drink nectar from narrow flowers. Male spinebills have waxy-black coloured heads. The chin is white, with a splotch of mustard-brown and black feathers in the middle, like a goatee. The females have a greyer head, with a paler 'goatee'. Both males and females have creamy orange underbellies, with two prongs of black feathers extending down from the shoulders onto the chest. Their backs are orange-brown and their wings black. The tail is dark, with some white feathers that are much more visible in flight than when these jumpy birds are at perch.
IMMATURE BIRDS	Young eastern spinebills have no prongs of black on their chest, and don't have a 'goatee'. Overall, they are much more muted in colour.
WHAT THEY EAT	Flower nectar – they only take the occasional bug when hard pressed for other food options.
WHERE TO START LOOKING	Spinebills stick to areas where they can dive into shrubs and bushes to hide between hurried feeding sessions. Try keeping an eye out in heathlands, bushland and dense gardens – any areas with plenty of trees that are flowering and laden with nectar. If you have a patch of grevilleas, bottlebrushes or kangaroo paws in your garden, try keeping a close eye out there.
SIMILAR BIRDS	New Holland honeyeater (*see* page 25, they share the same diet and have a similar habitat), crescent honeyeater (south-eastern Australia and Tasmania), tawny-crowned honeyeater (southern Australia). Also pictured opposite is the western spinebill (*Acanthorhynchus superciliosis*), found only in Noongar Country in south-western Western Australia. The western spinebill is similar in its habits to the eastern spinebill but is much more limited in its range.

YELLOW
WHITE-EYE

YELLOWER
BODY

OLIVE-
GREEN
HEAD

GREY
WINGS

SLIGHTLY
PINK - GREY
BELLY

WHITE
RING AROUND
EYE

Silvereye

Zosterops lateralis

Sometimes known as a 'waxeye' or, in my opinion, the way cooler name, a 'blightbird' (due to their ability to clear out pest insects by feeding on them), silvereyes are stern-looking, pragmatic little birds. They sensibly stay in thick cover, often in a large, gossiping colony, relying on their greenish-grey feathers to camouflage them among the vegetation. With their white eye-rings, they look like they're peering at you through thick spectacles, almost like a librarian glaring at you for speaking too loudly, or dozens of versions of Atticus Finch, chiding you in court for giving false testimony. As silvereyes are busy, speedy little birds, their colourful plumage often makes me think, 'Gosh! I've discovered a new species of bird!' when I first spot them racing around. It usually takes a moment or two to realise what I'm actually looking at. These gossipy little librarians are also found in New Zealand.

WHAT TO LISTEN FOR	Silvereyes usually call in a cacophonous group, making a set of high-pitched, 'tittering' chirps.
WHAT TO LOOK FOR	Silvereyes are tiny birds that are so named because of their white eye-ring. Their body colour varies depending on their geographic location, but the dominant impression is of a tiny, green-grey bird with this striking white eye-ring. The head and outer wings are green, while the back body and the tail are greyish-green. The sides of the body may have a 'blush' of pink. The chin and tail are framed with yellow, though this may be difficult to see consistently on your birdwatching ventures due to the variation in the birds' plumage across the country.
WHERE TO START LOOKING	Denser areas of vegetation, especially along the edges of creeks, ponds or lakes. Coastal heath or sections of bushes and scrub in less populated areas are good places to try. I rarely see them out in the open; instead they seem to hang in thickets of scrub and dense upper canopies, where they can keep away from the prying eyes of predators.
WHAT THEY EAT	Insects, nectar and fruit.
SIMILAR BIRDS	Thornbill species (*see* pages 41 and 51), yellow white-eye (pictured opposite; northern coastlines).

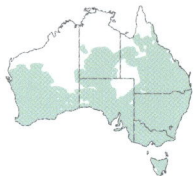

BUFF-RUMPED
THORNBILL
(note rust-coloured
face)

DARK
STRIP OVER
EYE

FOREHEAD
COVERED
WITH PALE
DOTS

PALE
UNDERBELLY

YELLOW
RUMP

Yellow-rumped thornbill

Acanthiza chrysorrhoa

Despite being tiny, defenceless birds, yellow-rumped thornbills seem quite happy grazing out in the open where there is sparse cover. They are very chatty and often tousle one another, engaging in tiny, chattering 'domestic feuds'. If surprised, they will flutter off in a flock to an area of cover – usually a nearby tree. They prove pretty hard to track with a camera or binoculars, as they perch for mere milliseconds before darting off to their next position. Sometimes it pays to stick around at a patch of noisy scrub and train your binoculars at it until something hops within range of your lenses. Usually I will see the 'wink' of a yellow rump among the flock that will clue me into taking a closer look.

WHAT TO LISTEN FOR	A loud, repetitive squeak, like two pieces of styrofoam being rubbed together. These birds live in large colonies, so you'll likely be able to hear them as a whole flock, squeaking and trilling.
WHAT TO LOOK FOR	Yellow-rumped thornbills are tiny pale brown birds (around ten centimetres long). Like the other thornbills (e.g. the brown thornbill, *see* page 51), they have round bodies with pale chest feathers. They have a dark strip over their tiny eye, and a dark forehead covered with pale dots. Their wings and tail are dark grey, leading down to a white tip. At the base of the tail (where the tail meets the body) there is a yellow patch – the nominal 'rump'. This patch is visible from certain angles when they are perched, but is most apparent when they fly in short bursts.
WHERE TO START LOOKING	I've mostly seen yellow-rumped thornbills on the edges of farmland, hanging as a small flock on the grassy verge of a country road, or perching on fence wires. Try heading along the edges of agricultural fields, outer suburbs, grassy paddocks, lawns and along fencelines where bushland meets farmland.
WHAT THEY EAT	Small insects and grubs.
SIMILAR BIRDS	Brown thornbill (*see* page 51), yellow thornbill (eastern Australia), striated thornbill (pictured on page 50). The most likely bird to trip you up is the buff-rumped thornbill (pictured opposite), which also has a range along the east coast, and has a similar yellow rump patch. However, the buff-rumped thornbill has a large rusty spot on its forehead where the yellow-rumped thornbill has a dark head with white spots.

WESTERN
YELLOW ROBIN

ADULT

GREY
CHIN

YELLOW
BELLY
STARTS
LOWER

WHOLE
BELLY IS
YELLOW

YELLOW
PARTIALLY
EXTENDS ON
TO RUMP

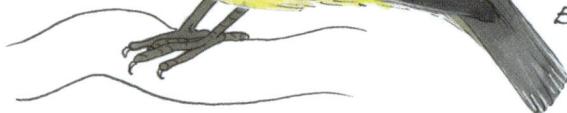

IMMATURE

WHITE
DOTTING ON
WINGS

MOTTLED
UNDERBELLY

Eastern yellow robin

Madaan [mah-darn] (Gumbaynggirr)
Eopsaltria australis

The eastern yellow robin is an inquisitive bird. It is usually seen solo, or in a mating pair that forages through the same section of bushland. It habitually swoops overhead to perch sideways on a vertical tree trunk, where it can get a look at whoever is walking past, twisting its head, beady-eyed. While other robins will happily perch on bare branches to puff up their breast, the eastern yellow robin is the only species I know that makes a habit of perching sideways on tree trunks like this. Despite their yellow bellies, they blend into the bush surprisingly well. They make me picture them as tiny film noir detectives, hiding under the canopy to investigate the latest goings-on in the forest. These little grey-backed birds can be hard to spot initially – until they show their yellow belly in a splash of bright colour, usually as they take flight. I hope you get a chance to see these curious little birds – just know they're watching you as much as you're watching them.

WHAT TO LISTEN FOR	A high, clear, piercing *de-deww-deww-deww*, descending in pitch, similar to the white-throated treecreeper (*see* page 205). The other call of the eastern yellow robin is a two-note pulse, usually, *pdeww-pdeww!*
WHAT TO LOOK FOR	The eastern yellow robin is a small grey, round-bodied bird, often seen in the understorey of wet bushland. The back of the bird is slate-grey, with darker wingtips and tail. The underbelly is bright yellow, though this underbelly is often surprisingly well hidden when this bird is at perch. In flight, a pale line runs along the curve of the outstretched wings. Further north on the eastern coast of Australia, the yellow underbelly of these birds is extended, forming a patch below and above the base of the tail in addition to the underbelly. This is particularly visible in flight.
IMMATURE BIRDS	Juvenile eastern yellow robins are chestnut brown with streaky pale feathers over their head and chest.
WHERE TO START LOOKING	Eastern yellow robins are versatile but don't seem to venture very far into urban areas. You'll have better luck in both inland and coastal bushland, rainforests or any thickly treed areas, as they like to stay under the cover of a canopy.
WHAT THEY EAT	Insects and grubs.
SIMILAR BIRDS	Golden whistler (*see* page 65). It should be noted that many female robins are often a similar grey to the back of the eastern yellow robin, so female flame robins (*see* page 45) or rose robins (pictured on page 44) may trip you up. There is also a similar-looking bird, the pale-yellow robin (a bird limited to sections of the New South Wales and Queensland coast). Also pictured opposite is the western yellow robin, which occupies the south-westernmost tip of Western Australia and the southern coastline of South Australia. This bird looks very similar to the eastern yellow robin, but has a greyer upper breast and chin.

ROSE ROBIN (♂)

NO 'LIGHTNING BOLT' ON WINGS

PINK CHEST

SCARLET ROBIN (♂)
(note larger white dot)

'CLEAN' COLLAR

WHITE 'LIGHTNING BOLT' ON WINGS

WHITE DOT ON FOREHEAD

'MESSY' COLLAR

RED-CAPPED ROBIN (♂)
(note red forehead)

FEMALES ARE GREY-BROWN OVER HEAD & WINGS

VERY BRIGHT ORANGE BELLY

PALE BELLY

Flame robin

Barradyal [ba-rra-dyal] (Wiradjuri)
Petroica phoenicea

Also termed 'flame-breasted robins', male flame robins sometimes have 'showdowns' where one male will try to intimidate another male out of claimed territory. I have been lucky enough to see a display like this on Mt Buffalo in Taungurung Country. Back and forth the two males hopped, one retreating while the other approached, daring the other to come forward. They puffed out their little bright chests, back and forth, twittering and showing off. Meanwhile, a female was happily grazing for insects among some nearby grasses, completely uninterested in the whole display. Given the ostentatiously coloured males, complete with a lightning bolt down the wing, I think of these energetic birds as small Ziggy Stardusts, swooping around the Australian bush. The nests they build are densely packed into a cup shape, sometimes interwoven with lichen.

WHAT TO LISTEN FOR	A piercing, high peeping and twittering *dee-dee-dewww, dredredwee!*
WHAT TO LOOK FOR	The flame robin is a small perching bird with a vivid orange chest. Males have a dark grey (almost black) body with jagged white 'lightning bolts' on the wings, as is characteristic of some of the other red robins (scarlet and red-capped robins). The head is also hooded in black, with a small white dot above the base of the beak. From chin to tail, the belly of the males is a bright, almost fluorescent tangerine colour. Females, by contrast, are grey-brown, with darker wings that have the same pale 'lightning bolts' as the male. There is also a pale white spot above the beak that is even smaller than that of the male. The breast is faintly rust-coloured, moving through to plain grey, and becoming increasingly white further towards the tail.
IMMATURE BIRDS	Juvenile flame robins look much like the female birds, but may have more 'rustiness' in their chest feathers.
WHERE TO START LOOKING	I associate flame robins mostly with the Victorian High Country, where, alongside ravens (*see page 7*), they seem to be one of the only birds that readily frequent the sparse snow gums at the tree line. In summer these birds seem to like mountainous, cold country where they can easily swoop in on insects, so if you are within the range shown, head to some nearby hills (to gain some altitude) and see if you have any luck! During winter they usually retreat further 'downhill' to lower altitudes, so you may have more luck at that time of year if you're closer to sea level. I often see them around Ngunnawal Country in Canberra on the low hills, as a fair bit of remnant bush still remains to 'sustain' them between suburbs. Bushland and open forests in higher country (in summer), or open paddocks, grassland, heathland and open bushland (in winter) will be your best bet.
WHAT THEY EAT	Insects.
SIMILAR BIRDS	The scarlet robin (pictured opposite; far south-west Australia and south-east Australia), red-capped robin (pictured opposite; a dweller of more arid, inland regions), pink robin, rose robin (pictured opposite). Both the pink and rose robin have belly colouring that starts lower than that of the flame robins. These robins also do not have the 'lightning bolt' of white down their wings that the flame robin has.

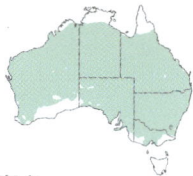

DIAMOND
FIRETAIL

GREY-BROWN
WINGS

♀

ORANGE
BEAK

SPOTTED
TAIL

ORANGE LEGS

MALES HAVE
ORANGE CHEEK
PATCH

♂

ORANGE
DOTTED PANEL
UNDERWING
(ONLY MALES)

GREY
BODY

IMMATURE

'TEARDROP'
ALREADY
VISIBLE

DARK
BEAK

Zebra finch

Muliyiin [mu-li-yii-n] (Wiradjuri)
Taeniopygia guttata

Zebra finches are colonial, usually hanging out in large flocks in dense scrub (e.g. acacia trees) or on the ground near water (e.g. on the banks of a dam). These birds are quite 'chunky' – they are big-beaked, round-bodied little fluff balls that peck rapidly at the ground to pick up seeds, then lift their head to scan their surrounds as they eat. As they feed out in the open, zebra finches will stay very wary of birds of prey, such as harriers (*see* page 189) or falcons (*see* Tails of birds of prey in the appendix, page 209), which may take advantage of their vulnerability while feeding. The groups can become extremely large where water and food is abundant; they will all perch in a tree as a flock, or feed on the ground in a huge, squeaky group.

WHAT TO LISTEN FOR	A high-pitched squeaking, kind of like a toy in the jaws of your enthusiastic dog, *eeeei-eeei*.
WHAT TO LOOK FOR	Zebra finches are small, striking birds and are often seen feeding in low shrubs or on the ground in more arid areas of the country. These birds manage to wear all the offcut material from the sewing box in one set of spectacular plumage. Males are grey-headed, with a bright orange, pyramidal beak (characteristic of finches). They also have two clownish – yet adorable – 'blush' circles on each cheek. The grey head descends in 'zebra' stripes to a creamy belly. The side-body is orange with a white polka-dot pattern. Finally, the tail is black with white horizontal barring. The small eye is reddish, with a black 'teardrop' of feathers descending vertically below the eye. Females are largely grey-brown, with the grey descending onto their chest, lacking the male's 'zebra' barring. The tail is spotted and they have the black 'teardrop', but they lack the other patterning of the males.
IMMATURE BIRDS	Young zebra finches have no patterning and are largely brown-grey with darkening at the wingtips and tail-tip. The beak and legs are brown-black.
WHERE TO START LOOKING	Zebra finches are widespread, excluding the southernmost and northernmost rainforest areas of Australia. They like to feed on drier, open ground where there's plenty of seed, so heading somewhere inland with open ground may prove worthwhile. These birds are also common aviary birds.
WHAT THEY EAT	Primarily seeds, but they may supplement these with various fruit at times. Finches, among a number of other species, were one of the animal groups in which naturalist Charles Darwin studied adaptation in the Galapagos Islands. The very wide, wedge-shaped beak that is characteristic of finches has adapted to make for efficient seed-grazing.
SIMILAR BIRDS	Diamond firetail (pictured opposite; south-eastern Australia), double-barred finch (pictured on page 72; north and eastern Australia), red-browed finch (*see* page 49).

BEAUTIFUL
FIRETAIL

IMMATURE

DARK BEAK
& NO
EYE BAND

RED
RUMP

OLIVE-GREEN
BACK

RED
RUMP

ADULT

RED
BEAK &
EYE BAND

GREY
UNDERBELLY

Red-browed finch

Bunyun [say the 'ny' in the middle as in 'onion': 'boonyoon'] (Gumbaynggirr)
Neochmia temporalis

Red-browed finches are tiny, energetic birds. They're colonial, meaning they hang out together in large groups, often in a dense thicket of vegetation. When breeding season comes around, a male bird will separate from the colony, hauling a long strand of grass as he goes. While this may sound like the beginning of the rose ceremony on *The Bachelor*, it's a little more nuanced (and adorable). The male, having carried off the long piece of grass, will find a nice visible perch on a branch or fence, and bob up and down on the spot, as if to emphasise the excellent grass-grabbing skills it has. The first time I saw this, I imagined the bird was saying something along the lines of: 'Look at this awesome piece of grass I found! I'm gonna build the best nest! Date me!' This display is so outrageously cute that, given the airtime, red-browed finch courtship would give other reality TV shows a run for their money. If you accidentally disturb a crew of red-browed finches, they will all take flight, making the flock look like a blur of winking red butterflies as they move over the ground.

WHAT TO LISTEN FOR	A high-pitched, layered piping, *dyeep-dyeep-dyeep* – often a group calls together.
WHAT TO LOOK FOR	The red-browed finch is a small olive-grey bird with a vivid red eye-band and matching red tail patch. The red beak is small and pyramid-shaped (perfect for seed-snacking!). The head and body are grey, while the back body and wings are olive green. The tail is grey-black. If you watch red-browed finches closely, you will see their brilliant red tail patch showing between their folded wings (this patch sits where the tail meets the body). This rump-patch is very visible as the bird takes flight.
IMMATURE BIRDS	Young red-browed finches are a darker colour overall, less vivid, with no eye-bar and a black beak instead of red.
WHERE TO START LOOKING	Try exploring the edges of bushland, scrub, dense thickets and hedges in bush-neighbouring suburbia. Like zebra finches (*see* page 47), red-browed finches tend to feed on grassy, open ground (always with a nearby bush or tree to duck into for cover when needed) or they hang out in low scrub, gossiping. Tree-lined grassy areas in the gardens of outer suburbs, along scrubby walking trails, golf courses, parklands and picnic areas are good places to start looking. Bushes around dams, the edges of farmland (where there are thickets), or along grassy walking trails in a rainforest are also places where I've encountered these finches.
WHAT THEY EAT	Seeds supplemented with insects and grubs.
SIMILAR BIRDS	Beautiful firetail (pictured opposite; south-eastern coastlines), star finch (Northern Territory, northern Western Australia and northern Queensland), diamond firetail (pictured on page 46), red-eared firetail (restricted to Noongar Country in south-western Western Australia), zebra finch (*see* page 47).

Brown thornbill

Acanthiza pusilla

The brown thornbill hangs out in thickets, singing and bustling around, and generally forages in sections of the canopy where they can grab insects from between the leaves at their leisure. So try keeping your eyes out near low bushes and short, dense trees in bushland – and listen for a lot of squeaking and scolding. When you eventually see a brown thornbill, you'll be struck by how *tiny* it is! But what it lacks in size, it makes up for in character, using song and trilling vocalisations to lure threats away from its nest. Like Tyrion Lannister, the brown thornbill is an oft-overlooked bird, which despite its limited notoriety, is constantly strategising, always using stealth and intelligence to avoid capture, rather than brute force. These birds will often scuttlebutt in a small, twittering colony, speaking to one another across adjacent bushes – they are quite vocal and will often be heard rather than seen. Their nests, like those of other thornbill species, are rounded little caves made of grasses, spiderwebs, twigs and downy feathers. The nests have a 'side' entrance rather than an entry at the top.

WHAT TO LISTEN FOR	These tiny birds alternate between a watery gurgling, harsher throaty cheeps and a clear, whistling *dew-dew-dew-dew-dewww-wo-wo-weeep!* As the call of the brown thornbill is so variable, becoming familiar with the 'tone' of their call may be more helpful in your outings than remembering any particular song.
WHAT TO LOOK FOR	The brown thornbill is a *tiny* brown bird mostly seen (or heard) in dense thickets. Only about ten centimetres long, brown thornbills are grey-brown, with vertical streaks extending down below the beak onto the pale breast, fading towards the belly. The 'forehead' of the brown thornbill has a distinctive rusty-brown 'splotch', which is a great help in distinguishing the species. The underbelly becomes more yellow towards the tail, which has a chestnut brown base.
	Note: As nondescript, small brown birds, brown thornbills are considered (in birdwatching circles) to be members of the 'LBB' club – namely, the 'Little Brown Bird' club (or 'LBJ': 'Little Brown Job'). 'LBB' or 'LBJ' denotes any species that is so brown, plain and small that it proves difficult to identify.
	Most small brown birds you see are likely to be *one* of the thornbills, but *which* one – that is the challenge. The hot tip I have for you in the field is this: carefully observe whether the vertical streaks on the breast extend up to completely surround the eye of the thornbill. If they do, you've likely seen a *striated* thornbill (pictured opposite), a very similar species to the brown thornbill, though they have a yellower belly. If the eye area is a more plain, unpatterned brown, and the streaks begin lower on the chest – it's likely you are looking at a *brown* thornbill. Geographical ranges can help you to narrow the field too – use species maps from this book, other field guides, eBird, or similar websites to assist you.
WHERE TO START LOOKING	Brown thornbills can be found in diverse areas of bushland where enough vegetation is available for cover – wet or dry bushland, rainforests, heathland scrub – and bushes on the edge of rivers or lakes, blackberry thickets, rural gardens and hedges.
WHAT THEY EAT	Insects and small grubs.
SIMILAR BIRDS	All thornbill species, but particularly the striated thornbill (pictured opposite), weebill (another tiny brown bird with a shorter beak, found across most of Australia, excluding Tasmania), white-browed scrubwren (*see* page 53), brown gerygone (east coast).

WHITE 'SHOULDER' ON WINGS

WHITE 'BROWS' FRAMING EYES

SOUTH AUS & WESTERN AUS FORM (DOTTED CHEST)

White-browed scrubwren

Sericornis frontalis

Despite being so tiny, white-browed scrubwrens are fierce birds, hopping and bouncing from place to place in small family units. They are energetic, and urgent in all of their movements, screeching as they duck in and out of the brambles that protect them, chiding one another as they move. In my backyard, a family of white-browed scrubwrens live in the thick tangle of ivy and trumpet vines that covers our fence. Over time, these birds have become more bold, and occasionally I will see them hopping around and perching on the tools we have scattered out the back as they screech out across the yard. These birds are so sassy and demanding in their behaviour, they always make for wonderful birdwatching.

WHAT TO LISTEN FOR

Varied, descending whistles, *dewwww, dewwww*. Its alarm call is a bouncing radio-static screech, a harsh *shreep-shreep-shreep*-ing. If you are near a thicket where white-browed scrubwrens are foraging, you are likely to hear this alarm call.

WHAT TO LOOK FOR

White-browed scrubwrens are small grey-brown birds. Their back is brown-grey, with a black patch on the outer edge of the wings, spotted with white. The underbelly is pale cream. The eyes are yellow with black pupils and are framed above and below with a brightish white 'brow' that makes these tiny birds look quite fierce.

Note: The colours of the white-browed scrubwren can vary markedly in intensity. I have seen white-browed scrubwrens that are a dark, chestnut brown, while at other times, I have come across paler, more grey scrubwrens with fainter brows. Look carefully for the yellow eye, the white spots on the 'shoulder' of the wing, and white brows – if you spot these, this is a good indication you have identified this bold little bird correctly.

WHERE TO START LOOKING

Dense thickets in bushland, garden hedges, blackberry patches, rainforests.

WHAT THEY EAT

Insects and grubs.

SIMILAR BIRDS

Thornbill species (*see* pages 41 and 51), yellow-throated scrubwren (limited range along the eastern coast), white-throated gerygone (a yellower, similarly sized bird of eastern and northern Australia) and the Tasmanian scrubwren, a closely related species that is found only in Tasmania. (The Tasmanian scrubwren has less vivid 'brows' and darker grey-brown plumage.)

FORKED
TAIL

WELCOME
SWALLOWS

FAIRY MARTIN

NO FORKED
TAIL

Welcome swallow

Banggu-bangguginy [bung-goo-bung-goo-giyn] (Gumbaynggirr); **bidjenambul** [bi-djen-am-bul ('dj' as in 'da<u>n</u>ger')] (Taungurung)
Hirundo neoxena

Welcome swallows, like other species of swallows, swifts and martins, are brilliant flyers, moving in acrobatic swoops to catch insects, or to drink from puddles. These birds are such excellent flyers that they will sometimes feed their young in midair, preferring to stay in motion rather than perch. Little flocks of welcome swallows may pause for breath by alighting on nearby fencelines or powerlines, where they can be seen in a contemplative row (this is one of your better chances for identifying these birds – look for a red face and black hood). Due to their almost non-stop flight, these birds are less directly reliant on bushland or vegetated spaces than many other birds. As such, welcome swallows have carved a niche for survival out of the most obscure edges of our urban spaces, building nests of clay and grass in unlikely places – under house gutters, against pylons or metal girders and under concrete bridges.

WHAT TO LISTEN FOR	A rapid clicking and high-pitched chirruping. A keening *dew-deew* is repeated throughout this bird's varied calls, though often welcome swallows are too distant to be heard, or may only be calling as they fly overhead, making their song seem faint or soft. It took me some time to associate the welcome swallow's call with the bird itself.
WHAT TO LOOK FOR	The sight of welcome swallows diving through the air will likely be familiar to most of us. They are tiny, acrobatic flyers, with an obvious forked tail. They also hold their wings in a horseshoe curve as they swoop and dive, making their silhouette in the air quite distinctive. When at perch, their waxy, blue-black head and back body can be clearly observed. This dark 'cap' extends into dark-brownish wings, while the face and throat are red, with a dark eye-mask. The belly is white. The grey beak is small, flat and relatively wide, and when perching, the bird tucks its small head and chin close against the body, giving it a self-satisfied look. These birds often huddle in a little crew on fencelines, where they look relatively nondescript.
IMMATURE BIRDS	Young welcome swallows have a similar appearance to adults, though more dilute in colour and 'fluffier', with a grey downy breast.
WHERE TO START LOOKING	Usually welcome swallows can be seen flying over open ground – especially around wet areas, where insects are likely to be gathered. Try the edges of agricultural land, roadsides, powerlines, fencelines, drainage ditches, ovals and parklands. These birds are common even in urban areas, so with some patience and luck you should be fortunate enough to spot some! You can try focusing your attention to the open sky over areas where there is water – if you see some small birds circling overhead, look closely. There's a good chance they will be welcome swallows.
WHAT THEY EAT	Insects, which they grab from midair – which is why they're often seen near bodies of water, where certain insects are found in greater numbers.
SIMILAR BIRDS	Barn swallows (a less common bird, restricted to northern coastlines), fork-tailed swift (widespread across the continent, it is black-bodied with a white rump patch), tree and fairy martins (pictured opposite), white-throated needletail, white-backed swallow.

♂

MISTLETOE
PATCHES

MALE HAS
VIVID RED
CHIN

BLACK
STRIP ON BELLY

♀

ALMOST CONSTANTLY
FEEDING ON
MISTLETOE FRUITS

BOTH ♂ AND ♀
HAVE A RED PATCH
UNDER TAIL

Mistletoebird

Dicaeum hirundinaceum

Mistletoebirds are so named because of their infatuation with the fruit of the various mistletoe species that grow across Australia. These birds are the muses of ecology teachers, because they give a prime example of symbiosis (the bird benefits the plant, just as the plant benefits the bird). It goes like this: the tiny mistletoebird will eat the dense, sticky seeds of a fruiting mistletoe plant. These seeds pass rapidly through the bird's digestive tract, providing the bird with some nutrition before being pooped out. As a result, the seed is deposited onto whichever branch the mistletoebird happens to be perched on. When the seed is passed by the bird, it is surrounded by a sticky, resinous coating – the combined effects of the seed's defensive covering and the chemical processing of the bird's digestive tract. Thus, once deposited, the mistletoe seed is well equipped to cling onto the branch and force its root-like vasculature into the host tree. Conditions willing, this new mistletoe plant will once again grow into a healthy specimen, flower, then fruit. In turn, a mistletoebird will readily eat this fruit, allowing the cycle to continue. These are active, mobile birds, almost always feeding, so tracking their progress through the canopy can be tricky at times.

WHAT TO LISTEN FOR	Chirruping, a very high pitched *whirrup-whee*.
WHAT TO LOOK FOR	Mistletoebirds are tiny red and black perching birds. <u>Males</u> are black over their head and wings, with a white belly underneath. Along their belly is a strip of black feathers running from their chin towards their tail. The throat of the male mistletoebird is a bright, near-fluorescent red, with an equally bright red patch under the tail. <u>Females</u> are almost entirely grey, with a pale underbelly. Like the males, they have a flash of red on the underside of their tail.
IMMATURE BIRDS	Young mistletoebirds look much like females, though the beak is orange-red where the female beak is grey.
WHERE TO START LOOKING	Mistletoebirds can live wherever there is a dominant stand of older trees, as they rely on the presence of mistletoe for food. Mistletoe is a parasitic plant group, which grows by invading a host tree with its own vasculature (imagine root-like structures invading the branch of another tree). These 'roots' absorb water and nutrients from the host tree, allowing the mistletoe to grow into a slightly odd looking branch, nestled among the 'true' branches of the host tree. If you scan a eucalyptus tree, often you may see an area of leaves that looks darker, more withered or droopier. If you spot one of these patches, it is likely to be mistletoe! Mistletoe develops its own foliage, and is thus able to flower and fruit, all while growing on its host. Mistletoe seems to occur more often in areas where there are bigger, older eucalyptus trees, so these are areas where you're more likely to see mistletoebirds. Try going along the edges of rivers where there are still old-growth native trees, or in windbreaks on farms – any areas where you can spot mistletoe growing is worth a scan with your binoculars.
SIMILAR BIRDS	Flame robin (*see* page 45), red robin (which is larger and rounder bodied), scarlet robin (also larger than the mistletoebird, pictured on page 44), striated and spotted pardalotes (*see* pages 59 and 61 respectively) (if you see a pardalote in silhouette, you might confuse this tiny bird with a mistletoebird as both occupy the upper branches of eucalypts).

CROWN DARK WITH PALE STREAKS

ABOUT 10 cm. LONG

YELLOW ABOVE EYE

TINY RED SHOULDER PATCH

NOTE DOTS ON CROWN & RED ABOVE EYE

RED-BROWED PARDALOTE (NORTHERN AUS & INLAND REGIONS)

Striated pardalote

Jumjulum [joom-jool-oom] (Gumbaynggirr)
Pardalotus striatus

Another name for the striated pardalote is 'pickwick', a testament to their cute vocalisations as they forage. These birds feed on sugary lerp that parasitise eucalyptus leaves. Unlike noisy miners (*see* page 21), pardalotes eat the larvae *inside* lerp as well as the sugary coating, and therefore play an important ecological role by controlling pests in eucalyptus stands. They also frequently use tree hollows for nesting, another reason they are likely to be seen in areas of old growth trees (where tree hollows have had enough time to form). They can be somewhat hard to spot, given their adorable leaf-shaped bodies, so you may need some patience as you peer into eucalyptus foliage looking for them. If you hear the call and think you know which tree they're calling from, with a bit of persistence, you will eventually be able to track them with your binoculars. Take an extra moment to be sure you are looking at a striated pardalote – their territory often crosses over with that of the spotted pardalote (*see* page 61).

WHAT TO LISTEN FOR	If you've ever done any bushwalking, you're likely to have heard the song of the striated pardalote, though you may not have known it. It gives a surprisingly strong, clear call for such a tiny bird. These birds produce a bell-like tone, usually calling in three-note pulses, *de-de-deww*. I find this call is tricky to distinguish from that of the spotted pardalote (*see* page 61), though the striated pardalote seems to sing at a lower pitch. These calls often carry a good distance from the canopy of eucalyptus trees.
WHAT TO LOOK FOR	Striated pardalotes are tiny yellow and black birds that, like the spotted pardalote (*see* page 61), like to spend their time in the uppermost foliage of native trees. Their upper back is pale brown, and the folded wings form a distinctive 'V' of dark plumage over the back of the bird. At the base of the tail is a yellow patch. There is also a 'cap' of dark feathers on the back of the head. The eye has a brow of white, underlined with black and there is a strip of yellow on the chin. The beak is short and stout.
WHERE TO START LOOKING	Striated pardalotes nest in tree hollows, so often areas of tall, old-growth eucalypt forest are worth a try. They sometimes venture into outer suburbs, but only where the trees are still thick and there is enough insect activity to sustain them.
SIMILAR BIRDS	Red-browed pardalote (pictured opposite; northern Australia and Central Australia), spotted pardalote (*see* page 61), forty-spotted pardalote (restricted to areas in Tasmania, pictured on page 60).

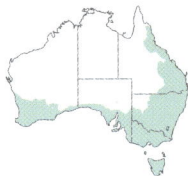

MALE HAS WHITE
DOTS ON HEAD

♂

YELLOW
CHIN

WHITE
DOTTING
ON
WINGS

FEMALE HAS
YELLOW DOTS ON
HEAD

♀

GREY
CHIN

YELLOW PATCH
UNDER TAIL

FORTY-SPOTTED
PARDALOTE
(ENDANGERED)

Spotted pardalote

Wijum-wijum [wi-joom-wi-joom]
(Gumbaynggirr)
Pardalotus punctatus

These little birds are also called the diamondbird – an appropriate name given the beautiful 'studded' patterning over their heads. Like the striated pardalote (*see* page 59), spotted pardalotes inadvertently help eucalypts by feeding on the parasitic lerp larvae that are deposited on the trees. I often see these beautiful birds feeding in the outer canopy of the eucalyptus trees, where they are almost identical in size to the leaves themselves.

They usually hang out in small groups or in mating pairs. However, sometimes during winter spotted pardalotes can be seen in Victoria's Mallee region moving in flocks of a hundred or more birds, foraging tree-to-tree through sections of bush. When it comes time to raise their young, these birds build a nest by burrowing a hollow in the side of a riverbank. For one (awesome) season, we had a pair of spotted pardalotes nesting in the backyard in our disused wood oven. Once they had raised their young, they never came back to the burrow – maybe they were sick of me ogling them when all they wanted to do was make a home.

WHAT TO LISTEN FOR	A *dew-dew*, repeated insistently while the bird feeds. Although these calls are surprisingly loud for such a teeny bird, spotted pardalotes are usually so high in the canopy that their voice is only a sweet echo heard over the bush. Sometimes they give a lower-pitched *pukk-* before the classic *dew-dew*.
WHAT TO LOOK FOR	The spotted pardalote is a tiny grey and yellow bird that hops around in the upper canopy of eucalyptus trees. Male spotted pardalotes have a vivid yellow chin and underbelly. They have a white brow over the black eye, while the head is capped in black and dotted with many small white spots. Like the head, the wings and tail are also black, dotted with white spots. Where the tail meets the body, there is a patch of orange-yellow. Female spotted pardalotes have a yellow-spotted head instead of white. Like the striated pardalote (*see* page 59), the spotted pardalote has a short, blunt beak.
WHERE TO START LOOKING	These birds like older eucalyptus forests with an abundance of insects to feed on. Try going into local parklands, along creeks and rivers, in campgrounds and national parks – these birds are common in many different kinds of bushland with established native trees across the country.
WHAT THEY EAT	Insects and lerp.
SIMILAR BIRDS	Forty-spotted pardalote (pictured opposite; restricted ranges in Tasmania), striated pardalote (*see* page 59).

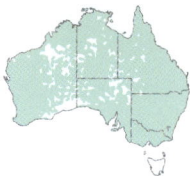

IMMATURE
(TRICKY TO DISTINGUISH FROM ♀)

BLACK-FRAMED FACE ▷

♂

WHITE CHIN ▷

RUST COLOURED BODY ▷

PALE CHIN ◁

♀

GREY WINGS ▷

STREAKED CHEST & BELLY ◁

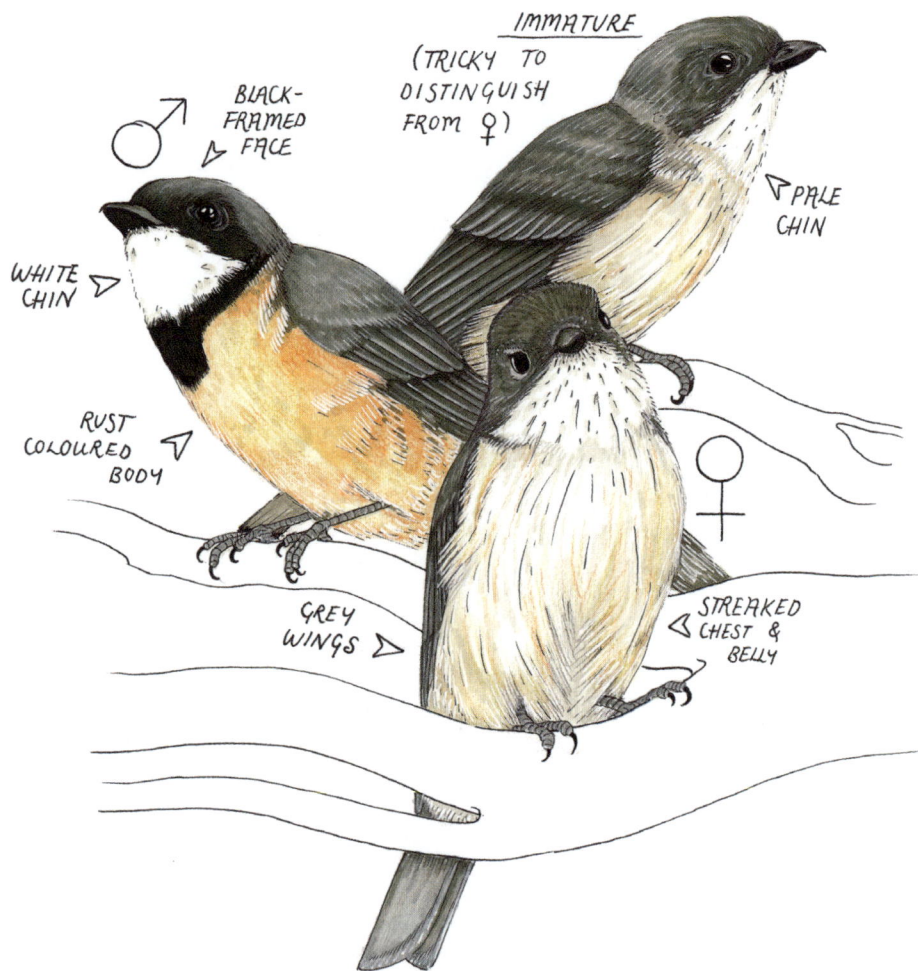

Rufous whistler

Pachycephala rufiventris

Rufous whistlers are named for their rusty coloured plumage (rufous is the common birdwatcher's term for this 'rust' colour). They are monogamous birds and are most often seen in pairs (as is the golden whistler, *see* page 65). I have been lucky to see them 'posing' on a branch as they sing, sometimes seesawing their body up and down between calls. Like the golden whistlers, these are photogenic little birds, though they seem a little less inclined to venture into more urban spaces (e.g. backyards). However, they remain incredibly vocal, singing with operatic enthusiasm – this, combined with their black neck 'tie' and orange waistcoats, makes me consider them the Pavarottis of the bush.

WHAT TO LISTEN FOR	The rufous whistler has varied calls, although most often it performs a series of trills, *deewit-deewit-deewahhh*. Like the golden whistler (*see* page 65), these birds are clear-voiced and sing frequently. Their longer calls are often interspersed with a repeated uprising whistle. This whistle sounds like the Doppler effect of a racing car – only played in reverse, and much sweeter in tone.
WHAT TO LOOK FOR	The rufous whistler is a small perching bird with a rust-coloured body and a dark head. Male rufous whistlers have a distinctive white chin patch, which is framed by a hood of black feathers, including a band over the eyes. The breast and belly is a pale rust colour. The upper body is grey, with darkened wing feathers. Female rufous whistlers are predominantly pale grey, with similarly dark wing feathers to those of the male. The underbelly is paler than that of the male and is overlaid with fine streaks running vertically down onto the chest.
IMMATURE BIRDS	Young rufous whistlers are an overall dilute grey with a faint blush of rust colour at their breast. Like the females, they have a streaked chest.
WHERE TO START LOOKING	Bushland, or any area with a good density of trees. Suburbs close to bushland will also be likely places, as well as the edges of farmland where it meets forest, rainforests, botanical gardens and parks in outer suburbs.
WHAT THEY EAT	Insects, seed and sometimes fruit.
SIMILAR BIRDS	Golden whistler (*see* page 65), olive-backed whistler, red-lored whistler. Note: The rufous whistler has the most widespread range of all the whistlers. Most others are restricted to tight ranges in coastal areas, so if you're lucky enough to see a whistler it may be worthwhile using your location to narrow down the possible species.

FOLDED WINGS FORM
BRONZE 'V' ON ♀

CRESTED
SHRIKE-TIT
(SIMILAR RANGE)

Golden whistler

Pachycephala pectoralis

Golden whistlers are *handsome*, and I mean 'handsome' in the old 1920s sense of the word, where it doesn't necessarily describe appearance, but suggests a kind of genteel, admiration-inducing poise. As they fly around in their mating pairs, golden whistlers brim with charisma and curiosity, a bit like Zelda and F Scott Fitzgerald circulating at a party. Just like the rufous whistler (*see* page 63), the males love to perform for attention, perching on bare branches as they sing. Males are particularly showy and confident in spring (the time of year they start to breed). The females are usually foraging nearby and seem to sing less often. While these birds usually stick to branches and the upper storeys of trees, they will sometimes fly to open branches to call, allowing you to get a better look at these handsome socialites.

WHAT TO LISTEN FOR	The characteristic song of the golden whistler is a fluttering repeated note, followed by a whipping whistle *whuh-whu-whu-whu-whu-dwuppp!* This whistler will also sing a cyclical, twittering few notes, followed by the same 'whip' conclusion, though this call varies often, as if these little birds were improvising just for the joy of it. I find the call of the golden whistler can be difficult to distinguish from that of the rufous whistler (*see* page 63).
WHAT TO LOOK FOR	The male golden whistler is a small bright yellow and black perching bird, and the brown-grey female will often be close by. <u>Male</u> golden whistlers have a black head with a vivid white throat patch. From the chin down, the belly is a lemon yellow colour. The wings and back body are grey. At perch, the tail has a slight fork shape. <u>Female</u> golden whistlers are nondescript in appearance (though not in character) with olive-brown-grey over their head and back body, and a paler cream underbelly. The underside of the tail has a very faint yellow patch, which can prove elusive to spot.
IMMATURE BIRDS	Young golden whistlers look similar to the adult females.
WHERE TO START LOOKING	Try looking for the golden whistler in rainforest, bushland, well-planted park edges, botanical gardens and green suburbs with native trees.
WHAT THEY EAT	Insects, grubs and, on occasion, fruit.
SIMILAR BIRDS	Rufous whistler (*see* page 63), mangrove golden whistler (northern coastline), crested shrike-tit (pictured opposite; has a similar range to the golden whistler), eastern yellow robin (*see* page 43). Note: Female whistlers can look a lot like the grey shrike-thrush (*see* page 15), only smaller. This has tripped me up many a time! Look for a faint bronze-coloured 'V' formed by the folded wings on the female (and juvenile) golden whistler. This will help you distinguish whistlers from the grey shrikethrush.

BLUE TAIL

NON-BREEDING ♂

♀ RED BROW

BREEDING ♂

IRIDESCENT CAP & CHEEKS

SPLENDID FAIRY WREN

Superb fairywren

Malurus cyaneus

Superb fairywrens hang out in small colonies that are made up of one breeding male, a kind of 'paterfamilias', if you will, with any number of female birds (and often some immature birds as well). Usually you will be able to spot several female and immature birds hanging in a thicket, with one spectacularly blue male among the mix. These fussy, trilling birds are always active and moving about, preening, singing and feeding. The restlessness of these birds makes me think of the Bennet family in Austen's *Pride and Prejudice* – they seem to have constant domestic arguments and are perpetually fussing over a handsome dude with a great estate. In flight, the tail of the superb fairywren extends out 'flat' beyond its body, trailing behind as the bird flits from place to place, almost as if it were a hindrance to the little wren's passage through the air (just as fashion in Austen's time stopped women from running anywhere at an 'unladylike' pace). Superb fairywrens build a nest that looks like a cosy 'cave' of fibrous grasses, twigs and spiderwebs, propped up in reeds or thick scrub.

WHAT TO LISTEN FOR	A fussy trilling, or high-pitched squeaking, usually from several scattered birds that are in the same area.
WHAT TO LOOK FOR	Superb fairywrens are tiny birds with iridescent blue and black feathers. They have the long, straight tails that are characteristic of wrens, usually sticking vertically upright when they perch. There are several forms of the superb fairywren that you may see: breeding males, non-breeding males and female birds. Though this makes matters a little more confusing, the most recognisable form is the breeding male with its striking blue plumage – if spotted, these handsome birds are unmistakeable. These breeding males have a vivid, iridescent blue cap, cheek patch and mantle across their shoulders. The rest of the head is black. The underbelly is pale grey to white, the wings are brownish rust–grey and the tail is dark, with a tint of blue. In non-breeding males, their 'intermediate' plumage (pictured opposite) is grey-brown and their underbelly pale, but the tail remains slightly blue. The females are pale brown with a pale underbelly and they have a small red band over their eyes.
WHERE TO START LOOKING	These beautiful, tiny birds are a familiar sight in agricultural areas, green suburbs and parklands. Some places to try looking are among reed clusters on riverbanks, scrubby bushland, hedges in green suburbs, heathland, blackberry thickets, beach scrub, farmland and open regions of grass where there is some vegetation to provide cover close by. These birds happily live in many environments, as long is there is enough scrub to house them.
WHAT THEY EAT	Insects.
SIMILAR BIRDS	Variegated fairywren (inland and across other parts of Australia excluding the northernmost and southernmost areas), splendid fairywren (pictured opposite; inland and western areas).

ABOUT 15 cm. LONG

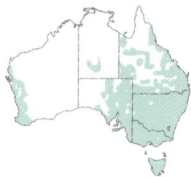

NOTE TAIL SHAPE ▷

DARK STREAKS ALONG BACK ▽

PALE EYEBROW ◁

note longer beak ◁

STRIATED FIELD-WREN ◁

Little grassbird

Megalurus gramineus

The little grassbird is a very shy bird that hides in thick vegetation. It sticks to areas over or near water, especially the reeds lining riverbanks or on floodplains where insect life is thick, and where they can hide well from predators. These birds are so stealthy that it can be very hard to spot them among grasses and reeds – they are the introverts of the bird world, sticking to their reed-filled homes, where they can pursue their art projects (insect eating and nest building) in peace and quiet. You're most likely to see them by scanning across the top of an area of grassland, waiting to see the bobbing flight of one as it moves between areas of vegetation, quickly ducking in and out of sight. It took me a long time to spot one, and getting a photo took even longer than that! However, they are common birds, and if you familiarise yourself with their call, you'll start to notice places where they are hiding just out of sight. Then, it is simply a matter of patience till you are lucky enough to see one of these cuties.

WHAT TO LISTEN FOR	A high-pitched, melancholy *put-wheee-wheet … put-wheee-wheet*. The sound of the little grassbird makes me think of a rusty Hills Hoist clothesline turning in the wind. Often you'll clue in to the presence of the little grassbird through the call rather than by seeing them, as their tiny voices carry well over reeds and grass, while they remain out of sight.
WHAT TO LOOK FOR	The little grassbird is a caramel-brown colour and usually hides among reeds. The tail is long and paddle-shaped, the wings are brown, and there are dark brown streaks running down the bird's back. The belly and chin is a creamy pale brown, with slightly streaky chest feathers. These birds have a distinctive pale eyebrow and a dark eye, which may be the only two things you spot if you manage to glimpse one among the reeds.
WHAT THEY EAT	Insects.
WHERE TO START LOOKING	Grasslands, reed beds, thick scrubland on the edge of waterways, bulrushes.
SIMILAR BIRDS	Striated fieldwren (pictured opposite; Tasmania and southern Victorian coastlines; these birds have a yellower belly, but are hard to distinguish at a mere glimpse), tawny grassbird (northern and eastern coasts; has less striated patterning and pink legs), golden-headed cisticola (pictured on page 70; northern and eastern coasts; smaller, golden, and has scratchy vocals), Australian reed warbler (*see* page 71; a bit bigger, crested, plainer, with less streaking).

SMALL CREST
MAY BE
RAISED

GOLDEN-HEADED
CISTICOLA

CREST
DOWN

PINKISH
BEAK

ALMOST
ALWAYS AT
PERCH IN REEDS
OR SHRUBS

PALE
UNDERBELLY

Australian reed warbler

Acrocephalus australis

The Australian reed warbler is also known as a 'reedlark', an apt name for a bird that spends so much time singing in the reeds. Like the little grassbird (*see* page 69), these birds are often very hard to catch a glimpse of, as they are well camouflaged in their reedy habitat – a brown bird among brown vegetation. However, unlike the little grassbird, the reed warbler is much more vocal and assertive, hopping out on perches to sing loudly, knowing it can easily duck within the cover of the reeds at a moment's notice (a risk the little grassbird doesn't seem to take as often). If the little grassbird is the introvert of the birding world, the reed warbler is the extrovert. Something about these chipper birds shouts of Crocodile Dundee, swinging out over perilous waters, uncaring of the dangers lurking nearby. In breeding season they construct nests that hover precariously over the water, propped up on a few reed stems. If you're at a wetland in summer in the warm months and you can hear alien-like, metallic bird calls among the reeds, you're very likely to be close to a reed warbler.

WHAT TO LISTEN FOR	The reed warbler's song is metallic and variable, but often contains a sharp *dyweep-du-dyweep* performed at several different pitches. Some of its calls can be almost robotic in quality, sounding less melodic than many of our other songbirds. If disturbed, the reed warbler may perform a short, white-noise bark.
WHAT TO LOOK FOR	The Australian reed warbler is a plain brown perching bird, almost exclusively seen among reeds or tall grasses. The adult bird is brown with a black eye and a pink beak. The head is adorned with a very small, fuzzy crest. (This crest isn't always visible, as the bird can opt to flatten it against its head.) The back body and folded wings are a slightly darker brown than the underbelly, but the overall impression this warbler makes is of a very plain bird. A combination of the habitat you're birdwatching in and this bird's strange, varied call will be what helps you to identify the reed warbler.
WHERE TO START LOOKING	Reeds, tall grasses, rushes, shrubs along riverbanks or water bodies. For those located in the south-east of Australia, the reed warbler has alternating seasonal movements – it flies north over the colder months during the non-breeding season, and south for breeding over warmer periods, so you may expect to see them more during certain times of the year, depending on your location.
WHAT THEY EAT	Insects.
SIMILAR BIRDS	Little grassbird (*see* page 69), striated fieldwren (pictured on page 68), golden-headed cisticola (pictured opposite; found in eastern and northern Australia in similar habitats).

BELT EXTENDS ON TO BACK OF HEAD

GREY BACK & BLACK WINGS

LARGE BLACK BELT

DOUBLE-BARRED FINCH (note double belt)

IMMATURE

NO BELT (OR A PARTIALLY DEVELOPED BELT)

'DOWNIER', MORE MOTTLED FEATHERS

DARK BROWN-GREY WINGS

ORANGE-BROWN EYES

SMALLER, BROWNER BELT THAN ♂

White-fronted chat

Epthianura albifrons

The white-fronted chat has an amalgam of characteristics. Its colouring is like that of a seabird, it moves like a shorebird as it forages on the ground, yet it perches like a robin in low scrub. To top it all off, these birds are actually classified as honeyeaters yet rarely feed on nectar. They are 'in-between' birds, seen mostly in open heathland or fields across the southern half of the country. These active birds sometimes pop up above the saltbushes to look about and give their short, babyish call, as if to reassure you they are still there. With their nun-like white masks and black hoods, I can't help but expect them to be gathered together by Whoopi Goldberg to sing a gospel number, à la *Sister Act* (1992).

When poised in scrub, they will look around, flipping their tail up and down the way you might flick a light switch. Sometimes they cruise in colonies, but more often in pairs, almost always where there is open ground or sand where they can pursue insects.

WHAT TO LISTEN FOR	A baby-like, squeaky *meep* or *bleep*, often in conversation with a fellow chat.
WHAT TO LOOK FOR	The white-fronted chat is a small black-headed bird with a white face, earning it the colloquial name 'white-fronted nun'. <u>Males</u> have a white chin and underbelly, which is separated by a 'belt' of black feathers. The wings are grey, darkened at the tips. The beak is straight and black, and the eye colour is variable (from yellow-brown through to orange). <u>Females</u> are browner overall, with a rusty tint to the brown back and wings. They have a less vivid breastband, which does not fully encircle the head as the male's band does. There is also a faint buff colouring to the side body of the females.
IMMATURE BIRDS	Young white-fronted chats are duller and browner, and do not develop the breastband until they become adults.
WHERE TO START LOOKING	Try heading out to drier pastures or sandy areas. I've often seen white-fronted chats along the edges of dams in otherwise dry farmland, among sand dunes, on inland salt flats, marshlands and some wet agricultural areas. If you know somewhere nearby that has saltbush growing, that's usually a good environment for trying to spot these birds. They largely pursue insects on (or close to) the ground, so make sure you scan that path and those low bushes ahead of you as you walk.
WHAT THEY EAT	Insects, grubs.
SIMILAR BIRDS	Double-barred finch (pictured opposite), white-winged triller (pictured on page 2), banded whiteface (found only in arid Central Australia).

LARGELY GREY

IMMATURE

FAINT 'RUST' COLOURING ON FEMALES

♂

RED 'CAP' ON MALES

♀

Red-capped plover

Girr-girr [geerr-geerr] (Gumbaynggirr)
Charadrius ruficapillus

Like other plovers, the red-capped plover runs over the ground more often than it takes to the air. It runs so quickly that its legs become a cartoonish blur as it bounces back and forth across the beach like a pinball, occasionally freezing to duck its head and pluck small insects from the sand. Given these birds live and nest almost entirely on exposed shorelines, they are very vulnerable both to birds of prey and more wily land-bound predators (such as foxes and feral cats). This vulnerability definitely shows in their character, as they seem to be constantly on edge, scanning their surrounds and pecking for insects as if late for an important date. If you imagine their red cap as a slightly ill-fitting waistcoat, it's easy to picture these rushed birds as the equally hurried White Rabbit from *Alice in Wonderland* (1951).

WHAT TO LISTEN FOR	A repeated, high-pitched *meep* that carries well over sand dunes, mudflats or saltplains.
WHAT TO LOOK FOR	Red-capped plovers are small white and chestnut-coloured shorebirds, who run rapidly on twiggy dark legs. The <u>male</u> red-capped plovers are white on their underbelly and face, and their legs are black. The head is adorned with a chestnut-red cap, which is framed with black, especially where it extends down past the cheeks, like one of those vintage 1950s swimming caps. The back body and folded wings are brown. The <u>female</u> red-capped plovers have a similar arrangement of colours but lack the red 'cap', instead bearing a continuation of their brown-coloured body onto their head, with some rust-coloured blush at the edges of their face.
IMMATURE BIRDS	Young red-capped plovers are white on their underbelly, and grey over the head and back body. They have no coloured markings, though they will moult into their adult plumage, sometimes with strange morphs in-between – designed specifically to trip up aspiring birdwatchers!
WHERE TO START LOOKING	Beaches, estuaries, sand banks, some inland water bodies, and marshlands.
WHAT THEY EAT	Invertebrates (insects and water-dwelling grubs) that live along the beach in sand, mud and shallow water.
SIMILAR BIRDS	These birds are also called the 'red-capped dotterel', dotterels being a similar-looking group of shorebirds (e.g. the red-kneed dotterel or the black-fronted dotterel). To further complicate matters, there are also *many* species of plover in Australia, though most of them are much more restricted in range than the red-capped plover. You might be tripped up by some of these other plovers (double banded, hooded), as these two species have a similar range to the red-capped plover. That said, the red-capped plover is one of the more common species among this similar-looking group of birds, and, as indicated above, is seen at inland lakes, mudflats and landlocked salt marshes. You may be able to eliminate some of the other potential species by checking where they are distributed.

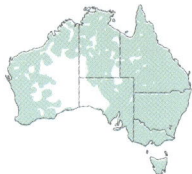

DARK CROWN

NON-BREEDING
PLUMAGE

YELLOW
EYE

BREEDING
PLUMAGE

PALE
CHIN

DOWNY
FEATHERS

WHITE
PATCH

RED
PANEL
ON NECK

IMMATURE

note
orange
beak

STRIPED FACE
ON YOUNG
GREBES

Australasian grebe

Tachybaptus novaehollandiae

Australasian grebes are great swimmers and usually prefer to get around by paddling rather than flying. When I've unintentionally surprised Australasian grebes, they tend to duck underwater to swim away, leaving me scanning the water to try and predict where they'll pop up again. These birds are such water dwellers, they even make floating nests. These nests look kind of like a drifting island of debris, made mostly of grasses and twigs. When raising their young, many grebe species will carry their chicks on the flat part of their backs between their wings. They'll cruise around the water carrying their babies until they're happily able to swim and dive on their own. Don't look this up on Google images (the photos are simply too cute for mortal eyes).

WHAT TO LISTEN FOR	A descending, shrill call, *trewwwww*, a little reminiscent of whale song.
WHAT TO LOOK FOR	A small, dark-coloured waterbird, the Australasian grebe has a longish neck and a duck-like posture. Like a number of other waterbirds, the grebe's appearance alternates between its breeding (springtime) and non-breeding (winter) plumage. When in breeding plumage, this bird has a black head that transitions to grey down the neck. The body is brown and the underbelly is pale, especially the downy, fluffy tail, which may be partially hidden under the water surface. The black beak has a white tip and a yellowish oval at its base that runs up towards the eye. At the side of the head is a strip of rusty red, fading as it descends down the neck. In its non-breeding plumage, the bird's body is also brown, but the head is capped only with black. The chin, cheeks and neck are white, and the beak becomes pale.
IMMATURE BIRDS	Young Australasian grebes are a mottled brown-black colour, with zebra-like white patterning over the face that descends partway down the neck.
WHERE TO START LOOKING	Try looking for grebes in almost any freshwater body – ponds, lakes, rivers and dams. These birds are common across Australia, except the most arid interiors. I rarely see them in brackish waters, so keep your eye out for small waterbirds when you're next near inland waters.
WHAT THEY EAT	Insects and small crustaceans, small water-dwelling critters.
SIMILAR BIRDS	Great-crested grebes (distributed across eastern and central north Australia) and hoary-headed grebes (another widespread grebe with a streaky head in breeding season – note: non-breeding hoary-headed grebes look very similar to non-breeding Australasian grebes).

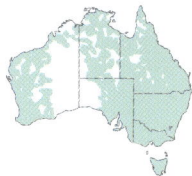

BLACK-TAILED
NATIVEHEN
(note beak
shape &
colour)

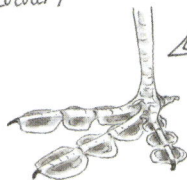

BROAD TOES
(good for both
wading &
paddling)

ADULT

IMMATURE HAS
NO FOREHEAD
SHIELD

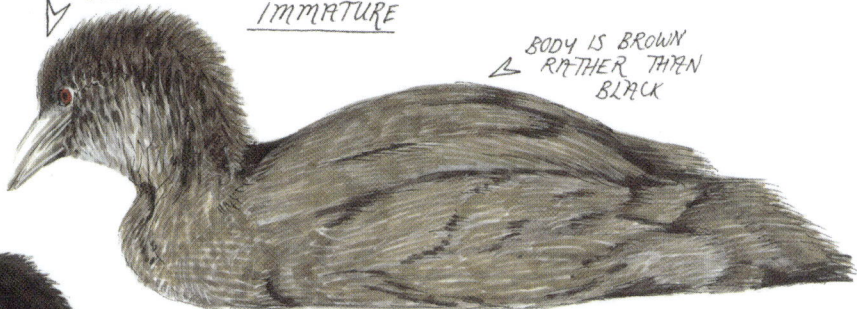

IMMATURE

BODY IS BROWN
RATHER THAN
BLACK

FACE
SHIELD
FROM
FRONT

BEAK EXTENDS
UP ONTO
FOREHEAD

ADULT

FEATHERS ARE DARK-
GREY TO BLACK

RED
EYE

Eurasian coot

Guuruwun [gooroowoon] (Gumbaynggirr)
Fulica atra

The Eurasian coot is part of the rail family, along with the Australasian swamphen (*see* page 91) and the dusky moorhen (*see* page 89). Rails are mostly long-legged, water-loving birds, and many of their Australian members fall under the catch-all name 'waterhen', given their shape and behaviour. This is an especially apt name for the Eurasian coot, which even pecks at the surface of the water when feeding, in much the same way as chickens peck at seed on the ground. For a wading bird, Eurasian coots are very comfortable paddlers, usually bobbing their head forwards insistently as they paddle. I have occasionally seen them in large flocks on larger bodies of water, and they will readily 'mix in' with other paddling birds. Often they will 'dolphin dive' to look for food, half-hopping in an arc to dip head first into the water. All too often, I have a slip of the tongue and call these birds 'Eurasian cutes' instead of Eurasian coots.

WHAT TO LISTEN FOR	A sharp, abrupt call, *clukk!* This sound carries very well over water and reminds me of the sound of a hammer on metal, or of someone striking a tent peg with a stone.
WHAT TO LOOK FOR	The Eurasian coot is a dark, hen-shaped wading bird, usually seen paddling in freshwater. It is mostly black, with a faint greyness to the feathers at the chest and lower neck. The eye is red and the beak is a white-grey, which extends up onto the head, like a small shield covering the bird's forehead. The legs are black. Female Eurasian coots have a slightly smaller forehead 'shield' than the males.
IMMATURE BIRDS	Young Eurasian coots look slightly browner than the adults, with a dark beak and no forehead 'shield'. Chicks are very fluffy, with brown feathers over their body, and exposed red skin over their face.
WHERE TO START LOOKING	These are relatively common birds, so if you head to any wetlands, riverbank, pond, reeds or water adjacent grasslands, you are likely to have some luck.
WHAT THEY EAT	Eurasian coots are omnivorous, taking plant matter and insects from water or from riverbanks. Like many other freshwater waders, these birds are territorial, so they'll have regular 'lurking grounds' where they try and hold their ground against other waterbirds.
SIMILAR BIRDS	Australasian swamphen (*see* page 91, note the colour and size), black-tailed native hen (pictured opposite; note its beak colour), dusky moorhen (*see* page 89, note the beak colour), Tasmanian native hen (restricted to Tasmania).

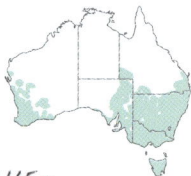

ROUNDED HEAD >

BLUE-BILLED DUCK ♀

NOTE BILL SHAPE

TAIL LIFTED UPRIGHT >

SQUARE-ISH HEAD >

MALE COURTSHIP DISPLAY (accompanied by calling & splashing)

♀

note: females are smaller >

LARGE WEDGE-SHAPED BILL

FAINT PATTERNING IN FEATHERS

♂

SITS LOW IN THE WATER >

MALES HAVE FLAP ON BILL

Musk duck

Biralbang [bi-ra-l-ba-ng], *waagabadha* [waa-ga-ba-dha] (Wiradjuri)
Biziura lobata

The musk duck provides an example of the strange and wonderful gifts evolution provides. During their courtship display, the males can partially inflate their face flap to impress a lady duck. In addition to inflating this flap, the males perform a ritual dance that's somewhere between a cabaret performance and a flamenco dance: they tuck their bill tight against their neck, fan their tail up in the air and splash water past their body. They accompany this splashing with their sharp, descending whistle. Pretty hot, I know.

These ducks tend to be 'low riders' when paddling: the body stays mostly below the surface, with only their head and neck lifted above the water (to my mind, musk ducks are the submarines of the Australian lake systems). Overall, they seem to prefer staying on the water, rather than grazing on land, feeling more comfortable diving and swimming to get around than waddling or flying.

WHAT TO LISTEN FOR	A sharp, high-pitched, descending whistle, *dewww*. (If you hear this call, you're actually hearing the males performing their 'courtship' dance. Apart from this performance, I've never heard these ducks make a noise!)
WHAT TO LOOK FOR	Musk ducks are medium-sized black ducks that float very low in the water. Their plumage, although dark, has a faint bark-like patterning that you might be able to spot through your binoculars. The underwing feathers are white, though you'll only get a chance to see this if you see musk ducks in flight. Their beak is much bigger, and more wedge-like, than most other species of duck, making them look distinctly chunky compared with other duck species. You'll be able to pick the <u>male</u> musk ducks straight away, as they have a large flap of leathery skin that hangs from one side of their beak. <u>Females</u> are similar in appearance, but do not have the face flap, and are much smaller than the males.
IMMATURE BIRDS	Young musk ducks look similar to adult females (young birds also don't have the face flap.)
WHERE TO START LOOKING	Although these ducks are relatively common, I've only spotted them in large flocks on big bodies of water rather than in ponds or smaller dams. Being diving ducks, they might prefer more established and deeper bodies of water where food is more abundant. Try heading to nearby lakes or large dams where there is plenty of other birdlife and you may have some luck.
WHAT THEY EAT	Musk ducks are omnivorous, diving underwater to retrieve crustaceans and invertebrates (e.g. snails) and some aquatic plants.
SIMILAR BIRDS	Freckled duck (especially the female freckled duck, which has a much longer, narrower and more curved bill than the musk duck), blue-billed duck (again, especially the female blue-billed duck, pictured opposite).

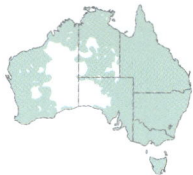

NORTHERN MALLARD (♀)

ADULT

NOTE LESS DEFINED 'BROWS'

WHITE 'BROWS' ON FACE

ADULT P. BLACK DUCK IN FLIGHT

TORTOISESHELL PATTERNED BODY

COLOURED PANEL IN WING

DUCKLING

Pacific black duck

Wirraal [we-raahl], **gilaawarl** [ghee-lah-worl] (Gumbaynggirr); **budhanbang** [bu-dha-n-ba-ng], **burangguwing** [bu-ra-ng-gu-wi-ng] (Wiradjuri); **dulum** [du-lum] (Taungurung)
Anas superciliosa

The Pacific black duck is a familiar sight in parks, lakes, wet golf courses and similar sections of urban greenery. I most often see them grazing in pairs, small families (of around three to five birds), or hanging in among flocks of mixed species on water. These birds are very regal with their long necks and delicate manner of paddling about. Even their Latin name *superciliosa* means 'haughty' or 'superior'. This royal-esque character helps me to distinguish them from the slightly smaller and plainer wood ducks (*see* page 85), and the patterned female chestnut teals (*see* page 87). Despite their monarch-like behaviour, when it comes to feeding in water, these birds are noisy and enthusiastic. They seem to enjoy guzzling through shallow, muddy areas where they can filter out algae and little invertebrates, making for a soundscape that is at odds with their otherwise sophisticated behaviour. These ducks tend to stay close to water, grazing and feeding in close range to their nesting site, which is a woven bowl among reeds and shrubs, or in a low tree hollow or stump.

WHAT TO LISTEN FOR	A sharp repeated quack, descending in pitch, like a wheezy laugh. These birds may also perform a monotonous quacking at even intervals, *shakk-shakk-shakk-shakk*. In flight, their wing feathers 'squeak', making a *whii-whii-whii-whi* noise. Around dusk I'm often alerted that they are flying overhead by the creaking of their wings. Adorable!
WHAT TO LOOK FOR	The Pacific black duck is a medium-sized waterbird with curved eyebrows on the face. The body is grey-brown with tortoiseshell-patterned feathers. The head is darker than the body, fading into black over the eyes and central forehead. On each cheek are two creamy bands of feathers, one above and one below the eye. Sometimes, depending on the position of the wings, a small panel of blue-green feathers can be seen. In flight, this panel is much more visible, as are the pale underwing feathers.
IMMATURE BIRDS	Pacific black ducklings are grey and fluffy without patterning, though they form their pale eye-bands early.
WHERE TO START LOOKING	The Pacific black duck is relatively common, so keep an eye out for them in any parks where there is nearby water, or try ponds, rivers, lakes, recently watered ovals or golf courses, where you might spot them waddling over the ground, or paddling in the water.
WHAT THEY EAT	These ducks are omnivorous, mostly feeding on algae and plants but also snacking on some invertebrates (e.g. snails) when the opportunity arises.
SIMILAR BIRDS	Australian wood ('maned') duck (*see* page 85; a smaller, paler duck – the male has a rich-brown head, the female has similar 'bands' on the face), female northern mallard (pictured opposite; these birds are an introduced species), grey teal (pictured on page 86), the female chestnut teal (*see* page 87).

♀

♂

NOTE WING
PANEL

'MANE'
(LONG NECK FEATHERS)

♂

♀

'EGGSHELL'
PATTERNING

Australian wood ('maned') duck

Gudharang [gu-dha-ra-ng], **guwiyarrang** [gu-wi-ya-rra-ng], **gunaru** [gu-na-ru] (Wiradjuri); biygmum [biyg-mum] (Taungurung)
Chenonetta jubata

If you can get close enough to properly see their patterning, you will notice that wood ducks have spectacular plumage, especially the speckled belly feathers. Being small 'brown' ducks that are common in suburbs, it is easy to bypass them without giving them the notice they merit – their patterned feathers may be subtle, but they are beautiful. Sometimes coupled wood ducks 'double date', grazing on lawns together. Occasionally they can be seen in larger family flocks of a dozen or more, though this is more often a 'family unit' of parents and their now-adolescent ducklings. Unlike other Australian duck species I have seen, I rarely spot wood ducks on the water. Instead, they are almost always meandering over land, grazing and exploring for nesting hollows. If they venture into water, it will usually be in shallower areas. When it comes time for nesting, the wood duck lays its eggs in a tree hollow, often several metres off the ground. After the ducklings hatch in the hollow, these young birds must undergo a 'baptism of fire', trundling out of the entrance of the tree hollow to drop several metres to the ground, where their parents await them.

WHAT TO LISTEN FOR
These ducks make the sweetest, softest repetitive *wack-wack-wack-wack-wack* as they browse through grass, usually conversing in pairs. They also give an alarm call, which is like the laugh of a supervillain, rising in pitch, *wahh-waaaahh-waaaahh*. This sound carries long distances from urban parks and local creeks, so you may recognise this 'laugh' when you next hear it. They will also readily hiss and chase those who come too close.

WHAT TO LOOK FOR
The Australian wood duck, or 'maned duck' as it is sometimes known, is a small brown duck that is often seen grazing on wet grass. The beak is relatively small for a duck, more of a delicate 'nose' than the wider, flatter bills of the Pacific black duck (*see* page 83), or the pyramidal beak of the magpie goose (*see* page 95). Both male and female birds have grey backs, but they differ slightly in appearance. The female is speckled like an eggshell along its entire underbelly, with a pale brown head and two faint white bands above and below the eye. The male has a grey underbelly and the head is a dark, rich brown without the eye-bands of the female. The male also has a dark, short mane of feathers along the back of the neck.

IMMATURE BIRDS
Australian wood ducklings are little grey-brown fluff balls, with pale underbellies and a pale white spot on each side of the body. Their heads are dark, with a 'blurred' version of the female's white eye-bands.

WHERE TO START LOOKING
The Australian wood duck is another common species of duck that cruises around areas of grass, suburban lawns, golf courses, waterways, creek banks, lakes and ponds – almost anywhere close to water and with good grazing (usually any area with grass gone to seed). These ducks often come to feed on grass seed in our front yard, especially if there's been recent rain.

WHAT THEY EAT
These ducks are generalist feeders, munching on grass seed, algae, and insects and occasionally gnawing away at tender greens in vegetable patches. I once watched them approach a new row of seedlings I planted in my backyard, but they were so sweetly *wack-wack-wack*-ing as they snacked on the row of baby cos lettuces, I didn't have the heart to stop them.

SIMILAR BIRDS
Pacific black duck (*see* page 83), freckled duck, hardhead duck.

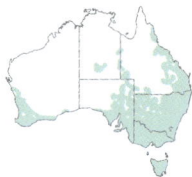

GREY
TEAL
↙ WHITE CHIN
REACHES UP
TO THE EYE

♀

WHITE
CHIN STARTS
LOW

RED
EYE ↘

♂

TORTOISESHELL
CHEST &
BELLY

IRIDESCENT PANEL
IN WINGS

↙ CHESTNUT
CHEST & BELLY

Chestnut teal

Anas castanea

Chestnut teals are monogamous birds, meaning they find a partner, 'put a ring on it' and stick together for the rest of their lives. Sometimes juveniles are seen in groups, loitering on lawns, but adults are mostly seen in breeding pairs, or with their ducklings. In springtime, pairs of chestnut teals can be seen 'real estate shopping' – namely, trundling through the parklands, scanning for a good place to build a nest, usually a hollow log or stump. If you happen to come across them several weeks after the real estate rounds are finished, you are likely to be rewarded with the sight of two chestnut teal parents shepherding a family of ducklings. Often I will be out looking at a flock of waterbirds at a local lake and presume that they are all Eurasian coots or a large flock of musk ducks. Usually a second, closer look over the flock will reveal a pair or two of chestnut teals, blended in among the hordes of other birds. It pays to look closely at large flocks on water. A unique species of bird can blend in among the crowd like Daniel Day-Lewis into a movie role.

WHAT TO LISTEN FOR	Chestnut teals make a raspy chuckle that descends in pitch, *weeeehnk-weenk-wenk-wenk*.
WHAT TO LOOK FOR	The chestnut teal is a medium-sized duck with distinctive red-brown plumage. <u>Males</u> have a black bill and metallic-green head (though the head may appear black if seen in the shade). The upper back is a deep chestnut brown, while the chest is lighter, a rusty-brown with tortoiseshell patterning running down the belly. Below the folded wings is a white panel of feathers, which separates the rusty underbelly from the black tail. <u>Females</u>, by contrast, are grey, with a darker brown head. Their upper chest fades from grey into brown tortoiseshell on the underbelly, and they have a dark grey back. In flight, both females and males have a section of metallic green, edged with white, on their wing.
IMMATURE BIRDS	Young chestnut teals are grey-brown and mottled, and are usually visibly smaller than adults.
WHERE TO START LOOKING	Try heading to local bodies of water – wetlands, lakes, rivers, ponds or dams. These ducks aren't bothered by a little bit of salt, so you could also try looking for them at river mouths and other areas of brackish water.
WHAT THEY EAT	Algae, grass seeds and soft vegetation from riverbanks, insects and snails.
SIMILAR BIRDS	Australian wood duck (*see* page 85), Australasian shoveler (males, when in breeding plumage; note that shovelers have a very large beak), grey teal (pictured opposite; note that the female chestnut teal looks very similar to the grey teal; the female chestnut teal has a grey chin where the grey teal chin is white, though this distinction is hard to make at a distance).

IMMATURE

DARK
BEAK

WHITE
PATCH
UNDER TAIL

ADULT

RED
FACE
SHIELD

RED
& YELLOW
BEAK

BODY
FEATHERS ARE
DARK BROWN-
BLACK

REDDISH
LEGS

Dusky moorhen

Dyilbal [dyi-l-ba-l], **dhularr** [dhu-la-rr], **dhinbun** [dhi-n-bu-n], **mililung** [mi-li-lu-ng] (Wiradjuri)
Gallinula tenebrosa

The dusky moorhen, like the Eurasian coot (*see* page 79) and Australasian swamphen (*see* page 91) is part of the rail family (a group of wading birds). The dusky moorhen looks very similar to the Australasian swamphen, only smaller, more slender and darker in colour. I usually see them standing on the banks of ponds or lakes, where they preen thoroughly between wading sessions, often sharing the same patch with Australasian swamphens and Eurasian coots. On the water, feeding is a messy, splashy affair, as these birds usually 'faceplant' their beak into the water and swish it side to side, as they try to break up the vegetation they so love to snack on.

As these birds are so common along suburban waterways and in parks, they can sometimes become very tame around humans. Once a very confused juvenile moorhen ran right up to my feet with big, puppy-like steps before it realised I didn't have any food to give it. Pretty adorable! Like some humans, the feet of immature dusky moorhens seem to grow faster than the rest of their body, making the youngest of these waders look a bit clumsy.

WHAT TO LISTEN FOR	An abrupt, sparse *peep!* The dusky moorhen will also occasionally chatter in a squeaky voice, almost like a lorikeet.
WHAT TO LOOK FOR	The dusky moorhen is a medium-sized wading bird with a hen-shaped body. These birds are mostly black with a small patch of creamy white at the tail. Their beak extends part of the way up their forehead into a bright red 'shield'. This shield fashionably matches the red legs. The very tip of the beak is yellow.
IMMATURE BIRDS	Young dusky moorhens have a grey-black beak, dark legs to match and a lighter body than adults (closer to dark grey than black). Like the Eurasian coot (*see* page 79), dusky moorhen chicks are small brown fluff balls with red heads.
WHERE TO START LOOKING	Try going to any nearby water body, be it a lake, pond, creek, dam, marshland, mangrove forest or irrigated fields – almost any place where there is water for wading and food for grazing. These birds are territorial, so will likely stick to a particular body of water where they habitually roost.
WHAT THEY EAT	Dusky moorhens are generalist feeders, grazing on aquatic vegetation, algae, insects and small crustaceans.
SIMILAR BIRDS	Australasian swamphen (*see* page 91), Eurasian coot (*see* page 79), black-tailed native hen (note the beak colour, as pictured on page 78), Tasmanian native hen (restricted to Tasmania).

RED
FOREHEAD
SHIELD

RED
EYE

FOREHEAD
SHIELD
MERGES
WITH
BEAK

DARK GREY
WINGS &
BACK

PURPLE-
BLUE
BELLY

WHITE PATCH
UNDER TAIL

PINK
LEGS

Australasian ('purple') swamphen

Biyawiiny [be-a-ween] (Gumbaynggirr)
Porphyrio porphyrio

As freshwater waders, the Australasian swamphen is usually seen grazing in the shallows, in wetlands or ponds, or picking over wet ground on riverbanks. These birds much prefer to stay on the ground or to wade in the water rather than fly, so they will often move off from any disturbance by foot rather than by taking wing. Thus, they are usually seen stalking around parks, creeks and gardens, chowing down vegetation. Their movements are very calculated and dinosaur-like, and they flick their tail repetitively as they walk (up and down like a light switch). This 'flashes' the white patch hidden under their tail, almost like a cancan dancer flashing their skirts.

WHAT TO LISTEN FOR	The Australasian swamphen makes a high-pitched, 'oinking' cluck, *hukk-hukk*. This swamphen may also perform a descending whistle, still with an 'oinky' sound to it.
WHAT TO LOOK FOR	The Australasian swamphen is a blue-purple wading bird with a chicken-like body. It walks on long reddish legs and has a large red beak, which extends onto the forehead in a 'shield'. The wings, tail and the underbelly are grey-black in colour, while the chest has violet-coloured feathers, which are particularly visible in direct sunlight. There is a panel of white under the tail, which is made visible when it flicks its tail up and down.
IMMATURE BIRDS	Young swamphens come into adult plumage fairly rapidly, though the red shield takes some time to develop. If you see a bird with a small, darker forehead shield, check against the similar birds listed below – it may be a Eurasian coot or dusky moorhen. But if the bird you're looking at has a bright blue-purple belly, it's likely an Australasian swamphen.
WHERE TO START LOOKING	The Australasian swamphen is another common wading bird that you should have some luck seeing at local wet parklands, lakes, ponds and creeks. If there is a reasonably well vegetated water source, even in relatively urban areas, these birds might be seen there. Water bodies with a good amount of reeds or shrubbery along the banks are useful places to scan from afar using your binoculars – especially if you hear oink-like honking and the crunching of undergrowth as these water-chickens shift around. They remind me of mini velociraptors, moving stealthily around the 'jungle' (aka Australian riverbanks and ponds).
WHAT THEY EAT	Mostly aquatic vegetation and shoots.
SIMILAR BIRDS	Dusky moorhen (*see* page 89), Eurasian coot (*see* page 79), black-tailed native hen (pictured on page 78), Tasmanian native hen (restricted to Tasmania).

VIVID
RED
BILL

SIZE OF
WHITE PATCH
VARIES

NECK IS
HELD STRAIGHT
IN FLIGHT

CYGNET

WHITE FLIGHT
FEATHERS MAY BE
VISIBLE

DARK
BEAK

IMMATURE
(NOTE DOWNY
FEATHERS)

Black swan

Guniibi [goon-ee-be] (Gumbaynggirr); **dhundhu**
[dhu-n-dhu], **ngiyaran** [ngi-ya-ra-n], **gunyig**
[gu-nyi-g] (Wiradjuri)
Cygnus atratus

Despite all appearances to the contrary, the black swan certainly isn't the 'evil twin' of the mute (white) swan of Europe. Though the name may conjure images of schizoid Natalie Portman in *Black Swan* (2010), these birds are usually quite gentle, gracefully looping their necks as they paddle through water, sometimes guiding a number of fluffy grey cygnets with them. When not raising young, these birds can be seen in huge flocks on lakes, or in flight, where you'll easily be able to spot their long neck and white-tipped wings. Given the size of these birds, flight in itself seems incredibly ambitious, yet they fly so beautifully, keeping their neck held out ahead of their body, long and static, with the wings slowly beating. It's little wonder these birds have inspired ballet choreography, as they seem to embody poise and decorum. When they are peckish, black swans will tip forward to dunk the entire front half of their body underwater, allowing them to extend their neck down to the algae-laden lake floor, with the tail and legs held up in the breeze. If they are eating dry food of some form (often bread from enthusiastic park visitors), they will dunk their beak in the water to 'wet' the food before they eat it – a habit that makes them seem perhaps slightly less graceful than their onstage portrayals.

WHAT TO LISTEN FOR	A low, nasal honking, *deww-dinkdeww*, or, if disturbed, a high-pitched trilling, similar to a silver gull.
WHAT TO LOOK FOR	Black swans are large, dark, long-necked waterbirds, with black plumage over their body and neck. They have a vivid red bill with a white patch at the tip, and in flight, their white wingtips can be seen. As they fly, their neck is stretched out ahead of them, long and straight (unlike herons and egrets, which keep a slight bend in their necks during flight).
IMMATURE BIRDS	Young black swans are greyer, while the babies – cygnets – are tiny grey fluff balls with black beaks.
WHERE TO START LOOKING	Black swans are relatively common birds, and are often seen in large flocks on water, sometimes intermixed with other breeds of waterbird. Try your local lake or pond, a dam, or if there's a floodplain or marshland nearby, these may also be places where you'll have luck seeing these elegant birds. The black swan doesn't migrate cyclically, but travels in nomadic patterns between water bodies, so it may not frequent your area for certain periods of time.
WHAT THEY EAT	Algae and water-growing vegetation.
SIMILAR BIRDS	Magpie goose (*see* page 95), and that's about it – black swans are pretty distinctive. There are also introduced mute (white) swans in some areas of Australia, but they are entirely white and very recognisable, especially to any of us who watched *The Swan Princess* (1994) growing up.

GLOSSY DARK FEATHERS OVER NECK & HEAD

FEMALE HAS SMALLER BUMP

♀

MALE HAS LARGER BUMP

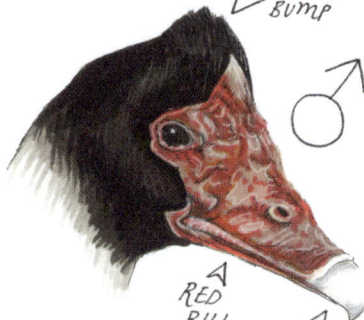

♂

RED BILL

WHITE BILL TIP

EYE LIGHT BROWN

SMALL (OR NO) BUMP ON HEAD

<u>IMMATURE</u>

BILL PINK

MALE HAS VISIBLE BUMP ON HEAD

WHITE BODY

DARK WINGTIPS & TAIL

ORANGE LEGS

SEMI-WEBBED FEET

Magpie goose

Anseranas semipalmata

Magpie geese are often seen in huge colonies on water, or flying together in a large flock. As you can imagine from their honking call, they can become quite cacophonous when in such a large group. Due to their 'in between' shaped feet (being only partially webbed), they seem most comfortable standing in the shallows of wetlands, rather than paddling beyond their depth. It's common to see an enormous flock of them standing together in the shallows of a wetland, honking away. Their calls echo a long way over water and definitely add to the atmosphere of a swampy area, especially in the more tropical areas of northern Australia. When nesting, these birds make a large shallow bowl of dry reeds and grasses propped up on vegetation. In the Northern Territory, magpie geese gather in such large numbers that they are seasonally hunted for sport and food. If you get to see a magpie goose – especially if it's out of water – try and get a look at its semi-webbed feet.

WHAT TO LISTEN FOR	Abrupt, short, airhorn-like honking.
WHAT TO LOOK FOR	The magpie goose is a large black and white goose. The long neck, head and wings are black and the body is white. (This combination of black and white plumage is termed 'pied' in the birding world, hence the common European name given to the magpie goose, the magpie-lark and the Australian magpie.) The red beak has a white tip. Females and males look largely the same, though males have a larger bulge on the top of their head. The legs are red and, unlike most waterbirds, magpie geese have long, strong toes that look more designed for walking than for paddling, with only slight webbing between these digits.
IMMATURE BIRDS	Young magpie geese have a dark upper back instead of white, which will begin to mottle as they transition into adult plumage. Additionally, they usually have a paler beak than adults. The very young geese are entirely brown and fluffy.
WHERE TO START LOOKING	Magpie geese will always be close to water, often in large flocks. If you are within the bird's range, your best bet will be to head to the largest local body of water nearby and have a look for large flocks of birds. These birds especially like vast, shallow areas of water, so often seasonal wetlands or floodplains are a good place to try. You may also have luck visiting dams and rivers.
WHAT THEY EAT	Vegetation from wetlands, grasses (roots, shoots etc.), some fruits – especially when they encounter farms (many news stories relay the woes of local mango croppers who have lost portions of their harvest to the hungry beaks and stamping feet of magpie geese).
SIMILAR BIRDS	Black swan (*see* page 93), grey goose (i.e. imported domestic geese). There is another goose species endemic to Australia – the Cape Barren goose – but these beautiful birds are entirely grey with a shorter, yellowish bill, so shouldn't cause too much confusion with the magpie goose.

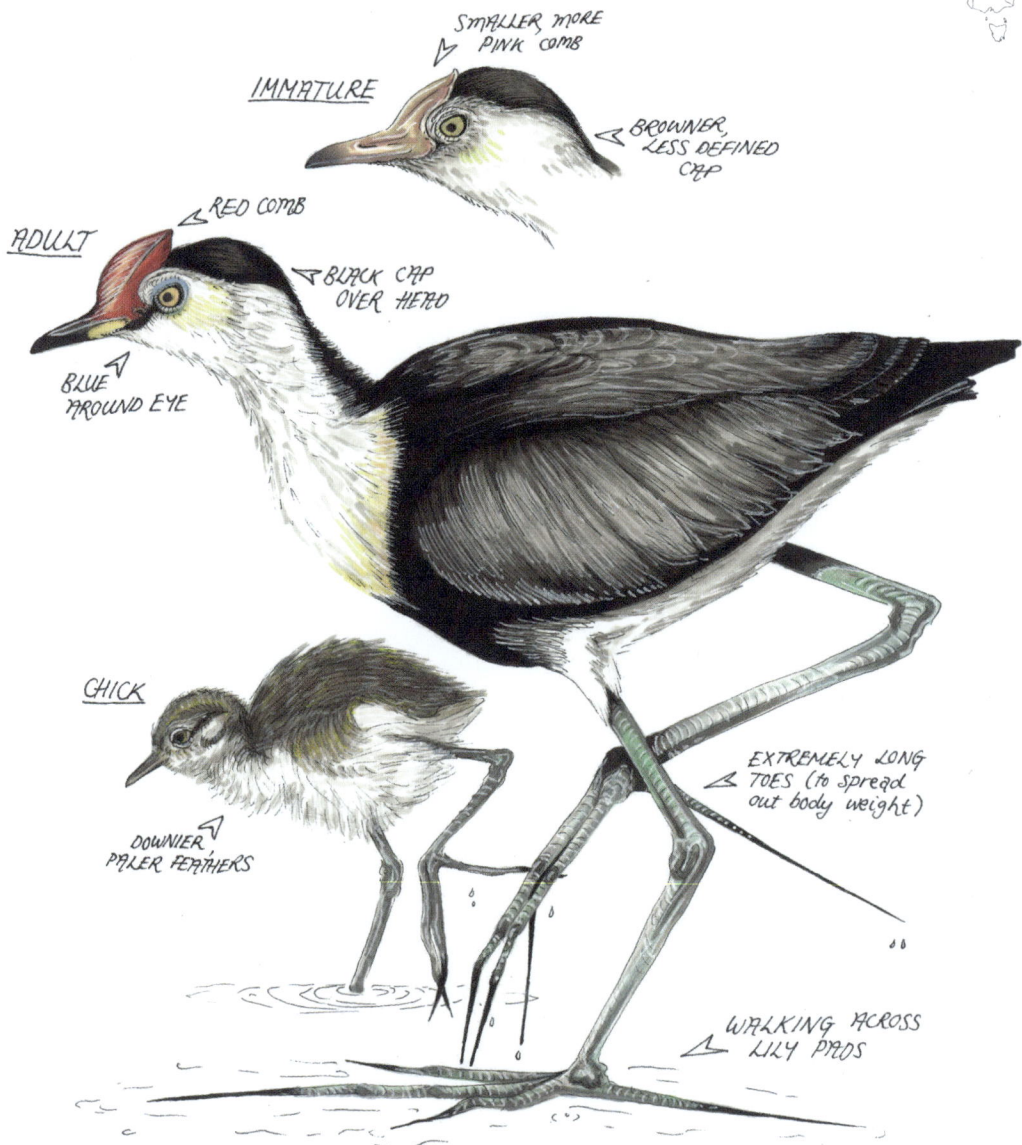

IMMATURE

SMALLER MORE PINK COMB

BROWNER, LESS DEFINED CAP

RED COMB

ADULT

BLACK CAP OVER HEAD

BLUE AROUND EYE

CHICK

DOWNIER PALER FEATHERS

EXTREMELY LONG TOES (to spread out body weight)

WALKING ACROSS LILY PADS

Comb-crested jacana

Irediparra gallinacea

The comb-crested jacana is able to walk across the surface of water using lily pads, a habit which has earned it the names 'lilytrotter', 'lotusbird' or even 'Jesus bird'. Its extremely long, spider-like toes help spread its weight as it steps onto floating plant leaves – it is both strange and wonderful to see a bird 'tiptoe' across the surface of a pond, rather than wading in the shallows.

Living almost solely on the surface of water bodies is a tenuous existence, especially in northern Australia, where crocodiles readily swim. Despite this, the comb-crested jacana is wily to the ways of predators and the father keeps a close eye on his young as they move over water (the mother comb-crested jacana usually isn't involved in parenting duties, leaving the father to do the hard yards of keeping the chicks safe). If the kids need to be moved, the father – in an adorable feat of toddler transport – will close his wings over the youngsters, pinning them in place. Then, with their bodies tucked safely under his wings, and only the chicks' lanky toes exposed, the father bird carries them over the lily pads to safer waters.

WHAT TO LISTEN FOR	Comb-crested jacanas make a piercing repeated whistle, descending in pitch. They can also produce a piercing, seabird-like chattering.
WHAT TO LOOK FOR	The comb-crested jacana is a surreal-looking, long-legged, large-footed wading bird – these birds remind me of something that might walk out of a Salvador Dalí painting. The adult birds are adorned with a red beak and red forehead shield, which forms a vertical 'fin' over the top of the head. The face is white, framed with yellow feathers that intensify at the base of the neck. The back of the neck and wings are dark and there is also a large band of dark feathers across the chest. The chin and chest are otherwise white. The legs are greenish-grey and the toes are very long and spidery. <u>Females</u> are larger than the males.
IMMATURE BIRDS	Young comb-crested jacanas have white bellies, but have no band around the front of the chest, and the wing feathers are a lighter brown than those of the adults. They have a smaller, paler beak and head 'fin'. The chicks are tiny and fluffy. Their backs are pale brown with some dark streaks running along the length of their body. From a young age they have long toes, making them look even more adorable as they pat-pat-pat over lily pads.
WHERE TO START LOOKING	To find a comb-crested jacana, visit local wetlands, or, at a push, well-vegetated ponds and lakes. They prefer areas with lots of water plants and vegetation, so floodplains and established water bodies are a great place to start – and will most likely be found in areas with conserved habitat (more likely reserves and habitat sanctuaries, not so much in suburban water bodies). As described above, jacanas like to use lily or lotus pads to help them make their way across the water, so areas where these plants grow in abundance are a great place to start.
WHAT THEY EAT	Water vegetation and insects.
SIMILAR BIRDS	Perhaps – at a squint – the dusky moorhen (*see* page 89, more in the southern and south-eastern range of the comb-crested jacana) or the Australasian swamphen (*see* page 91).

BODY IS MOTTLED, STREAKY BROWN

IMMATURE

LIGHTER 'CAP' THAN ADULT

BREEDING PLUMES

ADULT BODY IS PALE, CHESTNUTTY BROWN

DARK CAP & YELLOW EYE

ADULT

PALE SECTIONS ON WING & UNDERBELLY

YELLOW LEGS

STRIATED HERON

DARK BEAK

GREYER THAN NANKEEN N. HERON
(note dark 'cheekbone')

Nankeen night heron

Buraandaan [bu-raa-n-daa-n] (Wiradjuri)
Nycticorax caledonicus

These beautiful night herons are described as 'crepuscular' birds – which means that they hunt and socialise most actively during twilight and dawn hours. This is why they are often seen 'hanging out' in trees during daylight, waiting for the more mellow bookends of the day before they get moving. Like their relatives, the herons (*see* page 105) and egrets (*see* page 103), these birds stalk their prey through shallow waters, systematically and patiently pursuing their next catch. However, the nankeen night heron seems to prefer staying in murkier, more shady or reed-filled areas of wetlands and rivers where they can go about their snacking in peace. They can be quite difficult to approach, as they are wary and are able to move quickly along water bodies to escape bird-paparazzi. That said, these birds are something special to get a good look at – especially if you have a chance to see their two long nuptial plumes. Between these fancy feathers and the dessert-worthy colour scheme, these birds have an outfit worthy of the Met Gala.

WHAT TO LISTEN FOR	A single note, repeated, *treeew*, reminiscent of a bird of prey.
WHAT TO LOOK FOR	Nankeen night herons are large creamy-coloured waterbirds that usually perch on trees overhanging water. I like to think of the nankeen night heron as the 'dessert bird' because its colours are a mix of peach, hazelnut and cream (or maybe the colours of Neapolitan ice-cream). The underbelly of the bird is white. The head is topped with a dark brown cap that extends onto the back. The wings are pinkish-brown, descending to a darker brown towards the wingtips. The eye is yellow, and the beak a dark grey. When it is perched, the nankeen night heron appears to have almost no neck, but during flight, as with other herons, its neck extends partially. Its wings are almost owlish and 'voluptuous' when you see them in flight. Note: If you are able to see two long, white feathers that extend down from the cap, the bird is in 'breeding plumage' and is likely to be looking out for (or has been recently united with) a partner.
IMMATURE BIRDS	Young nankeen night herons are chestnut brown patterned with white streaks, and have a darkish patch over the head where the adult 'cap' will develop.
WHERE TO START LOOKING	I have one particular spot where I can reliably see nankeen night-herons, and it's in the branches of some native bushland overhanging a local lake. They tend to stay on the far side of the water, away from human activity. You may find it worthwhile to go to your local lake or river, and to try to head for one of the quieter sections to scan the trees. These birds are widespread but not in great numbers, so it may take a little patience to see one. Try anywhere near water bodies that have some decent tree cover, excluding the more arid areas of Australia.
WHAT THEY EAT	Mostly fish, frogs, small reptiles and insects.
SIMILAR BIRDS	Bittern species (shy, stealthy birds that usually stay low to the ground), white-faced heron (*see* page 105), striated heron (pictured opposite; northern and eastern coastlines), Australasian darter (*see* page 107).

LARGE
EYE

WHITE
EYE-BROW

DARKER FEATHERS
OVER BACK

LARGE-ISH
BEAK

VERTICAL
STREAKS ON
CHEST

BEACH-STONE
CURLEW
(note the enormous, more
yellow beak)

LONG
LEGS

Bush stone-curlew

Burhinus grallarius

The bush stone-curlew, for all its camouflage, looks like a mix of several bird groups. It has the posture of a wader, the head of a perching bird and the huge eyes of a predatory night bird. They're something of a polymath of the bird world, being fast runners and flyers, canny hunters and excellent (read: creepy) singers. The sound of the bush stone-curlew calling at night is truly something worthy of a Stephen King novel – disconcerting and shiver-inducing. Though they're less active during the day, if you do spot one while out walking, the bush stone-curlew will often freeze in position, relying on its bush-camouflaged plumage to keep it from harm (these birds would be unbeatable at musical statues). If directly threatened – especially when defending its young – the bush stone-curlew will lift out its wings, puff out its chest and try to intimidate the threatening party. They give a harsh, screeching noise from deep in their chest as they do this.

WHAT TO LISTEN FOR
The bush stone-curlew makes a mournful (and bone-chilling) 'whistle scream', a sound so haunting it has earned the bird the colloquial name 'murderbird'. This screech rises then falls, like someone playing a ghostly tin whistle. Usually these calls are heard at night.

WHAT TO LOOK FOR
The bush stone-curlew is a tall, long-legged, pale brown bird. The belly and neck are cream with brown streaks. The immediate face around the beak is cream coloured, extending into a brow over the large yellow eye. The legs are long with knobbly knees and are pale brown. The back of the bush stone-curlew is brown-grey with scalloped patterning, which also caps the head. In flight, two separate panels of white feathers can be seen on each wing. Overall, this bird is very well camouflaged in its preferred dry bushland habitats.

WHERE TO START LOOKING
The bush stone-curlew is more of an inland-dwelling bird, so try heading to open bushland or the drier sections of rainforest, open scrub or edges of grassy pasture. They will also sometimes head into more suburban areas, but inland bush is likely to be your best bet.

WHAT THEY EAT
They have a varied diet that includes insects, grubs, small reptiles and other small nocturnal critters.

SIMILAR BIRDS
Beach stone-curlew (pictured opposite; restricted to northern beaches and urban centres on the coast).

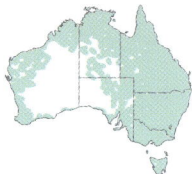

IMMATURE
(yellow beak)

NON-BREEDING
ADULT

BREEDING
ADULT

BLUE-ISH
BEAK

NECK
MAY APPEAR
SHORT WHEN
FOLDED

LONG FINE
NUPTIAL PLUMES
OVER WINGS

DARK
LEGS

NECK STAYS
FOLDED IN
FLIGHT

Great egret

Ardea alba

In the water, great egrets take slow, dainty steps on their long legs as they scan for food in shallower areas. Habitually they step, pause, scan with a beady eye, then take another step, a repeated rhythm that they use when hunting. Eventually, when a snack is sighted (usually a small fish or a frog), the bird will stab its sharp beak downwards to grab the meal.

Sometimes great egrets can be spotted hanging out in large colonies (usually in several poop-stained trees on the edge of a lake or estuary). During these 'colonial sessions', great egrets will form mating pairs for the breeding season, a process that relies on a courtship ritual between pairs. When it comes time to settle down for the breeding season, the male great egret captures the attentions of a female by doing a series of dance moves. Part of the courtship process is for the male bird to raise his long 'nuptial plumes' from the back of his body to perform a hopping dance, bobbing them about, making for a rather hypnotic display. The female, if interested, reciprocates with preening and several other minute behaviours to communicate her favour. Despite these large colony 'sessions' happening every year over the warmer months, I more often spot great egrets just solo or in a pair, stalking slowly through shallow waters in an estuary or marshlands.

WHAT TO LISTEN FOR	A guttural growl, similar to the jerky chortling that an Australian pelican makes (*see* page 115).
WHAT TO LOOK FOR	The great egret is a white, long-legged, long-necked wader. The body, neck and head are all white. The beak is yellow with a greenish tinge at the base – in <u>non-breeding season</u>, the beak is yellow-grey with a very faint green-blue tinge at the base of the beak; in <u>breeding season</u> the beak becomes darker, almost black, and the base becomes intensely green-blue. Both the male and female birds show breeding plumage. Also during breeding season, the great egret grows 'nuptial plumes'. These 'plumes' are long, hair-like feathers that drape over the back of the bird. In flight, the great egret tucks its neck into a 'u-bend' fold.
IMMATURE BIRDS	Young great egrets have a yellower beak where that of adults (during breeding season) is blue-green (pictured opposite). Between breeding and non-breeding times of year, this green colour may wax and wane, so distinguishing adults from youths can be very difficult.
WHERE TO START LOOKING	Great egrets stay close to water, so try visiting wetlands, edges of water bodies, rivers, marshlands, estuaries and well-watered pasturelands.
WHAT THEY EAT	Fish, frogs and insects – these birds are generalist snackers when it comes to small critters that live in wetlands.
SIMILAR BIRDS	The egrets are challenging to identify as they all look quite similar. There are four species you are most likely to confuse with the great egret: little egret (has a dark beak), intermediate egret (has plumes on its chest), cattle egret (its feathers are yellower, especially when in breeding plumage), eastern reef egret (has yellow legs). Note: The great egret is the largest of these birds, with a body length (beak-tip to tail-tip) of nearly a metre. With the added height of its long legs, this is a big bird, which will hopefully help you distinguish it from other egrets.

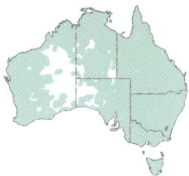

WHITE-FACED HERONS OFTEN HOLD THEIR NECK AT LEAST PARTIALLY FOLDED

IMMATURE

LESS WHITE ON FACE

PINKISH AREAS AROUND YELLOW EYE

ADULT

WHITE FACE

BLUE-GREY BACK & HEAD

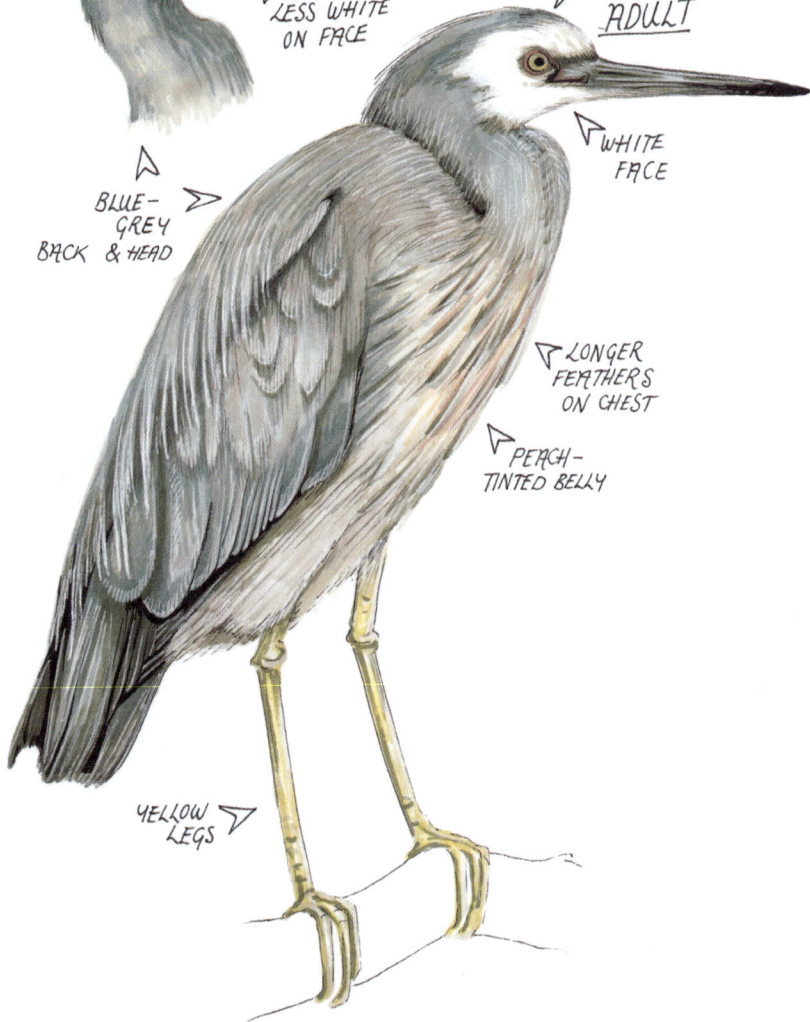

LONGER FEATHERS ON CHEST

PEACH-TINTED BELLY

YELLOW LEGS

White-faced heron

Garranygay [garan-gay] (Gumbaynggirr);
gandaru [ga-n-da-ru], **yambil** [ya-m-bi-l],
gungarung [gu-nga-ru-ng] (Wiradjuri)
Egretta novaehollandiae

Sometimes called the 'blue crane', the white-faced heron is a beautiful colour – though there is something a little mournful and Eeyore-ish about them. They seem to be alone so much of the time, picking their way through the shallows, and fleeing with gangly, flapping wings and legs at the slightest threat. I've mostly seen them alone or in pairs, carefully making their way through the shallows of a lake, river or estuary. As they move, they look left and right, scanning for food with careful precision. Eventually they will stab down to grab the creature they've spotted, much like the great egret does (*see page 103*). They are wary of humans and will readily flee if approached, despite being common in high-contact regions along coastlines and rivers.

WHAT TO LISTEN FOR	When startled, the white-faced heron makes a harsh, repeating call, *scccrahh-sccraahhh-scrrahhh*. It sounds similar to the white noise a construction truck makes when reversing.
WHAT TO LOOK FOR	White-faced herons are tall, grey wading birds. The neck and body are a cool grey, with a faint pinkish blush to the underbelly. They have a white 'mask' over the immediate face, a large dark grey beak and a yellow eye. During breeding season, the feathers over their neck and back become long and almost hair-like. In non-breeding season, these feathers are shorter and less obvious. The legs are yellow.
IMMATURE BIRDS	Young white-faced herons have a less defined white 'mask'; instead they have pale grey feathers around the face with only the beginnings of a white 'mask' appearing as they age.
WHERE TO START LOOKING	The white-faced heron is a relatively common waterbird, so try looking for these birds at your local wetlands, estuary, river, beach, lake or dam. It is worth keeping an eye out for them whenever you visit an area with a water source. They are so quiet and shy that they can often be overlooked, but stay observant and hopefully you'll be able to see them as they wade through the shallows.
WHAT THEY EAT	Fish, invertebrates, crustaceans, frogs and other small water-dwelling critters.
SIMILAR BIRDS	White-necked heron (a less common bird found across a similar range – note that these herons have a darker body and the entire neck is white).

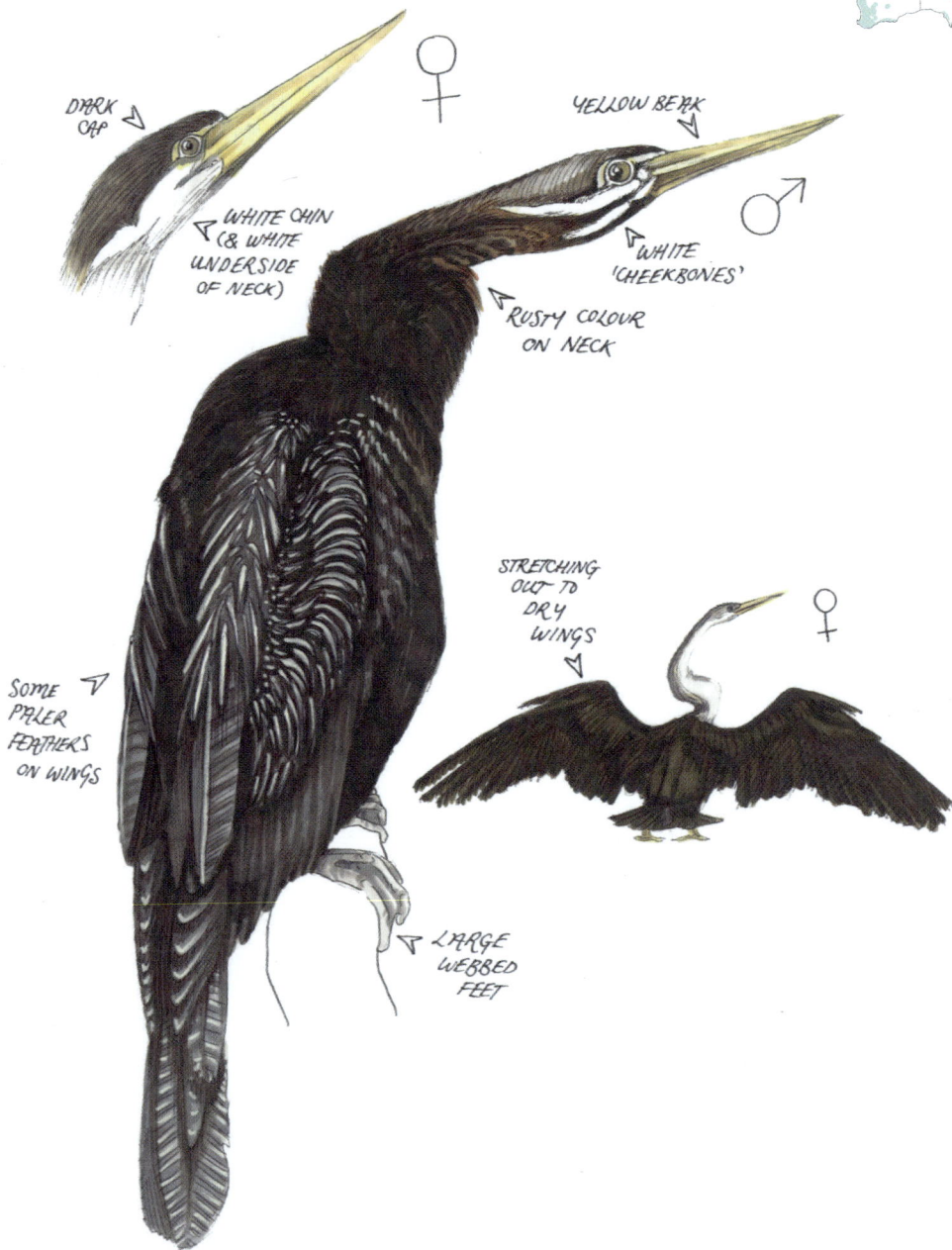

DARK CAP ᐳ

♀

WHITE CHIN (& WHITE UNDERSIDE OF NECK) ᐳ

YELLOW BEAK ↓

♂

WHITE 'CHEEKBONES' ᐳ

RUSTY COLOUR ON NECK ᐳ

STRETCHING OUT TO DRY WINGS ᐁ

♀

SOME PALER FEATHERS ON WINGS ᐁ

LARGE WEBBED FEET ᐁ

Australasian darter

Anhinga novaehollandiae

The Australasian darter is a shy diving bird that will quickly swim off if you approach it. They are excellent swimmers, and thus can pursue fish and crustaceans underwater with ease. Although being water-lovers, darters are excellent flyers (unlike their fellow waterbirds the cormorants, who look much more 'panicked' in the air). Darters are often seen at perch on a dead log in water, holding their wings outstretched to dry. Though some other diving birds – like little penguins – have special oil glands that waterproof their feathers, the darter lacks these glands, and therefore must dry off between diving sessions. Sometimes darters will swim across creeks or lakes with their head held above the surface of the water, much like a snake would. This behaviour has earned them the nickname 'snakebird'.

WHAT TO LISTEN FOR	Rapid, duck-like honking with a creaky tone to it, *gwek – ekk-ekk-ekk-ekk*.
WHAT TO LOOK FOR	The Australasian darter is a brown, long-necked diving bird. It has a yellow beak and a white 'cheek-bone' mark (a line extending horizontally below the eye and partially down the neck.) The tail is large and shaped like a paddle. <u>Males</u> are predominantly dark brown and they have a rusty splotch of feathers at the base of the neck. <u>Females</u> have a white underbelly, including the underside of their neck and chin. When these birds are flying, the tail is often 'fanned' and they hold a slight kink in their neck. If you get to see an Australasian darter in flight, you'll notice that the females have a crisp white underbelly, framed by the black wings and tail, while the males are entirely dark.
IMMATURE BIRDS	Young Australasian darters have a similar look to the females, but have mottled, pale brown feathers over their backs (unlike the dark feathers of the adult female).
WHERE TO START LOOKING	Australasian darters prefer freshwater regions, so they are less common to the seaside, though they will head down into estuaries where water becomes brackish. They are found on, in or alongside freshwater across Australia, except in arid inland regions in the west. Try your local creek, river or lake, especially sections where debris provides perches alongside or in the water.
WHAT THEY EAT	Fish, crustaceans and insects. These birds are excellent swimmers and divers and can easily grab prey underwater.
SIMILAR BIRDS	All cormorant species (e.g. little pied cormorant, *see* page 109), nankeen night heron (*see* page 99).

LITTLE PIED
IN FLIGHT

LITTLE
PIED

AUSTRALIAN
PIED

SLIGHTLY
HOOKED
BEAK

BLACK
BACK &
WINGS

DRYING WINGS
AT PERCH

WHITE
FACE &
BELLY

WEBBED
FEET

Little pied cormorant

Barrigurrun [bah-ree-goo-roon] (Gumbaynggirr)
Microcarbo melanoleucos

Often called the 'little shag', the little pied cormorant can also be found in New Zealand and other parts of Southeast Asia. These little divers will scour rivers and oceans in search of food. They are often seen perched on flood-deposited logs, or on jetties, with their wings lifted out on either side of them to dry off in the wind and sun. They may share these perches with other shorebirds, including their close relatives the little black cormorant and the Australian pied cormorant.

When they are in flight, there is something about cormorants that makes me think 'student pilot'. There is a panicked style to the flapping of their wings and their midair turns, especially when they are coming in to land. Not to say they aren't bold – sometimes I've seen cormorants fly in very stormy weather to reach their destination, showing grim determination as the wind buffets them around. These are common shorebirds so you should have some luck in seeing them next time you're near the coast.

WHAT TO LOOK FOR	The little pied cormorant is a medium-sized black and white waterbird. Like other cormorants, it has a sleek body that is almost 'oily' looking, with a narrow head that merges into a hook-nosed beak. The underside of the body is white, extending through to the face. The back of the little pied cormorant is black, with a cap over the upper part of the head. The beak is yellow, while the feet are large, webbed and black.
IMMATURE BIRDS	Young little pied cormorants are brownish where the adults are black.
WHERE TO START LOOKING	I most often see little pied cormorants on dead logs in estuaries or rivers. They usually stay near salty waters, so if there is a sea lagoon or inlet near you, try looking for them there. Like the Australasian darter (*see* page 107), they perch on dead logs or rocks to dry off, so areas with plenty of perches over the water are good places to begin looking.
WHAT THEY EAT	Fish, crustaceans and insects.
SIMILAR BIRDS	Australian pied cormorant (pictured opposite; this is a bigger bird with a dull beak), little black cormorant (similar range; entirely black), Australasian darter (*see* page 107).

DARK OVERALL WITH IRIDESCENT FEATHERS

GLOSSY IBIS

AUSTRALIAN WHITE IBIS

PINK STRIP UNDER WING

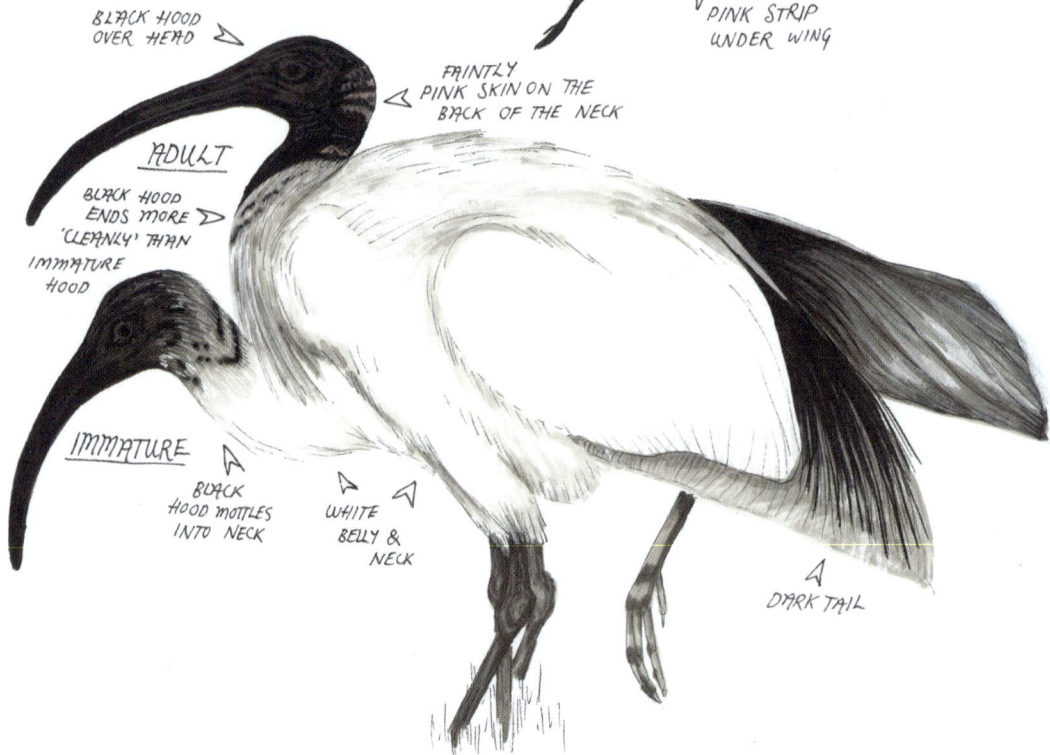

BLACK HOOD OVER HEAD

FAINTLY PINK SKIN ON THE BACK OF THE NECK

ADULT

BLACK HOOD ENDS MORE 'CLEANLY' THAN IMMATURE HOOD

IMMATURE

BLACK HOOD MOTTLES INTO NECK

WHITE BELLY & NECK

DARK TAIL

Australian white ibis

Threskiornis molucca

The Australian white ibis is a common wading bird, usually frequenting shallow areas of salty or brackish water. They efficiently filter through sand for food, delicately picking their way through swamps and marshlands. However, they are just as often seen wading through refuse at landfill sites, or raiding bins in urban parks. Sometimes termed the 'bin chicken', the white ibis has been the unfortunate beneficiary of Australia's waste depots. Populations of these birds have now flourished in urban areas. It's a bit sad that these birds have been so tainted by human industry, when in their natural context, these are birds we would otherwise appreciate for their awesomely weird appearance. Whenever I see an ibis stalking through shallow waters, I am reminded that these birds were often depicted in the hieroglyphs of ancient Egypt. It is surreal knowing we have denigrated creatures that were once so revered on the banks of the Nile. With their waxy black heads, they look like noisy friarbirds on steroids (*see* page 29), especially when seen in the water, scanning for food. In flight, the white ibis may be seen in enormous flocks, moving between feeding sites.

WHAT TO LISTEN FOR	Chicken-like clucking and honking.
WHAT TO LOOK FOR	The Australian white ibis is a large white wading bird with a black-hooded head and a black tail. The long, narrowing, curved beak of the white ibis is used for feeding in shallow water. The legs are long and black, with high knee joints. The black 'hood' on its head extends part of the way down the neck, giving the impression of the bird wearing a balaclava. The body has relatively long, white feathers that may appear 'bedraggled' or stained, depending on the local conditions. There is also a section of black feathers at the tail, which may or may not be visible, depending on the position of the wings. In flight, a strip of pink plumage is visible under the ibis's wings.
IMMATURE BIRDS	The young Australian white ibis has a more mottled grey head, which gradually fades into the white body, rather than having the abrupt 'hood' of the adult bird.
WHERE TO START LOOKING	Try visiting marshy areas in farmland, and beaches, ponds and dams. Any area where water is relatively available is a potential spot to see ibises, including parkland, urban lakes, golf courses, football pitches and other park-like areas.
WHAT THEY EAT	Usually small water-dwelling crustaceans, insects and mussels, though these birds have become generalists, taking scraps from bins, tips and dumpsters.
SIMILAR BIRDS	Straw-necked ibis (*see* page 113), glossy ibis (pictured opposite; an entirely black, iridescent variant of the ibis group, spectacular!), royal and yellow spoonbill (*see* page 117) species.

BLACK CAP
OVER WHOLE
HEAD

WHITE
UNDERBELLY

IRIDESCENT
WING
FEATHERS

'STRAW'
NECK

PINK LEGS

Straw-necked ibis

Jilawarr [jil-ah-warr] (Gumbaynggirr)
Threskiornis spinicollis

It took me a while to register that the straw-necked ibis is not the same bird as the Australian white ibis. They have similar behaviours, wading through water in enormous flocks or cruising through the air in crowded, honking flocks. These two species will also often graze in the same area without too much conflict, although the straw-necked ibis hasn't found such an 'urban niche' as the Australian white ibis. Along with the eastern cattle egret (a yellow-coloured egret, often seen among herds of farm animals), the straw-necked ibis is sometimes called the 'farmer's friend'. Both of these birds frequent pastures, where they eat some of the insects that would otherwise bother cattle and sheep or consume crops. The sight of a flock of straw-necked ibises wheeling in the sky is glorious to see, especially as they often gather in such enormous numbers – but be sure to scan the flock closely with your binoculars to make sure you are able to distinguish which species of ibis you're looking at.

WHAT TO LISTEN FOR	Bark-like honking, most often calling in flight.
WHAT TO LOOK FOR	The straw-necked ibis is a large black and white wader with the same long, downcurved beak as the Australian white ibis (*see* page 111). The beak and head of the straw-necked ibis are black. The uppermost section of neck is white, adorned with a 'mane' of fine, long feathers. The base of the neck and the entire back of the bird is an iridescent black colour (in <u>females</u>, this 'band' of dark feathers around the base of the neck will be bigger and darker than that of the male birds). In certain light, particularly at perch, the reflective substance of these feathers gives off a spectrum of colour, like an oil slick might. The underbelly is white, down to the tail, and the legs are red.
IMMATURE BIRDS	The young straw-necked ibis doesn't have any iridescence in its feathers, nor a decorative 'straw' mane on its neck. The legs also remain black until adulthood.
WHERE TO START LOOKING	Try similar areas to those where you might look for the Australian white ibis (*see* page 111). Any wetlands, lakesides, estuaries or irrigated farmland may prove worthwhile. These birds seem to stick more closely to fresh water than their less discerning relatives.
WHAT THEY EAT	The straw-necked ibis snacks on insects, crustaceans, vegetative matter, and waterborne invertebrates.
SIMILAR BIRDS	Australian white ibis (*see* page 111), glossy ibis (pictured on page 110), royal spoonbill (pictured on page 116).

ADULTS
(beak may be
more or less
pink)

MOTTLED
FEATHERS
ALONG BACK
OF HEAD

UNDERSIDE
OF BEAK IS A
STRETCHY MEMBRANE
(for fishing)

ADULT

IMMATURE
(note brown
feathers)

Australian pelican

Junggaarr [joong-gar] (Gumbaynggirr)
Pelecanus conspicillatus

I always seem to see Australian pelicans perched at docking areas on the very top of light poles. It often appears as if these birds are claiming some kind of judgemental authority over the jetty-side by staying up so high. When not perched at boat ramps or fishing areas, these birds will comfortably paddle in waters among silver gulls and other birds, sometimes scavenging on fish offcuts where they've been thrown by humans, following food where it is abundant. Despite having a very 'generalist' diet in principle, pelicans largely consume fish, sometimes working in groups to shepherd fish into a more concentrated school, where they can easily be scooped up.

As mentioned below, the Australian pelican has a distinctive way of flying. The way these heavy, large birds lift off from the surface of the water can be reminiscent of an Airbus A380 taking off from the tarmac. However, once in the air, they are very graceful flyers. They seem to find warm, rising currents easily, holding their wings out straight and wide as they cruise over the landscape with only the occasional tilting of their wings to steer. Sometimes they'll cruise in formation, creating diagonal lines in the sky as they move between bodies of water.

WHAT TO LISTEN FOR	A croaking, guttural honk, and a jerking *gwaaa-ek-eke-ekk*. This call sounds similar to the noise made when two boats tied to a jetty bump against one another.
WHAT TO LOOK FOR	Pelicans are large, pale shorebirds with enormous beaks and long necks. Their bodies are white, while the wings and tail are black-tipped. When the wings are folded against the body in the water, the back of the Australian pelican appears to have a panel of black feathers, though your gaze will likely be drawn immediately to their long, acutely triangular beak. This pink beak is hard on the top, but the bottom is a membranous gullet that can expand to hold one (or several) fish, which the pelican then 'slithers' down its long throat to its stomach, where the fish will be digested. The female birds are smaller than males. In flight, these birds have visibly huge bodies, and they often glide on the breeze with static, outstretched wings.
IMMATURE BIRDS	Young Australian pelicans have browner plumage overall.
WHERE TO START LOOKING	Try visiting water bodies almost anywhere in Australia – lakes, rivers, estuaries, even the occasional dam. These birds become quickly aware of where fish gutting commonly occurs, and hang in the water nearby, where they can collect an easy meal, so if there is a local jetty or designated fishing area, try visiting there.
WHAT THEY EAT	These birds are opportunistic in their eating. Though they usually hunt for fish or crustaceans, they will sometimes take small reptiles, fish guts from jetty sides, and even birds of other species – particularly vulnerable chicks.
SIMILAR BIRDS	Yellow-billed spoonbill (*see* page 117), royal spoonbill (pictured on page 116).

IMMATURE

ROYAL
SPOONBILL
(dark beak,
red eye)

PALER
(PINKER)
BEAK

NO
FRAME
AROUND FACE

DARK
'FRAME'
AROUND
FACE

ADULT
(BREEDING)

LONG, ROUND-
TIPPED BILL

IMMATURE

ADULT

LONGER
PLUMES ON
CHEST

Yellow-billed spoonbill

Murrugaya [mu-rru-ga-ya] (Wiradjuri)
Platalea flavipes

The yellow-billed spoonbill is often seen in large mixed colonies among royal spoonbills, ibises and other waders. They stalk through waters with their bill beneath the surface, sweeping it from left to right in large arcs, searching for food. Their bills are very sensitive to movement, so if they feel something shifting in the mud nearby, they wobble their bill back and forth to chase down their meal. They then lift their head to toss the food back into their throat – you may spot them doing this, if you catch them at the right moment! The long bill and slow movements of these birds are so thorough, they often make me think of someone raking sand in a Zen garden. They seem to go about their ritualistic feeding no matter the weather, so observing them is always a lovely opportunity to slow down and appreciate a quiet moment by the water in the company of birds.

WHAT TO LOOK FOR	The yellow-billed spoonbill is a large wading bird with a white body, long, grey legs and a long, yellow, spoon-shaped bill. Despite the bird's name, the bill may sometimes appear to be more pinkish-grey than yellow, though the colour may intensify during the breeding season. A faint line of black feathers frames the face in what is almost a square pattern, like the edge of a mask. In breeding plumage, the feathers on the front of the bird's chest are longer, forming a small 'mane' with a very faint yellow tint to it. Also during breeding season, the face may appear slightly pink-blue, though this can be tricky to spot from afar! In non-breeding plumage, the chest feathers are short and white, and the face resumes a similar colour to the bill, losing any blue-pink colouring.
IMMATURE BIRDS	Young yellow-billed spoonbills lack the black 'face frame' and have duller beaks.
WHERE TO START LOOKING	These birds feed as they wade, so they like to hang in shallow areas of water. Try looking for them in wetlands, bodies of water, dams, reeded areas on river banks, estuaries and inlets.
WHAT THEY EAT	Spoonbills use their paddle-like beaks to seek out water-dwelling invertebrates, smaller fish and crustaceans from below the surface.
SIMILAR BIRDS	Royal spoonbill (pictured opposite; has a black 'spoonbill' instead of a yellow one), Australian white ibis (*see* page 111), straw-necked ibis (*see* page 113) and great egret (*see* page 103).

ADULT
(northern form)

SMALLER MASK &
WATTLES

LENGTHY
WATTLES

IMMATURE

ADULT
(southern form)

IMMATURE
(note mottled
back and head)

ADULT

Masked lapwing

Didadida [di-da-di-da], **baldyarraydyarray** [ba-l-dya-rray-dya-rray], **balduridyari** [ba-l-du-ri-dya-ri] (Wiradjuri)
Vanellus miles

Lapwings tend to show off their long pins on football ovals, grassy verges, roundabouts and suburban lawns. I usually see them moving in pairs with limited regard for the danger of nearby cars. Often known as 'spur-winged plovers', or as my dad has said, 'those-bloody-birds-that-used-to-dive-bomb-me-on-my-way-to-school', these birds can be particularly crazed during spring breeding, when they are perhaps a little too proactive in their defence of their young. They nest on the ground, which makes them particularly vulnerable to predation by foxes and cats, so maybe they're uptight for a reason.

The yellow masking of the lapwing's head makes it look somewhat like a Casanova-esque Venetian seducer – albeit one that screeches like an agitated dolphin and flies away whenever you try to ask it to dance.

WHAT TO LISTEN FOR

It's quite difficult to do justice to the sense of sheer hysteria in the call of the masked lapwing. I most often hear them calling at dusk or just after nightfall. They give a gull-like screech, *geh-geh-geh-geh-geh-geh-geh*, which carries a long way. If you were to hear this call with your eyes closed and a coconut in hand, it might half convince you that you were relaxing on a beachside somewhere with slightly panicked bottlenose dolphins just past the breakers.

WHAT TO LOOK FOR

Lapwings are medium-sized birds that commonly prowl around the suburbs. Sometimes the masked lapwing hunches its head against its body, giving it a doleful kind of appearance. The pair of yellow wattles on its face only enhances this moody demeanour ('wattles' are droopy bits of skin, somewhat like those you see on a common chicken). These wattles are yellow and triangular, hanging well below the chin of the lapwing. They also extend upwards to merge with the beak, and to 'mask' the forehead (giving the bird its name). The remainder of the head is black and the underbelly is white. The wings and back are an olive-brown, and at the front of each wing 'shoulder', you might be able to see a small yellow spur. Note that in the northern half of the country, the masked lapwing has less black over its head and bigger 'wattles' on the face.

IMMATURE BIRDS

Young masked lapwings look more mottled and 'scaly' over their grey wings, as if you were viewing an adult lapwing through privacy glass. They also have smaller wattles, so look less 'masked' than the adults.

WHERE TO START LOOKING

These birds are likely to be found near water, in moist, urbanised environments, particularly in open areas of grass (e.g. a football pitch or school campus) and more expansive grassland areas. Try your local oval or golf course.

WHAT THEY EAT

These birds are omnivorous grazers, shifting between seeds, insects, worms and scraps.

SIMILAR BIRDS

Banded lapwing (these similar-looking birds are slightly less common. They have no masking, but they do have a white eye-band and a red strip above their beak).

COMMON
PIPIS

BRIGHT
ORANGE
EYE

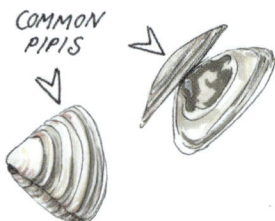

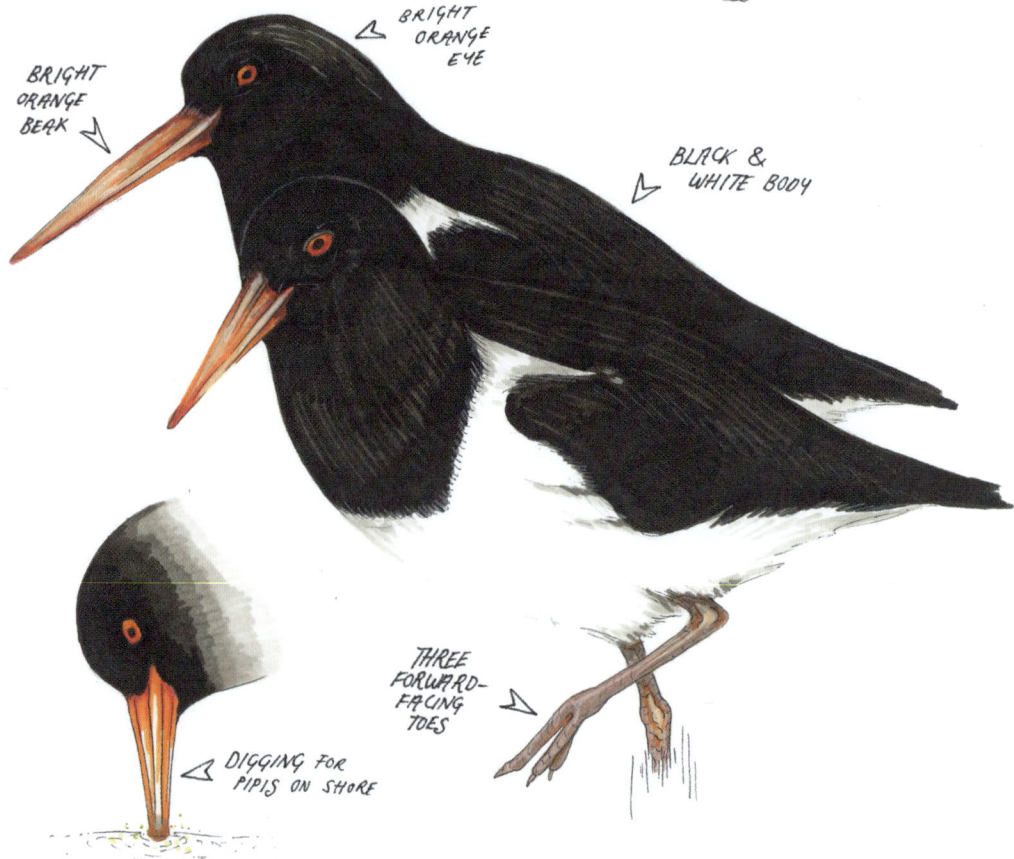

BRIGHT
ORANGE
BEAK

BLACK &
WHITE BODY

THREE
FORWARD-
FACING
TOES

DIGGING FOR
PIPIS ON SHORE

Pied oystercatcher

Haematopus longirostris

Usually if I get to see pied oystercatchers, they're cruising along shores in mating pairs, scouring the sand for snacks. They slowly stalk along the waterline, probing the sand with their beaks for goodies. Sometimes pied oystercatchers will head out on 'double dates', feeding alongside another pair of oystercatchers, and will occasionally form larger groups of their own kind, all scouring the shore and poking their beaks into the sand. I think of these birds as the treasure hunters of the bird world, using their beaks as if they were metal detectors, scanning the seaside for some buried 'gold' (a nice, juicy sandworm). These birds really do occupy the beachfronts just as we do – enjoying the shallows, walking along the beach, and sifting for fishing bait. They nest along open areas of shorelines too, crying out with their rapid squeaking alarm call to warn their fellows if birds of prey are overhead (especially, and most often, the white-bellied sea-eagle, *see* page 121).

WHAT TO LISTEN FOR	The pied oystercatcher makes a high-pitched, rubbery squeaking, *ee-eeh-eeh-eeh*. To me, it's reminiscent of a kid at a birthday party rubbing two balloons together.
WHAT TO LOOK FOR	The pied oystercatcher is a black and white shorebird with a vivid red beak. The head and body of the pied oystercatcher is black, excluding the white underbelly. Its beak, legs and eyes are an intense red-orange.
IMMATURE BIRDS	Young pied oystercatchers are a mottled grey colour where the adults are black. Their eyes and legs tend to be more grey than red.
WHERE TO START LOOKING	Pied oystercatchers tend to pick through shallows or right along the tideline on beaches and estuary shores. They seem to steer relatively clear of people, so try looking on sections of the coast where people don't hang out as readily, or go to your local beach at quieter times of the day.
WHAT THEY EAT	Rarely oysters, more often sandworms, sand-dwelling bugs, pipis and other small bivalves along shallow sandy shores.
SIMILAR BIRDS	Sooty oystercatcher (these birds are entirely black, but otherwise are similar), white-headed and banded stilts, Caspian tern (*see* page 127), masked lapwing (*see* page 119) and banded lapwing.

RED EYE RING

VIVID RED BILL

ADULT

SOMETIMES ARCHES NECK WHILE CALLING / PURSUING OTHER GULLS

DARK BEAK

IMMATURE

DARK FEET

MOTTLED FEATHERS

Silver gull

Gaawil [gah-will] (Gumbaynggirr)
Chroicocephalus novaehollandiae

Growing up, I always called silver gulls simply 'seagulls' – I wasn't really aware of any other seabirds, as silver gulls seemed to dominate shorelines and jetties so much. These birds often hang in enormous trilling flocks, usually facing into the wind (to minimise wind resistance to those relentless sea breezes). Sometimes they will cruise solo in search of food, and will end up 'lurking' in urban areas, surprisingly far from the seashore.

Despite being a familiar sight (and sometimes even an annoyance) in many areas of Australia, I think the silver gull makes for excellent birdwatching. These seabirds have very expressive and vocal behaviour, constantly screeching, chasing, flapping and intimidating one another. These are maybe the 'hangriest' birds in the world and will always be ready to fight for one more chip. Sometimes I wonder what kind of life the silver gull would live if it was isolated away from human influence – perhaps these birds are actually quiet-natured and affectionate away from the moral sway of fried foods.

WHAT TO LISTEN FOR	A growling, rattling call, throaty, repeated insistently, *tttrrrrrowwwwwr*.
WHAT TO LOOK FOR	Silver gulls are the classic 'seagull' – they are predominantly white, medium-sized shorebirds. Their legs and beak are red, while the wings are grey. The black wingtips can be seen folded against the tail, and are even more obvious in flight. The eye is a white iris with a black pupil, making them look slightly enraged. The tip of the beak is usually slightly darker than the rest of the beak, with older birds tending to have more intensely red beaks.
IMMATURE BIRDS	Young silver gulls have a more mottled grey and brown tint in their wings. The juvenile beaks are usually more yellowish.
WHERE TO START LOOKING	For a 'shorebird', the silver gull is extremely widespread and very common. You can see these birds nearly everywhere, excluding the arid central south-west. You're most likely to see silver gulls in places where they can readily get a feed, so try visiting areas near gutting tables or fishing jetties. Another option is areas behind fish markets or places where food is dumped, or any spot that is often frequented along the shoreline (especially places where people go to have picnics or readily unwrap fish and chips).
WHAT THEY EAT	As their 'tastes' have been influenced by human behaviours, silver gulls have formed a diverse diet. At jetties, the silver gull will eat fish guts, food scraps (especially those proffered by seaside-picnickers) and garbage bin debris, occasionally diverting from this fare to go on 'healthy eating' stints, where they consume actual fish, worms and crustaceans from the bay. Unfortunately, through human influence, they often end up eating or being trapped by plastic bags, bottle caps, the rings that hold a six-pack together, old netting or fishing wire. It's hard to be a silver gull. Everything looks like food, yet so little of it actually is edible.
SIMILAR BIRDS	Pacific gull (*see* page 125), tern species (*see* page 127).

IMMATURE P. GULL
BEAK

SKUA
BEAK ▷

BROWN
SKUA
(note beak
shape)

IMMATURE

YOUNG BIRDS
ARE ENTIRELY
BROWN

ADULT

RED-TIPPED
BEAK

DARK
WINGS

WHITE
BELLY

WHITE BAND
ON FOLDED WINGS

YELLOW
LEGS

Pacific gull

Larus pacificus

The Pacific gull will often stand contemplatively in the shallow waves with its head turned into the wind, or will stalk along the shoreline feeding. I almost never see these gulls in groups – they seem to prefer coming into the shore alone. You may have a good chance of catching sight of them as they fly along a shoreline between feeding sessions. They're double the size of silver gulls (*see* page 123), so be prepared to see a pretty big wingspan as they cruise overhead.

Pacific gulls are well equipped for a life on the high sea – they actually have their own tiny desalination plants, right at the base of their beak. These glands have adapted to allow them to exude excess salt from their body, an attribute that is found in many seabirds. This makes surviving on salty water and salty seafood for long periods of time much easier, as they can maintain a healthy balance of salts in their body while remaining well hydrated. These big seagulls generally nest on remoter areas of the coast, but you're likely to see them eventually as they come in to rest or feed on a shoreline near you.

WHAT TO LOOK FOR	The Pacific gull is a large seabird, coloured mostly white with grey-black wings. The beak is large and yellow, with a red tip; the beak widens slightly at the end, then narrows to a curved point (excellent for cracking into the molluscs these birds love to eat). The underbelly and head are white, while the back of the bird is dark grey, nearly black. There may be a patch of white visible across the back of the Pacific gull when perched – this is formed by the white wingtips, which are more visible in flight. The tail is white with a black band across the tip.
IMMATURE BIRDS	Young Pacific gulls look quite different to the adults, as they are a mottled brown colour over their entire body, while the legs are pale brown. The beak is dark brown.
WHERE TO START LOOKING	Try anywhere along the southern coastlines of Australia, particularly sections of seashore or estuaries where there aren't too many people. Unlike the silver gull (*see* page 123), these birds rarely come inland on waterways.
WHAT THEY EAT	Pipis and other molluscs, and fish.
SIMILAR BIRDS	Kelp gulls have a very similar appearance to the Pacific gull, but they have a slightly different range. The kelp gull is much less frequently seen, but if you do see a bird you think might be a Pacific gull, look closely. In kelp gulls, only the *underside* of the beak-tip is red, and they have a second 'band' of white on the wings above the first, with vivid white dots down the tips of the wings. These details are specific to the kelp gull, so will help you distinguish it from the more common Pacific gull. The skua, a large brown shorebird, looks quite similar to immature Pacific gulls (pictured opposite; this bird has a narrower, dark beak and dark legs).

DARKER
WINGTIP

DIVING
POSTURE

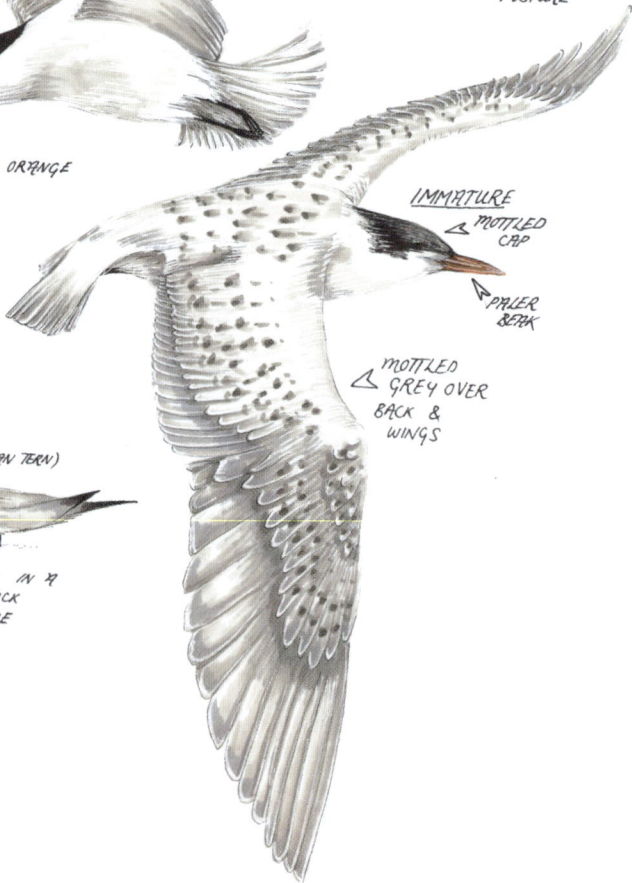

BLACK
CAP

ADULT

BRIGHT ORANGE
BEAK

IMMATURE

MOTTLED
CAP

PALER
BEAK

MOTTLED
GREY OVER
BACK &
WINGS

(SILVER GULL) (CASPIAN TERN)

OFTEN SEEN IN A
MIXED FLOCK
ON SHORE

Caspian tern

Hydroprogne caspia

The Caspian tern is mostly solitary or found in very small parties of their own kind, rarely forming the large same-species flocks that other tern species do. Most often, I will see a lone Caspian tern among a horde of little or fairy terns and silver gulls on coastal inlets, as if the Caspian tern were trying (and failing) to blend in. This huge, red-beaked bird will sit moodily among the mass of noisy seabirds that surround it, its size and bright 'fluoro' beak making it easy to spot. These birds are quite widespread but in sparse numbers, so it may take a few visits to appropriate habitats before you spot one.

The Caspian tern is one of the few tern species that visits inland water bodies in Australia. Most other pelagic birds (seabirds) are quite restricted to coastal waters, excluding the adventurous silver gull (*see* page 123).

If you're lucky, you may be able to spot a Caspian tern while it is hunting. To hunt, terns will commonly 'hover' in place above a shallow area of water. It stays in position by fluttering its huge wings as it scans the water for fish. When an appropriate sea snack has wandered into the shallows where they cannot easily dive away, the tern will fold its wings and dive to grab them from the water.

WHAT TO LISTEN FOR	A rasping 'chuckle', descending in tone. This call reminds me a bit of a wet scourer on the bottom of an empty metal pot. In flight, these birds will give a more piercing, gull-like shriek.
WHAT TO LOOK FOR	The Caspian tern is a white ocean bird with a vivid orange beak, and is often perched on seashores among other seabirds. This species is the largest tern in the world, with an enormous wingspan. It has a white chest and belly, with grey wings, and a black 'cap' over the head. The large beak is a vivid shade of orange, one of the best markers of this species – along with its large size. In flight, the bird's wingtips are black. The feet are also black and are usually tucked in tight against the body once the Caspian tern takes to the air. When the tail is folded, the tail feathers form a fork. If you get to see one perched on the beach, the Caspian tern appears to be very long-bodied with disproportionately short legs for its size.
IMMATURE BIRDS	Young Caspian terns have a white underbelly and chest, with the remainder of the body a mottled grey colour. They have darker mottling over the upper half of the head forming an early version of the adult 'cap'. The beak will also be darker than that of the adult birds.
WHAT THEY EAT	Fish.
WHERE TO START LOOKING	Caspian terns spend time hunting offshore, or come in to rest on the shoreline of beaches, inlets or lakes, usually remaining on waterways that are close to the coast (though they will occasionally visit inland lakes and rivers). Your most likely place to spot one is along a beach or estuary where there are already large numbers of other flocking seabirds, such as silver gulls (*see* page 123) or smaller tern species.
SIMILAR BIRDS	Fairy tern, little tern, common tern, whiskered tern (like the Caspian tern, the whiskered tern is also occasionally seen on inland lakes; it is smaller and greyer). Most tern species exhibit the same characteristic long body shape and short legs. Make sure to look for the biggest tern on a shore, and if it has a bright orange-red beak and black feet, that will be the Caspian tern you're seeing!

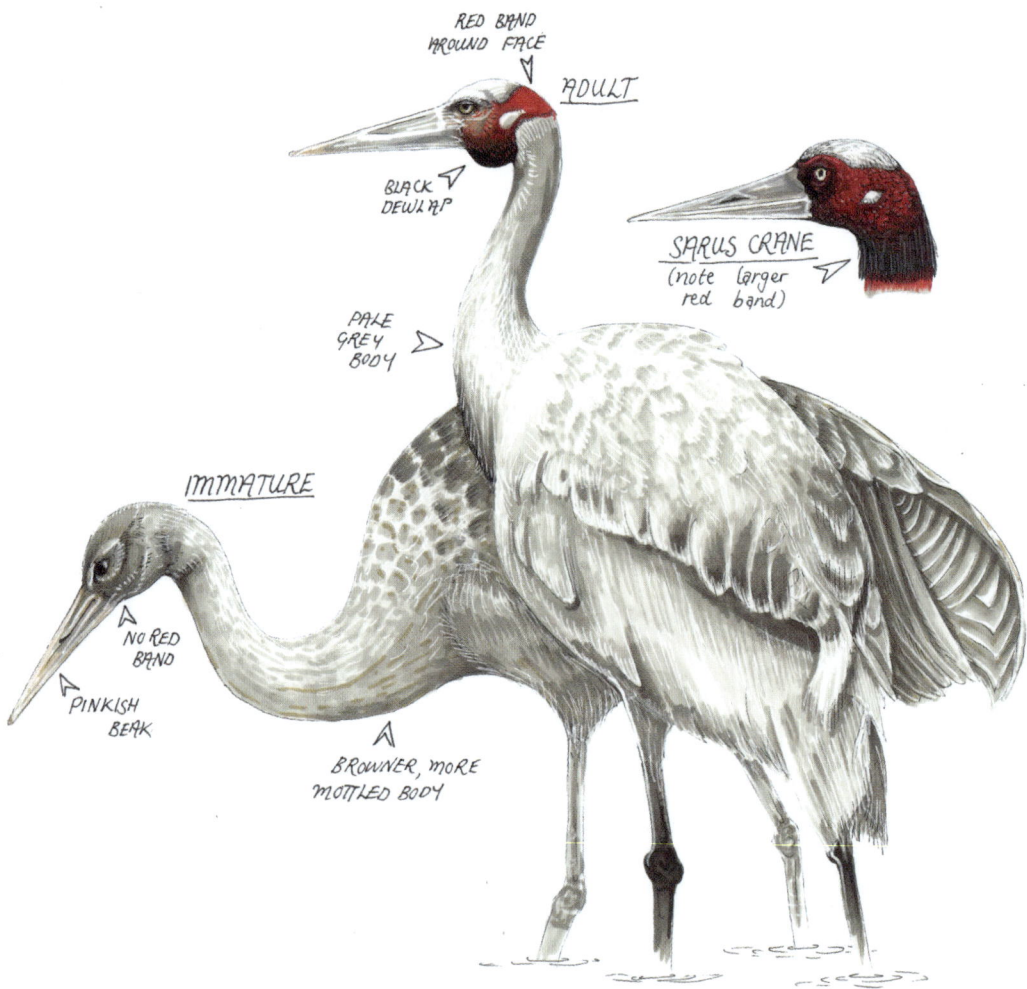

RED BAND AROUND FACE

ADULT

BLACK DEWLAP

SARUS CRANE
(note larger red band)

PALE GREY BODY

IMMATURE

NO RED BAND

PINKISH BEAK

BROWNER, MORE MOTTLED BODY

Brolga

Barlawi [bar-lah-we] (Gumbaynggirr); **garorrk** [ga-ro-rrk (rolled 'r')] (Taungurung)
Grus rubicunda

Brolgas are also known as the 'native companion', a name that likely caught on because these birds are monogamous (that is, they choose a mate that they stick with for life). As a result, they are often seen hanging out as a pair of 'companions'. The brolga not only appears graceful when picking its way through shallow wetlands, but also performs a strange, ballet-esque mating dance with its partner. When the time comes for nesting, these birds bow to one another and then leap into the air, flaring their wings out, and dropping to the ground to bow again. They repeat this, sometimes pausing to hold their beaks together before continuing their dancing. Both male and female birds perform for one another, making these courtship dances entrancing to watch. Take-offs are a gangly and clumsy affair (who could blame them, with legs that long?) – but the brolga is graceful in flight, with its neck elongated, unlike the herons (*see* pages 99 and 105) and egrets (*see* page 103), who usually fold their neck in flight.

WHAT TO LISTEN FOR	Brolgas make a trill-like honking. Often this sound is made as a call-and-response between a female and male.
WHAT TO LOOK FOR	Brolgas are large, graceful wading birds. Standing over a metre tall, they have a long, narrow body with predominantly grey colouring. A red band wraps around the head and eyes. The beak is a large pinkish-grey wedge. Beneath the chin is a black 'dewlap' (the scientific term for excess skin under the chin). The wingtips and underside of the wings are darker grey than the rest of the body.
IMMATURE BIRDS	Young brolgas take some time to develop the red 'headband' that the adult birds have. They are entirely grey, and may be visibly smaller than mature brolgas.
WHERE TO START LOOKING	Try looking for brolgas in wetlands, marshlands, flooded pasture and any other inland bodies of water – these birds are most commonly spotted wading through such areas. They are prominent even at a distance given their enormous size. Take a moment to appreciate their slow, methodical movement though the water. They seem unhurried in their activities, and become almost hypnotic to watch as they shift their long bodies around.
WHAT THEY EAT	Brolgas are generalists (you can think of them as 'grazers'). They nibble on vegetable matter, tubers, marsh plants, insects, crustaceans, frogs and small reptiles.
SIMILAR BIRDS	Sarus crane (pictured opposite; the sarus crane is taller, has red legs, a different arrangement of red on the head, and is restricted to northern Queensland).

IMMATURE

NO BLUE VISIBLE YET

ADULT

BLUE NECK

LONG SHAGGY FEATHERS

WINGS (vestigial)

STRONG LEGS

Emu

Gugaamgan [goo-gahm-gun] (Gumbaynggirr);
dinawan [di-na-wa-n], **gawumaran, nguruwiny**
(Wiradjuri); **barramul** [barr-a-mul] (Taungurung)
Dromaius novaehollandiae

Emus are rebellious – they're the birds that refuse to be put into the 'identity' box. They do not fly, traversing instead by walking. They've been moulded by the evolutionary funnel of Australia, travelling by foot over long distances. Their legs are long and their feet are clawed to defend against predators (they're known to give vicious kicks if threatened). Their eyes have two sets of eyelids and long eyelashes that protect from heat and sand. If their eyes look opaque, that's them closing the inner eyelid, but not the outer. So cool! Their long, shaggy-looking feathers actually result from double feathers (also known as 'afterfeathers' – that is, each 'feather' is actually a pair of unstructured, hair-like strands, unlike the single feathers on flying birds (*see* The structure of feathers, page xix). There is something really mysterious and ancient-looking about emus – but despite their fierce-looking feet and their sheer size, they are gentle, slow-moving birds that are a special sight to be savoured when you do finally spot one.

WHAT TO LISTEN FOR	Emus do not sing, but actually make a growling, drum-like noise, *krrumm-krrrum-krumm*, almost like a purring from deep in their chest. I've heard a pair 'drumming' like this to one another in Gariwerd (the Grampians, Victoria) and I felt very lucky to be overhearing a conversation between these beautiful, lumbering creatures.
WHAT TO LOOK FOR	The emu is Australia's biggest bird, standing around 150–170 centimetres tall. These birds have a large, domed body covered with shaggy feathers, and have a long neck and even longer legs. Their feathers are mostly brown-grey but are topped by finer black feathers, giving an overall impression of the emu being covered by hair. The body has a flattish 'hem', where these feathers fall to an even length, emphasising the dome shape of the body. Their two small wings are termed 'vestigial' – meaning, these wings have very gradually become smaller and less useful to the species, 'forgotten' by the forces of evolution. The neck arches upwards into a flattish head dominated by a triangular beak. A panel of blue skin runs down either side of the neck, while the head is dark.
IMMATURE BIRDS	Young emus are darker-skinned on the neck, lacking the exposed blue skin of the adults. Emu chicks are striped black and brown fluff balls.
WHERE TO START LOOKING	Despite being relatively difficult to see (depending on your location), emus are surprisingly widespread across Australia. They tend to avoid urban and suburban areas, as well as very dense forests or rainforests, preferring open bushland, mallee (drier interior scrublands), agricultural pastures interspersed by bushland, and national and state parks.
WHAT THEY EAT	Emus are generalists, mostly eating seeds, softer plants and insects. They often disperse seeds beneficially for native species, as they pass them undigested during their travels. However, this process goes for all plants – emus can also assist the spread of introduced weeds.
SIMILAR BIRDS	I'm hard-pressed to imagine someone mistaking another bird for an emu, except farmed ostriches in agricultural regions (ostriches are a bird endemic to the African continent). Another extremely large bird is the southern cassowary of Queensland.

NESTING
MOUND
(usually
sand-
covered)

TORTOISESHELL BACK

PALE
LINE
UNDER
EYE

DARK
VERTICAL
STRIP ALONG
NECK

STRONG FEET
FOR WALKING &
DIGGING

Malleefowl

Yunggaay [yu-ng-g-aay] (Wiradjuri)
Leipoa ocellata

The malleefowl is an endangered bird with curious nesting methods. When the season for brooding eggs arrives, the male malleefowl builds a large mound of sand and leaf litter to 'nest' the eggs in. (The female malleefowl heads off soon after breeding, hopefully walking in time to the Destiny's Child song 'Independent Women Pt 1'.) Ideally, the nesting site has been formed in a clearing where sunlight helps to warm the mound. In addition to the warming effects of the sun, the leaf litter in the pile begins to break down (composting), releasing a small amount of heat as a by-product. In a ritual carefully refined by evolution over millennia, the malleefowl monitors and adjusts the volume of the sand and leaf litter over the eggs to ensure they neither grow too cold, nor cook in the excessive heat of too much sun or composting. This is basically the outback equivalent of making a souffle on Masterchef – the stakes are high, the clock is ticking, and a few missed steps will spell disaster.

Malleefowl are complex, beautiful creatures. They are large and quiet, cruising in very specific and limited habitats. Despite their small population, they are sometimes seen in large numbers at the edges of roads where grain has spilled from truck beds. Imagine seeing a whole pod of these glorious, endangered birds, all in the one place! Unfortunately, their numbers are continuing to decline due to decreased habitat, harsher conditions and introduced pests such as foxes and feral cats. I cannot overestimate what a treat it is to see malleefowl. Their patterns are incredible, their motions slow and measured. These lumbering birds seem such a relic from a pre-colonial era that I can't help but think of them as a walking Shakespearean play: beautiful and tragic.

WHAT TO LOOK FOR	Malleefowl are large (reaching nearly 60 cm in length), brown-grey birds that are usually seen picking through scrubland. The head of the malleefowl is quite small, while the body is large and oblong, with strong legs. The head and body are grey-brown. The wings are covered with a tortoiseshell pattern of black and chestnut brown. The top of the back and the area under the chin is faintly rust coloured, while the underbelly is a paler grey. A dark vertical strip runs along the length of the neck. The eye is dark, with a pale line underneath it.
WHERE TO START LOOKING	The malleefowl is a threatened bird with relatively low numbers. Your best chance of seeing one is to head for dry eucalyptus woodlands, most particularly areas of mallee. Mallee is a type of bushland found in drier inland regions of southern Australia. These areas are characterised by sparse scrub and low rainfall. The name comes from a group of trees (mallee gums) that commonly grow in these conditions (these eucalyptus trees grow as a handful of slender trunks from a central root-knot called a lignotuber. Because of this peculiar growth habit, these trees look like large shrubs, and are quite recognisable).
	If you head to an inland national park in Victoria or southern Western Australia, you may have some luck. Keep scanning ahead of you, as these birds are quiet and very well camouflaged! You may also encounter some nesting mounds (see description above). Usually they will be a couple of metres across and covered by sand, so sometimes they remain well disguised among the equally sandy surrounds.
WHAT THEY EAT	True generalists, they eat a wide variety of foods – seeds, fruit, insects and vegetation.
SIMILAR BIRDS	You'd be hard pressed to find a similar species! Quail species (*see* page 135) may occupy similar areas, but are far smaller birds. The Australian brush-turkey (*see* page 137) has similar nesting habits but occupies different ecosystems from the malleefowl.

TASMANIAN BROWN QUAIL (note yellow eye)

TORTOISESHELL PATTERNING (note vertical white streaks)

FINELY PATTERNED CHEST & BELLY

MAINLAND BROWN QUAIL (note dark eye)

MOSTLY STAYS VERY CLOSE TO THE GROUND

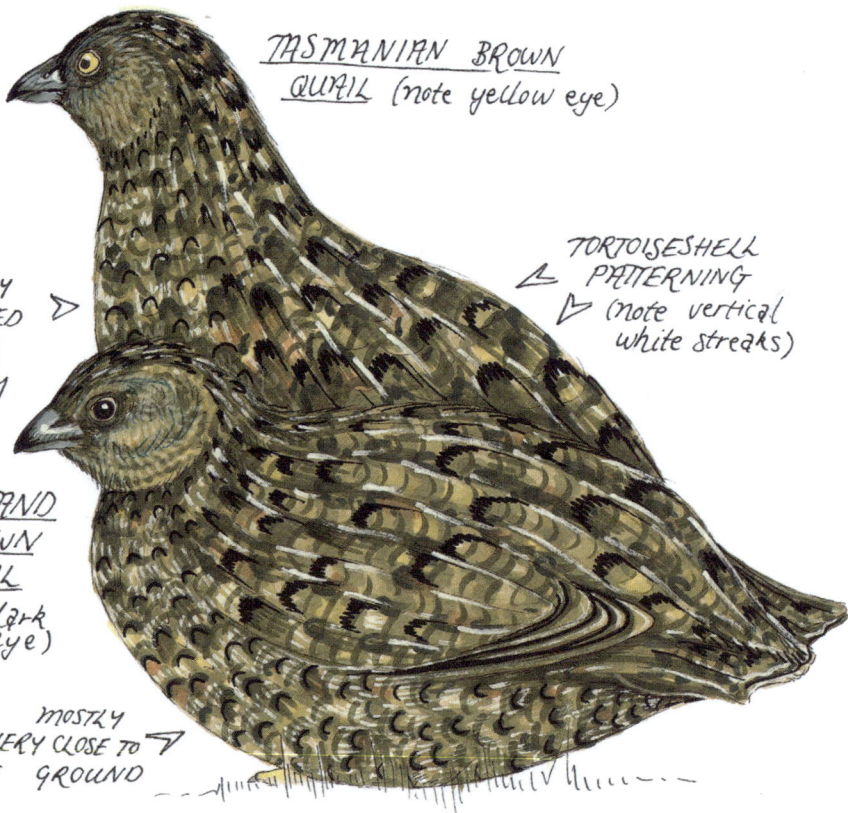

Brown quail

Driibin [drii-bin ('ii' as in 'sl<u>ee</u>p')] (Taungurung)
Coturnix ypsilophora

Also called 'swamp quail' due to their love of wetlands, brown quails are crepuscular (meaning they are largely active in the early morning and early evening). This is when you'll most likely see them darting about, grazing with urgency in small 'coveys' (flocks) of four or more birds. These birds rarely fly, preferring to run over the ground like little zooming footballs, occasionally flapping their wings to gain an extra burst of speed. In more undisturbed areas of habitat, these birds may gradually form little 'tunnels' through the grass, which indicate the paths they regularly take. If startled, the brown quail will take off and fly in shorts bursts to get away. As a ground-dwelling and ground-nesting species, it is particularly vulnerable to predation by foxes, feral cats and predatory birds. As a result, it is extremely wary and shy, and almost always sticks to areas with thick cover. Usually the best look you'll get at one is a flurry of brown feathers as it flies away from you.

WHAT TO LISTEN FOR	A high, piping *duweep-dyipp*, repeated at intervals to mournful effect.
WHAT TO LOOK FOR	Brown quails are small, round (and adorable) ground-dwelling birds. They have tortoiseshell patterning and white streaks along their backs. The face is a pale brown, as is the underside of their chin. The chest is rust-brown with fine, horizontal barring along the belly. The eye is dark. Note: Tasmanian brown quails have a yellow eye, instead of the dark eye of the mainland brown quail (though eye colour is often hard to pick from a distance).
IMMATURE BIRDS	I have never managed to spot a young brown quail. It's probably better this way, because if I did see one, I would probably undergo instant spontaneous combustion at the intolerable cuteness of it. However, immature brown quails are likely to look similar to immature domesticated quails – downier (fluffier) feathers and paler colouring overall.
WHERE TO START LOOKING	Brown quails can prove *very* tricky to spot. These birds are incredibly wary and shy of people, so they usually have 'bobbed' away through the undergrowth before you even realise they are there. If you're visiting wetlands with dense undergrowth, wetter areas of crops (e.g. ditches near wheat or triticale pasture), thick native grasses (e.g. spinifex) or grassy open areas in wetter bushland, try keeping an eye out for them. Heading out during dawn or at twilight can also increase your likelihood of seeing these shy birds.
WHAT DO THEY EAT	Seeds, grasses and insects.
SIMILAR BIRDS	Painted buttonquail (south-west and eastern Australia), stubble quail (widespread, excluding northernmost Australia), king quail (limited ranges in northern and eastern Australia).

VERTICALLY FANNED TAIL

RED HEAD & NECK

NORTH QUEENSLAND FORM (PURPLE 'COLLAR')

EAST COAST FORM (YELLOW 'COLLAR')

STRONG FEET (FOR WALKING & DIGGING)

ORANGE-FOOTED SCRUBFOWL

Australian brush-turkey

Gilgunyjan [gil-goyn-jun] (Gumbaynggirr)
Alectura lathami

Australian brush-turkeys are slow-moving, ponderous birds. generally quiet and shy, racing off by foot when startled. When picking through leaf litter for grubs, these birds will use their large feet to move debris around, and will regularly lift their heads to scan their surrounds for danger.

When it comes to mating, the Australian brush-turkey is a free-loving bird, with males mating with multiple females, and vice versa. Like the malleefowl (*see* page 133), the male Australian brush-turkey builds a large nesting mound in which (if he is lucky enough) he will eventually incubate his eggs. The female birds then visit these mounds both to mate and to lay their eggs, after which they set off again to roam the bush. As the brush-turkey is found in the more tropical, eastern areas of Australia, the mounds are built mostly of leaf litter, which is piled over the eggs. As the leaf litter starts to decompose (compost), heat is released as a by-product. This heat serves to warm the eggs (and, more so, the tiny developing brush-turkeys inside them). It turns out brush-turkeys are scholars of chemistry! As with other mound-building birds, the eggs are vulnerable to intense heat or cold, so the male must be vigilant at checking the temperature of the mound by sticking his beak into the pile. By adjusting the amount of leaf litter on the mound, the bird will avoid cooking the eggs, or allowing them to go cold.

WHAT TO LISTEN FOR	The Australian brush-turkey makes a guttural, insistent gulping noise that sounds a bit like a frog. It may also make a mellow, low call, *whooom*, almost like an owl call.
WHAT TO LOOK FOR	The Australian brush-turkey is a large ground-dwelling bird that looks a little bit like a large black chicken, with a brightly coloured throat. These birds are predominantly dark-brown to black, and they have a large tail that fans vertically (like an axe head) instead of horizontally, like most other birds. The exposed skin on their bald heads is bright red. At the base of the neck is a yellow, fleshy 'collar' (note that in the northern tip of Queensland, the brush-turkey has a pale purple 'collar' instead of yellow). These birds walk on long, strong legs and have large claws – excellent for sorting through leaf litter and for building their nesting mounds.
IMMATURE BIRDS	Young Australian brush-turkeys have more feathers over their heads, so their faces and necks look a bit darker. The 'collar' of young birds is also smaller.
WHERE TO START LOOKING	Brush-turkeys tend to stick to denser, wetter bushland where there is decent shrub cover for building nesting mounds. They do sometimes wander into suburban and urban areas, but usually stick to areas with decent vegetation. Try heading to areas of local rainforest or wetter bushland, especially areas along gullies or riverbanks, picnic grounds or campgrounds, or try your local botanical gardens.
WHAT THEY EAT	Australian brush-turkeys aren't too picky about what they eat. They take insects from among the leaf litter in forests, and also eat fruit and seeds. They will also scavenge a bit in urban areas.
SIMILAR BIRDS	Orange-footed scrubfowl (pictured opposite; found along northern coastlines, the orange-footed scrubfowl is a smaller bird with a prominent crest), black-tailed native hen (pictured on page 78; a smaller bird with a widespread range).

STAMPS
FEET WHILE
SINGING

MALE PERFORMS
FROM UNDERNEATH A
VEIL MADE OF HIS
TAIL FEATHERS

DARK BROWN FEATHERS
ALLOW THEM TO BLEND
INTO THE
SCRUB

FEMALE TAIL IS
DENSER & HAS NO
ORNAMENTATION

LARGE, STRONG
FEET FOR DIGGING
THROUGH LEAF
LITTER

MALE TAIL HAS TWO LARGE,
STRIPED FEATHERS, & MANY
FINE WHITE FEATHERS

PALER
GREY-BROWN
UNDERBELLY

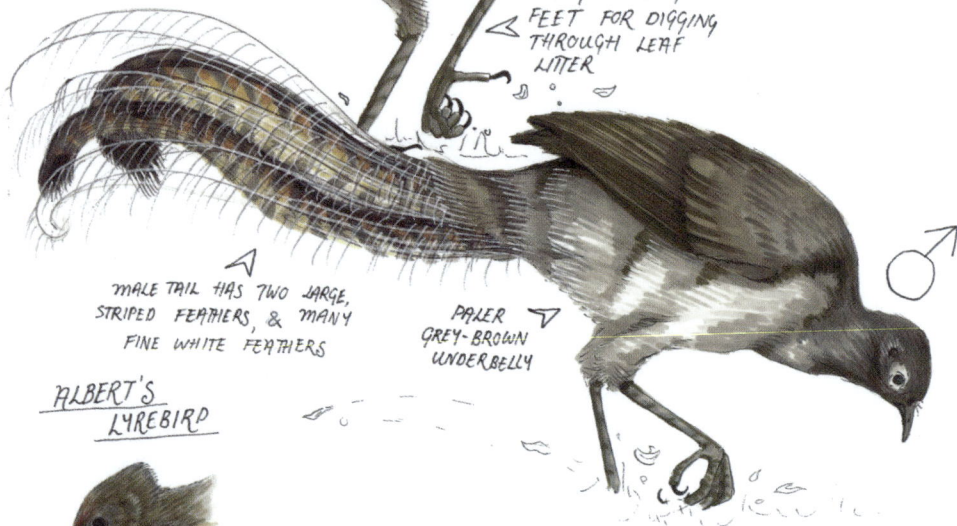

ALBERT'S
LYREBIRD

NOTE RUSTY
ORANGE CHIN

Superb lyrebird

Jaawan [jah-won] (Gumbaynggirr); **dyagula** [dya-gu-la] (Wiradjuri); **buln buln** [buln buln] (Taungurung)

Menura novaehollandiae

Despite their overlong tails, superb lyrebirds are surprisingly adept at staying hidden among rainforest shrubbery. Like the superb fairywren (*see page 67*), superb lyrebirds are polygynous – meaning one male courts several females. Once, when walking in Melbourne's Dandenong Ranges, I was able to hear a series of different bird calls all coming from the same spot amongst the bracken. I crept over towards the noise and peered through the shrubbery to see a male lyrebird, alone in a small circular clearing he had made – his 'stage'. As I watched, he lifted his tail up and over his body like a bride's veil, then proceeded to sing in the voices of many other birds – the laughing kookaburra (*see page 161*), golden whistler (*see page 65*), eastern whipbird (*see page 141*) and yellow-tailed black-cockatoo (*see page 179*). This performance, to my joy, was accompanied by the stamping of his large feet. He was dancing and singing in his own self-made theatre. As he danced, his long, veil-like tail shimmered, topping off this mesmerising display.

Male lyrebirds will spend much of their time performing this mimicry and dance as 'practice', singing year round, regardless of the breeding season. The female birds are more secretive than the males, finding secluded areas to build their nests, where they will eventually lay (most often) a single egg per season.

WHAT TO LISTEN FOR

The superb lyrebird is most widely known for its impeccable mimicry of other bird songs. If you're lucky enough to see a lyrebird during its courtship display, you'll also hear a repeated metallic sound, kind of like the bouncing of a metal spring, which the male birds make as they dance.

WHAT TO LOOK FOR

The superb lyrebird is a large ground-dwelling bird with a long, ornate tail. Their bodies are a dark chestnut brown, with a paler, grey-brown underbelly. Males have long, delicate tails, comprised of two broad, striped feathers that frame several white, filamentous feathers. Though this fancy plumage makes fast movements through dense bushland more difficult, these tails prove essential in their courtship displays (see above). While the males have a flashy tail, females have a long, denser tail of brown feathers. The feet of both the male and female lyrebird seem disproportionately large for the bird's size, but these hefty claws make them very efficient at digging and sorting through leaf litter and soil for food.

WHERE TO START LOOKING

Try going to areas of wet bushland (places where it rains regularly). Superb lyrebirds are most often heard singing in rainforest or heavily wooded areas, especially in gullies. These ecosystems tend to have a good layer of leaf and wood debris on the forest floor, which the superb lyrebird relies on for adequate food. As the male lyrebirds like to find a nice high perch from which to sing (so that their performances will carry a good distance), slopes alongside deep gullies are good spots to keep an eye (and ear) out. Places like the Dandenong Ranges in Victoria, denser bush along the east coast, New South Wales' Blue Mountains, and in the forests of the Australian Alps are well worth trying. Otherwise, head to shadier sections of forest in the closest hilly reserve to you – and keep an ear out for rustling, and the bird calls of five or more different species coming from the one place.

WHAT THEY EAT

Lyrebirds pick through leaf debris for insects, grubs and even small yabbies and scorpions.

SIMILAR BIRDS

Albert's lyrebird (pictured opposite), a rare species found in an isolated patch of coastline where the Queensland and New South Wales borders meet.

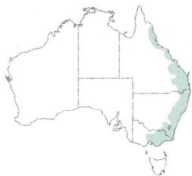

AUSTRALIAN
LOGRUNNER (♂)
(entire chest
is white)

WESTERN
WHIPBIRD
(note chin
panels)

PALER HEAD
WITHOUT CREST

IMMATURE

BROWN
EYE

SMALL
CREST

ADULT

LARGE
WHITE CHIN
PANELS

LONG DARK
TAIL

Eastern whipbird

Psophodes olivaceus

Eastern whipbirds, despite their striking appearance, are shy, stealthy birds. They can be *very* hard to spot, especially given their proclivity for thick, low-lying shrubs. They are often found in pairs, foraging close to one another. Sometimes the only help you'll get with identification is a flash of their white cheek patch as they slip away, à la Humphrey Bogart into the fog at the end of *Casablanca* (1942). Finally getting a look at an eastern whipbird is a real treat, as these birds scurry and clamber through the bush in a distinctive way, like little stealth-chickens on a mission. This, along with their habit of calling back and forth as a mating pair, makes for an awesome show. A number of times I have been happily 'trapped' on a trail, listening to a male whipbird calling on my left, and a female replying from my right. Glorious!

WHAT TO LISTEN FOR	The eastern whipbird produces a very distinctive song, which sounds like an approaching *whiiiii*, rising in pitch, followed by a piercing *cracck!* This is the call classically performed by a male. Most often, when you hear this call, the *cracck!* will be followed by a firm *dweep-dweep!*, which is the female's reply. In this way, the couple can keep in contact as they forage separately through an area of scrub.
WHAT TO LOOK FOR	The eastern whipbird is a medium-sized olive-green bird that is usually heard rather than seen. The bird's dark head bears a crest, which is sometimes flattened to the head. Its tail is dark and long, nearly the same length as the body again. Its chest has a bib, which is a continuation of the black-hooded head. There is a bright white patch on the cheek, one of the best distinguishing markings on this otherwise well-camouflaged species.
IMMATURE BIRDS	Young eastern whipbirds tend to be a more dilute chestnut colour, with no cheek patch, and a paler head.
WHERE TO START LOOKING	Eastern whipbirds like to stick to areas of dense thickets or low branches where they can pick through leaf litter away from prying eyes. Low alpine bushlands all the way down to coastal forests and rainforests are all great places to try listening out for them (hearing them is the best way to try and get close enough to catch a glimpse of them). I have sometimes heard eastern whipbirds in thicker, wetter parklands in the outer suburbs of cities where there is plenty of undisturbed shrubbery, though national parks, bush reserves and state parks on the east coast are the most likely places where you will spot these birds.
WHAT THEY EAT	Insects and grubs from the forest floor.
SIMILAR BIRDS	Logrunner (pictured opposite; only seen on the east coast in New South Wales and southern Queensland), superb lyrebird (*see* page 139), western whipbird (pictured opposite; this bird is the mirrored cousin to the eastern whipbird, seen only very sparsely in areas near Adelaide and in a patch of Noongar Country in south-western Western Australia. These birds are very rare and secretive).

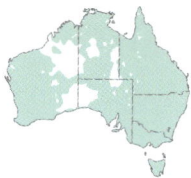

BRUSH
BRONZEWING (♂)
(note rust
colour)

WHITE
CHEEK-
BONE

DARKER FOREHEAD
THAN MALE
♀

IRIDESCENT
WING-
PATCHES

GOLD
FOREHEAD
PATCH
♂

PINKISH
CHEST

Common bronzewing

Wuuga [like 'sugar' with a 'w': 'wooga']
(Gumbaynggirr); **waba** [wa-ba] (Wiradjuri)
Phaps chalcoptera

Bronzewings are shy and flighty birds. They usually stick to higher, open branches in relatively open bushland, or peck their way across the forest floor. Once they suspect there is a threat present, if they don't flee immediately, they will remain wary for a time, so it's worthwhile freezing and remaining very still and quiet when you first spot one. They will eventually relax and continue pecking their way over the ground, allowing you to get a better look at them. Their colours truly are beautiful when you can get a lengthy glimpse of them. During courtship displays, a male will bob up and down while approaching the female, ducking his head quickly to tap his beak on the ground. The female may reciprocate with a few bobs, but most of the performance is done by the golden-crowned male, as if giving his queen due deference.

WHAT TO LISTEN FOR	A sparse, low *ooh*, repeated – somewhat soothing, like a soft, low recorder note. Carries through the bush.
WHAT TO LOOK FOR	Common bronzewings are large pigeons that have a similar body shape to a rock dove (aka the feral pigeon, a classic bird you see in city centres – *see* Introduced birds in the appendix, page 208). However, common bronzewings are more voluptuous and have a brownish, tortoiseshell-like colouring to their back body. They also have an iridescent wing patch where the feathers look like rainbow-coloured fish scales, reminding me of the children's book *Rainbow Fish* by Marcus Pfister. The underbellies of these pigeons are a pinkish-grey and their heads have a beautiful curl of white above and below their eye. Males have a large 'splotch' of yellow colour between these brows on their forehead. Females have a less obvious 'splotch'.
IMMATURE BIRDS	Young common bronzewings have more faded looking 'brows' and are less defined overall in their patterning and colour.
WHERE TO START LOOKING	The common bronzewing is widespread but very shy. These pigeons seem to prefer open bush where they can easily trundle around at ground level, but they still happily frequent most areas of Australia. I most often see common bronzewings in open areas adjacent to bushland, along walking trails in dry bush, on backroads and in people's yards – especially in suburbs that are alongside the bush.
WHAT THEY EAT	Seeds and fruit.
SIMILAR BIRDS	Brush bronzewing (pictured opposite; these beauties are smaller and have a range confined to the more coastal regions of south-eastern Australia; their bodies are a richer rust colour and they also have a dark band behind their eye), flock bronzewing (a rare species seen in the arid zones of Australia).

BANDING OVER WINGS

LONG FEATHERS ON HEAD

MOTHER-OF-PEARL' PANELS IN WING

PINK FEET

TOPKNOT PIGEON

Crested pigeon

Guwabadhu [gu-wa-ba-dhu], **willingga** [wil-li-ng-ga], **barrawang** [ba-rra-wa-ng] (Wiradjuri)
Ocyphaps lophotes

People in south-eastern Australia will occasionally call the crested pigeon a 'topknot pigeon', which can cause confusion, as the topknot pigeon is also the name for the more tropical coast-dwelling topknot pigeon (yes, this bird bears a bundle of man bun-esque feathers on its head). A number of times I have been disappointed when, after a bit of digging, I have realised the neighbour has in fact spotted the most common pigeon in the suburb, not a far-flung exotic bird of coastal New South Wales. That said, the crested pigeon is a hilarious bird that is always entertaining to watch. It *exudes* sassiness, albeit a kind of dopey sassiness. These pigeons peck seed with a powerful urgency, heads bobbing frantically as they graze. The crest loads their every motion with extra intensity. If you're lucky, you might get to observe a male performing a seductive courtship dance for a female, in which the male bobs down on its little legs, lifts its tail, continuing to bob while rhythmically closing the tail, cooing for attention.

WHAT TO LISTEN FOR	When in flight, these pigeons will whistle like a vortex, *whee-ee-ee-ee-ee-ee-e*. This noise is actually created by the movement of air over the wings of the crested pigeon, rather than being a true 'song'. However, they can also make an insistent, crooning *crroohh-croohh-crooohh*. This is especially made by the males when pursuing a female.
WHAT TO LOOK FOR	The crested pigeon is a medium-sized (around 30 cm long) grey pigeon with a tuft of feathers sticking up from its head like a tiny Eiffel Tower. This distinctive pointed crest is composed of several thin, dark feathers extending above the head for a couple of centimetres. The rest of the plumage is largely grey, while the back body, including the wings, is a tawnier brown-grey. There is tortoiseshell black banding over the feathers, and a small section of mother-of-pearl panelling on the outside of the wings, reflecting green, bronze and red. The eye is pink, matching the feet.
WHERE TO START LOOKING	The crested pigeon is a common bird and often frequents suburban lawns, especially where seed is put out. It is also often found at the fringes of bushland, in gardens and urban parks, and on nature strips. Where food is abundant, these birds will graze comfortably among peaceful doves, galahs and other common suburban species.
WHAT THEY EAT	Seeds.
SIMILAR BIRDS	Topknot pigeon (pictured opposite; eastern coastline), spinifex pigeon (this bird is found in the arid interiors of central, north and north-west Australia).

CAMPHOR LAUREL

SLATY GREY BACK & TAIL

♀ PINK EYE & BEAK

♂ GREYER UNDERBELLY

WHITE HEAD & UNDERBELLY

PINK FEET

White-headed pigeon

Columba leucomela

These birds are striking, when you manage to spot them, especially with their size and two-toned colouring. These birds are real tree dwellers – despite their size, they're very shy and excellent at hiding in upper foliage. You're most likely to see these birds from below, as they habitually remain on the higher branches of fruiting trees, so look for a large, white-bellied, dove-shaped bird. They like to stay in the canopy and indulge in fruit all day, usually only flying directly to the next fruit tree, rather than spending much time in the air. If you ever get to watch them calling from a perch, you'll be able to see them swell up their neck, frog-like, and then release their call, as if they need to 'charge up' before they can sing. To me, they are quite regal and solemn-looking, and their love of figs and other rich fruits makes me think of them as toga-wearing Roman emperors.

WHAT TO LISTEN FOR	The white-headed pigeon makes a deep, two-note *wooooh-whoo*, something like a diurnal boobook (*see* page 191). These birds call very softly, so it can be hard to figure out precisely where the bird is calling from.
WHAT TO LOOK FOR	The white-headed pigeon is a large, voluptuous white and grey bird that sticks to the canopy of fruit trees. It is a little larger than your usual 'rock dove' (the common 'feral' pigeons that are so successful in urban areas – *see* Introduced birds in the appendix, page 208). <u>Males</u> have a white 'hood' (head, upper back and chest). The back body, including the tail, is slate grey. The feet, beak and eye-ring are pink. The belly shifts from dark grey under the tail through to white. <u>Females</u> are mottled grey over the head and underbelly (where the male is pure white).
IMMATURE BIRDS	Similar in appearance to the females, the young white-headed pigeon is generally mottled grey over the head and underbelly, and is darker overall than the adults. It also has a dark eye (instead of pink).
WHERE TO START LOOKING	The white-headed pigeon loves fruit, so try heading for areas that are planted with fruit trees – especially plants with soft, fleshy fruits (e.g. figs and the berries on introduced camphor laurels and privet plants). You may also have luck in rainforest areas and other sections of bush along the eastern coast, particularly gardens with well-tended fruit trees.
WHAT THEY EAT	Fruits.
SIMILAR BIRDS	Wonga pigeon (has a greyer body with distinctive patterning), topknot pigeon (pictured on page 144; this pigeon has a saucy up-do that you can't miss).

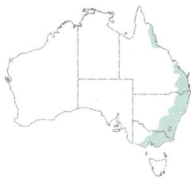

BOWER BUILT
BY MALES
(usually hidden
amongst scrub)

♀

VIVID
BLUE
EYE

BRONZE-
OLIVE
FEATHERS

'TORTOISESHELL'
PATTERNING
ON UNDERBELLY

♂

VIVID BLUE
EYE

BLUE-BLACK
BODY

REGENT
BOWERBIRD
(male)

Satin bowerbird

Jiirrgan [jeerr-gun] (Gumbaynggirr)
Ptilonorhynchus violaceus

Satin bowerbirds are one of several species of bowerbird in Australia, including the spotted, regent, golden and western bowerbirds, each with their own distinctive behaviours and courtship displays. Adult satin bowerbirds live in harems, with one male courting several females at once. The male satin bowerbird, when it comes time to court a female, will build a 'bower' (pictured opposite) from twigs and debris. The bird then collects blue objects – feathers, pebbles, flowers and, unfortunately, blue plastic – to decorate his bower and surrounds. (Other species of bowerbirds go in for different colours and objects.) Having decorated his patch with blue, the male bird calls out for female company in a hoarse, wheezing voice. Once a female is drawn in, she nestles into the bower to watch him perform. The male bowerbird begins a strangely robotic and elaborate dance, with bowing, wing flapping and head-bobbing dance moves, also performing the grasshopper-like call. All going to plan, the female bowerbird will be impressed enough to mate with the male.

Despite making a big show of courting several females at a time, the male bird will always be the first to fly off if we disturb them, usually hissing as it retreats. Meanwhile, the female and juvenile bowerbirds are usually tearing up brassicas from people's garden beds, hopping around like little dinosaurs.

WHAT TO LISTEN FOR	A raptor-like, descending whistle, *drrrrrriiiwwwww*, or a soft hissing, especially if disturbed in undergrowth. Females are often heard giving a radio-static screech. When a male performs a courtship dance for a female, he makes a grasshopper-like trilling. I have also been lucky enough to see adult males mimicking other birds, likely another component of their courtship displays.
WHAT TO LOOK FOR	The satin bowerbird is a voluptuous, glossy bird, about the size of the Australian magpie (*see* page 1). The males are dark blue (though they appear black in the shade) and females are a beautiful olive green. <u>Females</u> are a reflective green-bronze on their backs, with cream and green-brown tortoiseshell patterning on their underside. Their beak and legs are a similar bronze-green to their back. <u>Males</u> are a very deep, dark violet colour, so dark as to almost be black. In sunlight, their reflective feathers look more like a deep blue-violet colour, very much like satin. Their pale blue eyes stand out vividly among their dark feathers.
IMMATURE BIRDS	Young satin bowerbirds look similar to the adult females. If male, they will gradually moult into the dark violet colour as they mature. I have often seen juvenile male birds gathering bower materials and practising calls before developing their adult coats, though, so things can get a little confusing.

GREEN
CATBIRD

SATIN
BOWERBIRD (♀)

COMMON
BLACKBIRD

SATIN
BOWERBIRD (♂)

WHERE TO START LOOKING

Satin bowerbirds like to dwell near the ground, where they can build their courtship bowers (*see* page 149). They tend to hop and 'scoot' over the ground, but like to have nearby areas of cover to duck into. Try heading into local bushland, rainforest, thick gardens, overgrown areas and well-treed parklands. They particularly like to stick around in gardens if there is fruit available year round, but will stick to areas that have some low bushes or thickets where they can hide themselves.

Satin bowerbird males will usually choose a somewhat secluded spot to build their bower and scatter their blue objects – a location where they can carry out their seductions in (relative) solitude. Often you can discover a bower after spotting an area of scrub where there is a particularly dense scattering of blue bottle tops (a favourite of the satin bowerbird), blue bread tabs, foil, blue pens or blue straws.

Your likelihood of seeing a satin bowerbird really depends on how lush the gardens are in your area. I am fortunate to live in a suburb with lots of greenery and fruiting trees, so I often see female satin bowerbirds either tearing up the broccoli greens in our veggie patch, or 'rocketing' smoothly between backyards, like little green footballs. I often see males on the ground near their bower, meekly retreating to the trees, as if embarrassed by their courtship displays. I love these weird birds.

WHAT THEY EAT

Insects, fruits and some vegetation (i.e. the pak choy from the veggie patch; they *love* brassicas). This season, we've also been having trouble with the female bowerbirds getting into the raspberry patch, where we can see their little heads bobbing in and out of sight as they happily decimate the berry harvest.

SIMILAR BIRDS

(At a glance) Australian raven (*see* page 7), eastern ('common') koel (*see* page 195) and the common blackbird (pictured opposite; also Introduced birds in the appendix, page 208) are similar to the male satin bowerbird, while the green catbird (pictured opposite) and spotted catbird (both limited to the north-eastern coastlines) are similar to the female satin bowerbird.

Rainbow bee-eater

Dira-yurrun [dirra-yoorroon] (Gumbaynggirr)
Merops ornatus

Rainbow bee-eaters are often seen in pairs, perched on fences, powerlines or upper branches. They fly with swooping, gliding turns, flapping their wings sparingly, though they often wait to sight prey while they sit on a fenceline or bare branch. When feeding from such a perch, they swoop out, grab the insect, then quickly return to the perch. Their colours are spectacular, their long tail and colouring making them look like they belong in the tropics of the north. After having their meal, they often chirrup in conversation with their partner (or small flock), and fluff up their beautifully coloured feathers. Despite their proclivity for high perches and hunting insects in the air, rainbow bee-eaters actually dig burrows in the earth to serve as nests, rather than crafting a nest in a tree.

The first rainbow bee-eater I saw was on a long walk in Ngarigo Country, during my earliest days of more dedicated birdwatching. As I crossed what was a patch of (now regenerating) farmland, I saw a small bird swooping in and out of the cover of a tree on the edge of the river. When I brought my binoculars up, I could see this bird was a glorious gradient of colour, with a long, ornate tail. It was special to see such a colourful, tropical-looking bird in familiar surrounds.

WHAT TO LISTEN FOR	The rainbow bee-eater makes a high-pitched, frog-like chirrup, often in pairs or threes. This may be interspersed with lower, throaty chirrups.
WHAT TO LOOK FOR	The rainbow bee-eater is a striking, multicoloured bird with a black eye-band, often seen perched on bare branches or on fence wires. The back of the bird transitions from green through to turquoise, then darkens into black wingtips and tail-tips. The tail itself extends into a pair of long, very thin antennae-like feathers. The beak is long and curved, almost like that of a honeyeater, and they have a band of black feathers across the eye. The head is yellow and orange with a small amount of turquoise 'staining' on the forehead. The throat bears a band of black, like a little bow tie. <u>Females</u> have shorter 'antenna-feathers' extending from the tail.
IMMATURE BIRDS	Young rainbow bee-eaters are green-blue overall, with a dark eye-band and dark wingtips. The tail lacks the long 'antennae' feathers of the adults, and they do not have a 'bow tie' across their throat.
WHAT THEY EAT	These birds feed on insects, and particularly enjoy munching on bees and wasps. Insects are caught midair in efficient, swooping circuits from perches.
WHERE TO START LOOKING	I usually see rainbow bee-eaters loitering at the edges of cleared pastoral land. Try walking along the edges of open forest or bush reserves, agricultural land and windbreaks, or near cattle pasture where insect populations are high.
SIMILAR BIRDS	Dollarbird (*see* page 155; doesn't have the darker colouring, is shorter and has a red beak).

REDDISH
BEAK
∨

DARK
∨ BEAK

IMMATURE

ADULT

DARKER
◁ BODY

TURQUOISE ∨
BELLY

◁ WING SPOTS
VISIBLE
IN FLIGHT

Dollarbird

Jadadany [judda-dain] (Gumbaynggirr);
dunabanban [duna-ban-ban] (Wiradjuri)
Eurystomus orientalis

Other names for the dollarbird include 'dark roller' and 'dollar roller', making me picture this blocky, 'buff' bird as a kind of money-hustling character. These birds are thickset, and at perch their dark heads give them a brooding look. They make only short, sharp trips to grab insects from midair before resuming their perch to munch their catch. When they have their wings outstretched in flight, the pale circles on each wing are very visible, like a silver coin on each outstretched limb. With their demeanour and their varied names, I remember these birds by thinking of them as a tiny feathered Tony Soprano. When they call at perch, the feathers under their chin stick out like a little gullet. They are usually only seen solo or in pairs, and, like the rainbow bee-eater (*see* page 153), they seem to benefit from hanging out on irrigated pastureland where insect numbers are high.

WHAT TO LISTEN FOR	Dollarbirds make a harsh, short scraping noise, *quiiipp*, sort of reminiscent of a laughing kookaburra call without the 'chuckle'.
WHAT TO LOOK FOR	The dollarbird is a chunky, dark-coloured bird with a red beak. The lower body of the bird is a turquoise-blue colour, while the head and tail are black. The beak is bright orange, as are the feet. In flight, two pale blue dots can be seen on the underside of the outstretched wings (at a glimpse these may appear white).
IMMATURE BIRDS	Young dollarbirds have darker colouring overall, particularly the head, with no orange beak.
WHERE TO START LOOKING	I've mostly spotted dollarbirds when I've been in smaller areas of bushland adjacent to towns; the birds have been perched on powerlines or a high branch where they can easily spot insects. Try looking for them in open bushland, on the edges of sparser rainforest (e.g. trees at the edge of national park picnic grounds), in the trees along the banks of rivers or on farmland where there are remnant trees. The dollarbird migrates to Australia from Papua New Guinea and Indonesia in the hottest months of the year, though some of the Australian population makes a more localised migration for the hotter months. As a result, populations will fluctuate, so you may only be able to see dollarbirds during the warmer months of the year.
WHAT THEY EAT	Insects.
SIMILAR BIRDS	Rainbow bee-eater (*see* page 153), common myna (*see* 'Introduced birds' in the appendix, page 208).

CROWN &
BACK ARE
AQUAMARINE

ADULT

YELLOW
BROW

WHITE
COLLAR

UNDERSIDE
OF BEAK IS
CURVED

IMMATURE

RUSTIER
CHEST
FEATHERS

PALE
UNDERBELLY

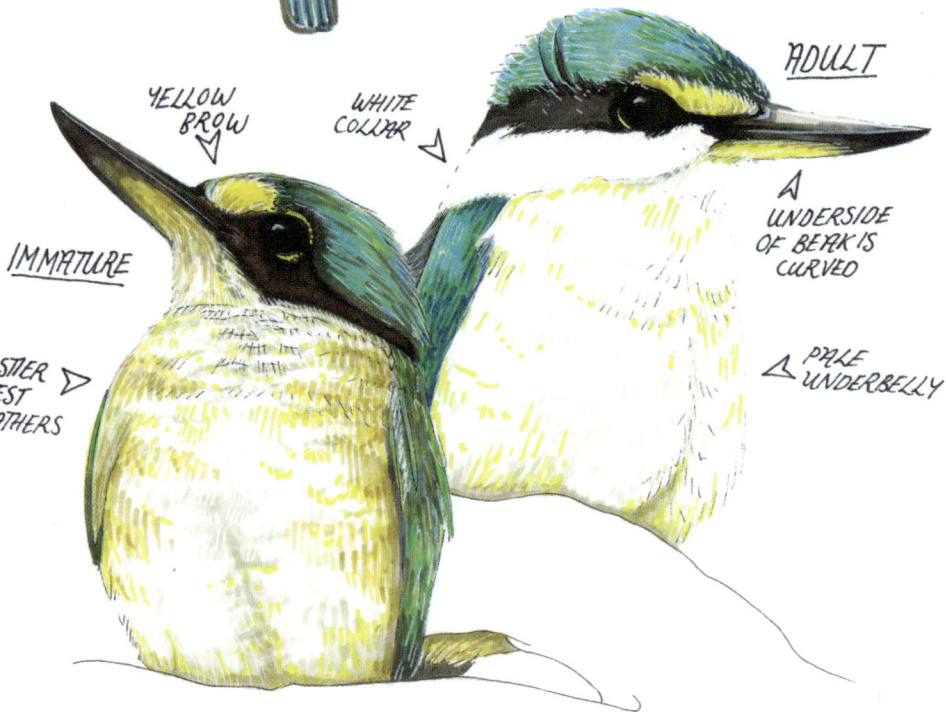

Sacred kingfisher

Dhaalirr [dhaa-li-rr] (Wiradjuri)
Todiramphus pyrrhopygius

Although the sacred kingfisher has a large beak that seems to be the perfect implement for fishing, these birds are actually more adapted for hunting on dry bushland. The sacred kingfisher will only rarely hunt fish, instead preferring to take large insects from the thick-fissured bark of eucalyptus trees or small reptiles from the forest floor. With their sword-like beak and little eye-masks, I think of the sacred kingfisher as the Zorro of the Australian bush, pouncing on their prey with a flourish. These kingfishers will sometimes dig a nest in a riverbank, excavating a small burrow in which to lay and incubate their eggs. In open bushland, sacred kingfishers will sometimes take advantage of tree hollows and nest in those, rather than digging a burrow. Yet again, I find the thought of birds heading underground to nest strange, and yet this is precisely what some kingfishers, pardalotes (*see* pages 59 and 61), short-tailed shearwaters (muttonbirds) and a number of other species do! Birds really can do it all.

WHAT TO LISTEN FOR	The sacred kingfisher makes an incessant but slightly throaty *eep-eep-eep* noise. You can often hear this call carrying through the trees when walking through open bushland. They also make a high-pitched trill, which (I think) sounds like it should come from a much smaller bird.
WHAT TO LOOK FOR	The sacred kingfisher has a long, knife-like beak when seen in profile, reminiscent of the laughing kookaburra (*see* page 161). However, this bird is smaller than the kookaburra, being only about 20 centimetres long from beak-tip to tail tip. It has aquamarine wings and tail, and a dark-grey band across its eyes, like a grey version of Zorro's mask. There is also a small 'eyebrow' of yellow above each eye. The underbelly is a creamy yellowish colour. Despite the eclectic mix of yellows and blues on this bird, I find it can be hard to spot among eucalyptus foliage, especially as it is often perched up high. I mostly recognise them first in silhouette, or when they are swooping to grab prey, as they are one of the few species in Australia with such distinctive beak-to-body proportions.
IMMATURE BIRDS	Young sacred kingfishers are more rust-coloured and dilute in their colouring, with a browner beak and a somewhat 'lankier' aspect to their proportions.
WHERE TO START LOOKING	Unlike the azure kingfisher (*see* page 159), the sacred kingfisher happily heads away from water and cruises through open bushland looking for insects. Try heading out to the closest open bush reserve or national park. These birds stay on upper branches, usually going from tree to tree to grab bugs and other small critters. Keep an ear out for a high-pitched *trilll* carrying through the trees. If you hear that, there's one nearby!
WHAT THEY EAT	Insects, grubs and small reptiles.
SIMILAR BIRDS	Azure kingfisher (*see* page 159; these birds are smaller and a vivid sapphire blue), the laughing kookaburra (*see* page 161; a close relative, the laughing kookaburra has a similarly proportioned body and beak, but is larger and distinguishable by its creamy colour and its laughing call), collared kingfisher (found along the coastline in the northern half of the country; these birds have a white belly where the sacred kingfisher has a creamy yellow belly.)

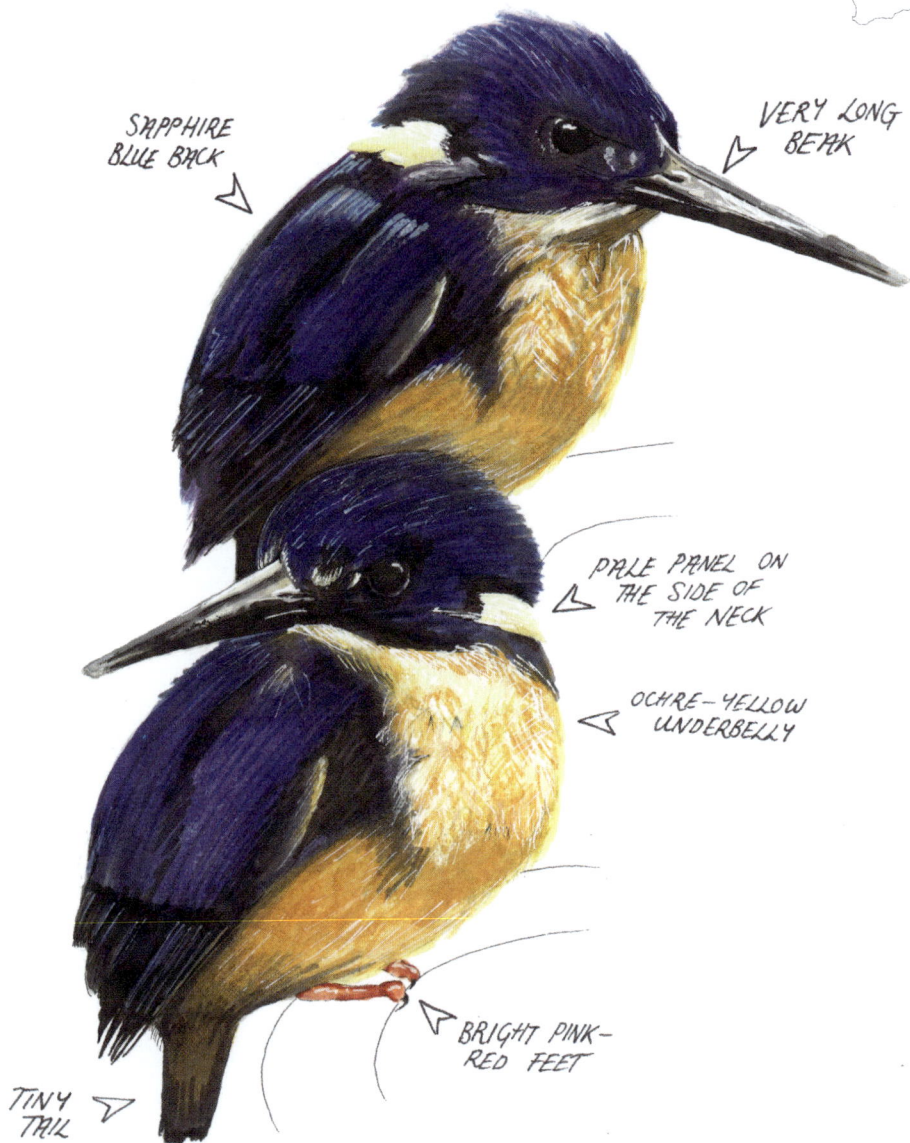

SAPPHIRE
BLUE BACK ▽

VERY LONG
BEAK ▽

PALE PANEL ON
THE SIDE OF
THE NECK ▽

OCHRE—YELLOW
UNDERBELLY ▽

BRIGHT PINK-
RED FEET ▽

TINY
TAIL ▽

Azure kingfisher

Birrangbirrang [bi-rra-ng-bi-rra-ng] (Wiradjuri)
Ceyx azureus

Azure kingfishers are small, vivid-coloured birds that always seem to stay close to water. These birds mate for life, digging out a burrow in a riverbank in which to incubate their young. Together the mating pair will defend their breeding territory – that is, the local section of bush surrounding their nesting burrow – from threatening birds. When paddling, I've seen them flitting ahead of me along the creek, keeping a couple of metres distant, almost leading me along the waterway. This is likely the azure kingfisher attempting to guard its breeding territory (though I like to think they're keeping me company). These birds like to sit on branches overhanging water so they can quickly dive down to catch fish (and boy, are they quick!). If the sacred kingfisher (*see* page 157) is the Zorro of the birding world, then I like to think of the azure kingfisher as a mini Inigo Montoya of *The Princess Bride* (1987). They are speedy, skilful and entertaining to watch ('prepare to dive!'). If you're lucky enough to see an azure kingfisher in full sunlight, these tiny birds really are a glorious splash of colour.

WHAT TO LISTEN FOR	A piping, very high-pitched *peep-peep-peep*.
WHAT TO LOOK FOR	The azure kingfisher is a small, nearly tail-less bird with a large beak. The proportions of the azure kingfisher are quite distinctive – it is large-headed with a small body, and has a *very* long, very sharp beak. The head and back body, including the tail, are a vivid sapphire-blue. The underbelly fades from cream at the chin to an ochre-yellow on the underbelly and underside of the tail. The feet can vary from pinkish through to bright red. There is also a small patch of yellow at the shoulder.
IMMATURE BIRDS	Young azure kingfishers are more mottled in their colouring, with the yellow shoulder patch visible quite early.
WHERE TO START LOOKING	I've been lucky enough to see these birds several times while kayaking on small creeks on Gunaikurnai Country in East Gippsland. Usually there will be a 'flash' of bright blue and ochre at the edge of your vision as an azure kingfisher flits by you, and sometimes that's the best look you will get! When perched – especially on the banks of dim or shaded waterways – these little birds can be tricky to discern, but in flight they are much more obvious. Try heading to watercourses in bushlands (particularly smaller, denser creeks or streams) and rainforests. Any body of water with plenty of overhanging branches and other good perching spots is a good place to start.
WHAT THEY EAT	Fish, reptiles and crustaceans.
SIMILAR BIRDS	Sacred kingfisher (*see* page 157; this kingfisher is larger than the azure), buff-breasted paradise kingfisher (north coast of Queensland), little kingfisher (northern coastlines; these birds have a white belly instead of an ochre-coloured one), forest kingfisher (northern coastlines; again, these birds have a white belly instead of an ochre-coloured one).

CHESTNUT HEAD PATCHES

LARGE BEAK (note curved underside)

note white section in wings

BLUE PATTERNING IN WINGS

BARRED TAIL

Laughing kookaburra

Gaagum [gah-goom] (Gumbaynggirr); **gugubarra** [gu-gu-ba-rra] (Wiradjuri); **durarong** [du-ra-rong] (Taungurung)
Dacelo novaeguineae

The laughing kookaburra is a well-known bird, partially due to its call, which is performed to define its territory. When a crew of kookaburras laugh on a branch, they are warning off other birds, or making an alarm call after they've noticed a possible threat. These birds are very intelligent and will quickly become wily to the ways of humans in campgrounds or parks. Once when I was harassed for some food by kookaburras at a campground, three or four birds seemed to be triangulating around my tent, calculating my movements. They were perched strategically in the three eucalypts that cornered my campsite and were watching me with all-too-knowing eyes. I had the strong feeling they'd done the same thing to many other campers before me. (Soon after, one nicked an entire Weet-bix out of the breakfast bowl. Cue the *Mission Impossible* theme.) Laughing kookaburras use tree hollows for nesting and are fierce when it comes to defending areas against other large birds, such as the Australian magpie (*see* page 1).

WHAT TO LISTEN FOR	Laughing kookaburras make a hoarse, repeated *hoo-hoo, haa-haa* and *hee-hee*. They sometimes perform a throaty growl, and many other variant calls, but their signature 'laugh' is the most familiar (and distinctive) sound they make. Young laughing kookaburras may be heard hoarsely practising their laugh, an even wheezier and sparse version of an adult laugh.
WHAT TO LOOK FOR	The laughing kookaburra is a big kingfisher (about 45 cm long), often heard chuckling from the canopy of the bush. The head is proportionally large to the size of the body, like that of the azure kingfisher (*see* page 159) or sacred kingfisher (*see* page 157). The laughing kookaburra's beak is large with a curved underside, like the hull of a boat. The upper half of the beak is a dark grey-brown, while the lower half is a lighter cream colour. The head and front body are cream. The head is patterned with a chestnut-brown eye-band that wraps around the back of the head. There is also a narrow patch of chestnut-brown plumage on the top of the head. The back and wings of the laughing kookaburra are brown, with blue scallop patterns across the wings (most obvious when they are perched). In flight, panels of white can be seen on the outstretched wings. The pale tail has dark horizontal bands across it.
IMMATURE BIRDS	Young laughing kookaburras are a bit darker and more 'blended' in colour overall. They have more chestnut-brown patterning over their entire bodies, particularly the chest and head, as if they were slightly dusty.
WHERE TO START LOOKING	Laughing kookaburras are common in more open bushland, but are also well adapted now to survive in relatively urbanised areas. Try looking in parks or camping areas, or along the local nature trail or creek. They often sing in the morning and evening, so going out at these times may help you to find them by following the sound of their laughing.
WHAT THEY EAT	True generalists, the laughing kookaburra will eat reptiles (I've seen them perched with a snake hanging from their powerful beak – gulp!), fish, larger insects and grubs, and sausages out of the hands of unsuspecting campers.
SIMILAR BIRDS	The blue-winged kookaburra (similar, but its range only crosses over in Queensland). Most kingfishers are similar in shape but none share the size of the kookaburra.

Laughing kookaburra   161

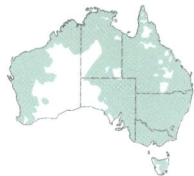

SOMETIMES
LIFTS SMALL
CREST

BLUE
AROUND
EYE

BEAK IS
TUCKED CLOSE
AMONGST FEATHERS

A
LARGE
BEAK

LONG-BILLED
CORELLA
(note dark
pink feathers)

Little corella

Ngarruk [ngarr–uk ('ng' as in 'si<u>ng</u>')] (Taungurung)
Cacatua sanguínea

The little corella often roosts and flies in large flocks, sometimes carpeting trees as a huge family. These birds are regularly seen grazing on nature strips and roadsides, and will happily do so among other parrots (e.g. sulphur-crested cockatoos and long-billed corellas). Given they're a similar size and colour to the sulphur-crested cockatoo, they can sometimes be overlooked when mixed in among other species. Despite initial similarities, with a closer look you'll be able to see the reddish-pink staining under the feathers of the little corella, a feature which earns them the colloquial name 'blood-stained cockatoo'. They are very playful, often pausing while grazing to 'wrestle' with fellows in their flock, and bleating ceaselessly to one another as they munch through grass rhizomes with relish. Overall, the little corella reminds me of the quieter sibling in a pair of kids – especially if you imagine a sulphur-crested cockatoo being the boisterous, attention-hungry sibling.

WHAT TO LISTEN FOR	The little corella makes a quavering, bleating noise, much like a sheep. This is often sung in a deafening chorus when they move as a flock. The little corella may also perform a harsh screech, though this call has less intensity than that of the sulphur-crested cockatoo (*see* page 165).
WHAT TO LOOK FOR	The little corella is a medium-sized cockatoo (around 35 cm long) that is largely white. The feathers at the throat and around the eye have faint pinkish staining, which is especially visible when the feathers are lifted or spread by a breeze. Pink feathers are also visible around the beak. The eye is framed in a blue ring and the beak is grey. A tinge of yellow is visible under the tail, and under the wings of the little corella when in flight. These birds will occasionally lift a small white crest on their head.
WHERE TO START LOOKING	Little corellas love to graze on open ground, especially on grassy lawns and ovals. Try going to the local footy pitch or university campus where there are decent lawns. They will also hang out in open bushland, on agricultural pasture and in rainforests. They need tree hollows for nesting, so they usually remain in areas where there are well-established stands of trees nearby.
WHAT THEY EAT	Seeds, fruit, tubers and crops. These birds are excellent at digging and pulling up tasty underground roots and rhizomes ('rhizomes' are horizontally growing roots that connect between growth points, like those seen in kikuyu grass, a common turf species). As such, little corellas sometimes decimate sports pitches when feeding in large flocks.
SIMILAR BIRDS	Long-billed corella (pictured opposite), western corella (larger than the little corella).

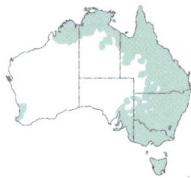

CREST
FOLDED

LARGE
STRONG
BEAK

CREST
RAISED

MAJOR MITCHELL'S
COCKATOO

Sulphur-crested cockatoo

Gayaarr [gay-ahrr] (Gumbaynggirr); **muraany** [mu-r-ine] (Wiradjuri); **ngarruk** [ngarr-uk ('ng' as in 'si<u>ng</u>')] (Taungurung)
Cacatua galerita

Sulphur-crested cockatoos are character-rich birds, being all at once boisterous, noisy and playful. They will hang out and fly in *huge* flocks, cruising between trees and performing clumsy (yet impressive) aerial manoeuvres. Sulphur-crested cockatoos can swoop in to clutch onto a powerline, perform a complete 360 degree loop, then fly off again, happy as Larry. I would be more impressed with the aerial stunts these birds perform if they didn't seem so blatantly unintentional. Sulphur-crested cockatoos love to chew and tear apart tree bark (even branches themselves, when they're particularly bored). In the absence of that, they're known to destroy other less organic and more industrial objects, like windowsills or outdoor furniture. They are very intelligent and long-lived birds, and when grazing, will strategically place a single 'watchbird' in at tree that will perform a warning call if a predator is spotted while the flock grazes. They do this at my local park, where they pick over the grass alongside little corellas (*see* page 163), galahs (*see* page 167) and the occasional wood duck (*see* page 85).

WHAT TO LISTEN FOR	Extremely loud, raptor-like screeching. The calling of the sulphur-crested cockatoo is cacophonous in a flock, sometimes growing so loud it makes me want to cover my ears.
WHAT TO LOOK FOR	The sulphur-crested cockatoo is a large white bird with a dark grey beak and feet. The head is adorned with a large yellow crest of finger-like feathers, which the bird can raise up or lower against the head. The eye is black.
WHERE TO START LOOKING	Requiring tree hollows to nest, sulphur-crested cockatoos flourish in many regions, from dry, sparse bushland to areas of wetter rainforest. Pretty much anywhere with well-established stands of native trees and seed nearby is a potential place for you to see some of this raucous species. They sometimes congregate in large flocks to feed on the ground, especially in open grassy areas. Try going to local football ovals or parklands to see if you can hear their screeching, then follow the sound!
WHAT THEY EAT	Seeds, fruits, flowers, seeds and some insects. These birds can be pests, given their ability to decimate food crops. They often come and land on our sunflowers, which usually spells disaster for the flowers (unless I can run outside with my arms flapping before the damage is done).
SIMILAR BIRDS	Little corella (*see* page 163), long-billed corella (pictured on page 162), Major Mitchell's cockatoo (pictured opposite; mostly restricted to arid interiors).

WESTERN GALAHS HAVE A PINK CAP OVER HEAD

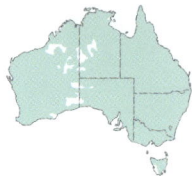

EASTERN & NORTHERN GALAHS HAVE PALE CAPS OVER HEAD

MALES HAVE DARK EYES

FEMALES HAVE PINK EYES

GREY WINGS & BACK

PINK UNDERBELLY & CHEST

Galah

Eolophus roseicapilla

Galahs will usually congregate in open areas to graze in a large flock – parks, ovals, agricultural fields, grassy verges or nature strips. They happily share grazing areas with sulphur-crested cockatoos (*see* page 165), long-billed or little corellas (*see* page 163), with sometimes the odd Australian raven (*see* page 7) or Australian magpie (*see* page 1) lurking around. When it comes time for nesting, galah pairs will seek out appropriately-sized tree hollows for laying and brooding their eggs. Once, a pair visited a gum tree beside our verandah. This particular gum tree had a large hollow filled with a bracket-fungi growth and the pair laboriously tried to scrape out the fungi using their beaks to create a nesting hollow for themselves. Alas, they opted for a different hollow – such searches will go on during the breeding season, as the competition for tree hollow real estate is fierce.

WHAT TO LISTEN FOR	A low, gurgling chuckle, interspersed with higher *deet-deets* – imagine an amalgam of the call of the crimson rosella (*see* page 169) and the sulphur-crested cockatoo (*see* page 165). Galahs most often give a piercing, double-note whistle, *dit-dit*, which carries well from the high branches where they often perch.
WHAT TO LOOK FOR	The galah is a medium-sized pink and grey cockatoo. The feathers over the cheeks, back of the neck and underbelly are a rosy pink. In the east of Australia, the feathers over the head are white, while in the west, the galah has pale pink feathers over its head. These feathers can be raised into a crest, which you'll be able to spot if you watch these birds for long enough – they often raise it during antics with other members of their flock. The back of the galah is grey, darkening slightly at the wingtips. The tail, beak and feet are also grey. The eye is black. Note (if you can get a clear enough look) that <u>females</u> have a pink iris and <u>males</u> have a dark iris.
IMMATURE BIRDS	Young galahs have mottled colouring over their chests and, in the east, take some time to develop the white 'cap' of the adult. The pink plumage and grey wings are paler overall.
WHERE TO START LOOKING	Galahs can be seen in a large range of urban areas, especially where there are remnant trees. As galahs nest in tree hollows, older stands of native trees are likely places for them to frequent, but they are found in many places, particularly if there are areas only a short flight away with plenty of seed or fruiting native trees. If you head to spots where you've often seen sulphur-crested cockatoos, these are likely places to also see galahs. Along riverbanks or in trees near lakes or creeks, in your local park, sports ground, university campus or on dam banks or farmland – there are many places to see them, but if your local park still has native trees planted (e.g. eucalyptus trees), that might be the best place to start.
WHAT THEY EAT	Seeds, flowers and fruit.
SIMILAR BIRDS	Little corella (*see* page 163), long-billed corella (pictured on page 162), Major Mitchell's cockatoo (pictured on page 164).

EASTERN ROSELLA

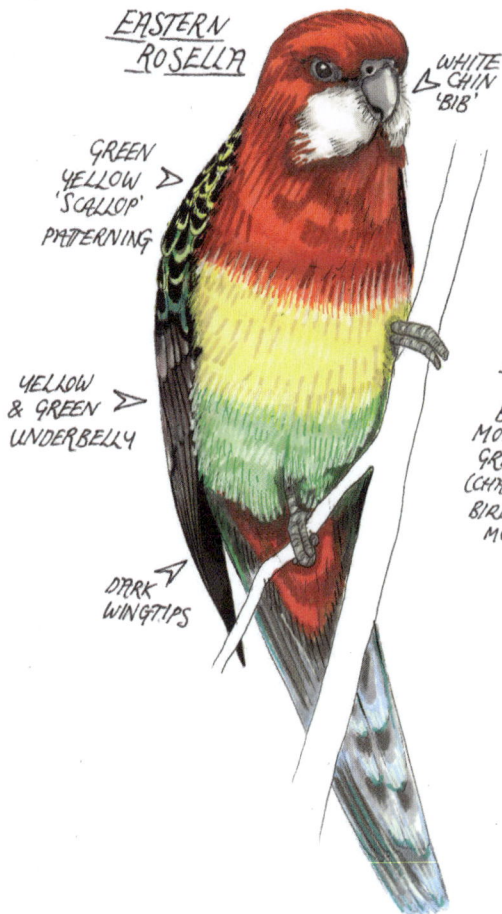

WHITE CHIN 'BIB'

GREEN YELLOW 'SCALLOP' PATTERNING

YELLOW & GREEN UNDERBELLY

DARK WINGTIPS

CRIMSON ROSELLA

BLUE CHIN 'BIB'

BLACK 'SCALLOP' PATTERNING

ADULT

IMMATURE

BODY IS MOTTLED GREEN (CHANGES AS BIRD MOULTS)

BLUE EDGED WINGS & TAIL

Crimson rosella

Jambaarriny [joom-bah-rriyn] (Gumbaynggirr);
bulanbulan [bu-la-n-bu-la-n] (Wiradjuri)
Platycercus elegans

Rosellas are widespread along the eastern coast of Australia and are commonly seen in well-planted suburbs and backyards. Rosellas love to pick the young olives off the trees in our yard, so if you know of a nearby stand of fruit trees or flowering plants, these sweet birds may sometimes visit for a snack. (Or, if rosellas visit your own garden, you might catch a glimpse as they delicately nibble through the plants you worked so hard to grow. Not speaking from personal experience or anything.) Crimson rosellas populate eucalyptus forests and urban green areas alike, as long as there are established stands of trees around, or enough bird seed to entice them away from their usual arboreal haunts. They cruise in family units, chattering sociably as they feed. They also 'trundle' on foot along the grassy verges of roads, where they can munch easily on grass seed. In areas where these birds are common, their repetitive bell-like *cheque please* call echoes out clearly and sweetly through the bush.

WHAT TO LISTEN FOR

These beautiful parrots most often perform two clear, bell-like notes, *whipp-whupp*, or *cheque please*, repeated sweetly from the tree canopy. They may also sing a slightly longer run of notes, with the same clarity, *dyipp-whip-whiup*. When feeding they will make chattering, squeaky conversation with their fellows.

WHAT TO LOOK FOR

Crimson rosellas are small, striking, blue and red parrots. Adults are bright red and have a blue 'bib' under the beak, covering the chin. The leading edges of the wings are also blue. The back is red, with black scallop patterning. The wingtips and tail are dark blue and the beak is pale grey.

IMMATURE BIRDS

Young crimson rosellas are a dark green and will erratically moult into the adult red and blue as they age. Many times I've spotted a juvenile crimson rosella in moult and have been mistakenly convinced that I'm seeing a 'new' species of parrot. Often their partially blue chin and red head is a tip-off, as these tend to appear first as they age.

WHERE TO START LOOKING

Crimson rosellas are common birds that can be spotted on lawns, in local parks, woodlands and suburban gardens, or varying types of bush along the south-eastern coast of Australia. Try heading to the nearest park or nature reserve, especially if you have noticed that the grass there is going to seed. These birds love to feed on the seeds of the winter grass or weeping grass on lawns.

WHAT THEY EAT

Seeds, flowers and fruit.

SIMILAR BIRDS

Eastern rosella (pictured opposite), which has a similar range to the crimson rosella, but is also found in Tasmania. Alongside the eastern rosella, several other species – and subspecies – of rosella exist across Australia, so you can see these parrots in a spectacular array of colours, depending on where you live. The green rosella is restricted to Tasmania, whilst the northern rosella sticks to the northern coast of Western Australia and the Northern Territory. The western rosella is found in southwest Western Australia. The pale-headed rosella is found along the northern New South Wales and Queensland coastline.

RED HEAD & BELLY ▷

♂

GREEN WINGS ▷ & BELLY

IMMATURE

♀

GREEN HEAD & UPPER CHEST ↗

RED BELLY ▷

MOTTLED RED & GREEN HEAD ◁

RED-WINGED PARROT ↴

LONG TAIL ▷

King parrot

Gaangan [gaah-ngun] (Gumbaynggirr)
Alisterus scapularis

The king parrot is slightly less common and more gentle in character than the sulphur-crested cockatoo and the galah, but frequents similar areas in fringe suburbs with plenty of bushland around. King parrots will occasionally graze among these other species but are more often seen in pairs, feeding on seeds on the ground or fruits in gardens. Our local king parrots definitely seem 'sneakier' than the other parrots – they manage to peck at fruits through netting, crawl in among the raspberries, and generally gnaw their way across the garden. Maybe they can be sneakier because they voice their attitudes much less frequently than other parrots: what will take galahs and sulphur-crested cockatoos twenty enormous raptor screeches to say, the king parrot says with one intense cheep.

However much frustration they might cause in the garden, their curiosity makes king parrots engaging birds. They often come to land on our verandah, even though we do not put seed out for them. They land on our clotheshorse and chatter sweetly, swivelling their heads to check us out with one eye, then the other, and hopping along the railing on their stubby legs. They are beautiful, cheeky birds.

WHAT TO LISTEN FOR	A single, long, enthusiastic *cheep!*, repeated sparsely. This call is quite similar to the single-note call of the galah (*see* page 167). King parrots also chatter in squeaky voices when in flocks or when feeding.
WHAT TO LOOK FOR	King parrots are medium-sized red and green parrots with long tails. <u>Males</u> are bright red over the head and the belly. Underneath the tail the red blends into dark green scallop patterning. The wings are deep green, with a line of paler feathers running down the 'shoulder' towards the wingtips. The tail looks as if it is a very dark green, but in sunlight you'll see that the feathers are actually blue. When the parrot is in flight, you might spot this same blue colour at the leading edge of the wings. <u>Females</u> are hooded with green over the head instead of the red of the male, but they still have a red underbelly. They also have a duller beak instead of the more orange-red beak of the male. In both males and females, the eye is a large black pupil surrounded by a yellow ring. These birds often tilt their head to peer one eye at potential food sources, as if they're trying to see into your popcorn box in a dark movie theatre.
IMMATURE BIRDS	Young king parrots are a mottled pale green colour – as if someone took the colours of the adult and swirled them together.
WHERE TO START LOOKING	King parrots seem to hang out in thicker bushland or rainforest where there is likely to be good seed and fruit available for feeding. They also frequent lawns in the outer suburbs and may be found in botanical gardens or more 'lush' suburban gardens. Try heading to well-forested areas along the east coast (often in altitudes where the weather is humid).
WHAT THEY EAT	Seeds, fruit and flowers. (Often local king parrots steal tomatoes and other fruits right off the plants before they're fully ripe from our garden, but I'm immobilised by their adorably cheeky chattering every time!)
SIMILAR BIRDS	Crimson rosella (*see* page 169). The red-winged parrot (pictured opposite; found in the north-eastern areas of Australia) may trip you up, but is much greener and lighter than the king parrot. The eclectus parrot has similar colouring, but is much more 'robust', and is limited to only a small section of the northern Queensland coastline.

MULGA PARROT (♂)

GRAZING
AMONGST GRASS ➘

♂ ➘

RED
RUMP ➘

♀

NO
RED RUMP ➘

♂

VIBRANT BLUE-
GREEN HEAD &
WINGS ➘

RED RUMP
MAY BE ONLY
PARTIALLY VISIBLE ➘

YELLOW
BELLY ➘

♀

FEMALES ARE
GREEN-GREY ➘

A
SMALL
FLAT
BEAK

Red-rumped parrot

Burrany [bu-rr-ain], wurri [wu-rri],
gunungburdyang [gu-nu-ng-bu-r-dya-ng],
burranygaang [bu-rr-ain-gaa-ng] (Wiradjuri)
Psephotus haematonotus

Red-rumps, as they are often affectionately called, have fooled me many a time. These common parrots have such spectacular colours that I often find myself thinking they're another species of inland parrot, like the mulga parrot (pictured opposite) or the swift parrot. Despite red-rumps being a common bird, it is always worthwhile getting a good look at them through your binoculars, as their colours are quite beautiful. I find that the males are so striking in colour that the more muted females are easily overlooked amongst the grasses they love to graze on. That said, the females are equally beautiful, just in a more understated way. These pairs are often seen fastidiously grazing through grass together, and usually only retreat to the treetops for a momentary reprieve, or to scout for nesting hollows.

I mostly see red-rumped parrots feeding on the ground in small flocks, where they'll waddle through longer grass, grazing on seeds. They only keep their heads down for short periods of time, then pop up to scan the surrounds while munching away. They're usually pretty shy and it doesn't take much to accidentally 'flush' them out and lose your chance of having a good look. If you're lucky, you may get to see these birds scouting out a tree hollow to nest in.

WHAT TO LISTEN FOR

An insistent twittering, *wewwewwewewwweww*. When in groups, red-rumped parrots will also chatter like a rainbow lorikeet (*see page 177*), interspersing this with more squeaky whistles.

WHAT TO LOOK FOR

The red-rumped parrot is a small turquoise parrot, often seen grazing on the ground. The <u>male</u> has a turquoise face and a bright green chest that fades to a yellow underbelly. The back body is a turquoise-tinted grey, with dark blue wingtips. The beak is small and flattish, but with the characteristic pointed 'hook' of all parrot beaks. The tail is also a vivid green. There is a patch of red nestled high on the rump, often concealed under the folded wings. The <u>female</u> has a similar colour scheme to the male, but is much duller overall, with a more olive-brown wash to its feathers. The female also lacks a red rump patch.

IMMATURE BIRDS

Young red-rumped parrots are similar in colour to females.

WHERE TO START LOOKING

I have most often seen red-rumped parrots in drier, slightly more inland areas of grass or open bushland. However, they also graze along the edges of Merri Creek in Naarm (Melbourne) or at Cotter Dam on Ngunnawal Country (Canberra), so heading to areas of grass at local watercourses may be a good place to start, even if you're in an urban area. They love grazing in taller grasses where they can stay hidden, so, unfortunately, you may sometimes scare them off before you get a good look. Ovals, golf courses and farmland are common places to find them, and if you're travelling through the countryside, try keeping an eye out in drier inland areas, where they can munch on native seeds and find adequate tree hollows for nesting.

WHAT THEY EAT

Seeds and small fruits.

SIMILAR BIRDS

Mulga parrot (pictured opposite; look for a faint pinkish-red splotch on the back of the head, which is characteristic of the mulga parrot), swift parrot (a critically endangered bird, the swift parrot is a migrant to southern Victoria from Tasmania at certain times of the year).

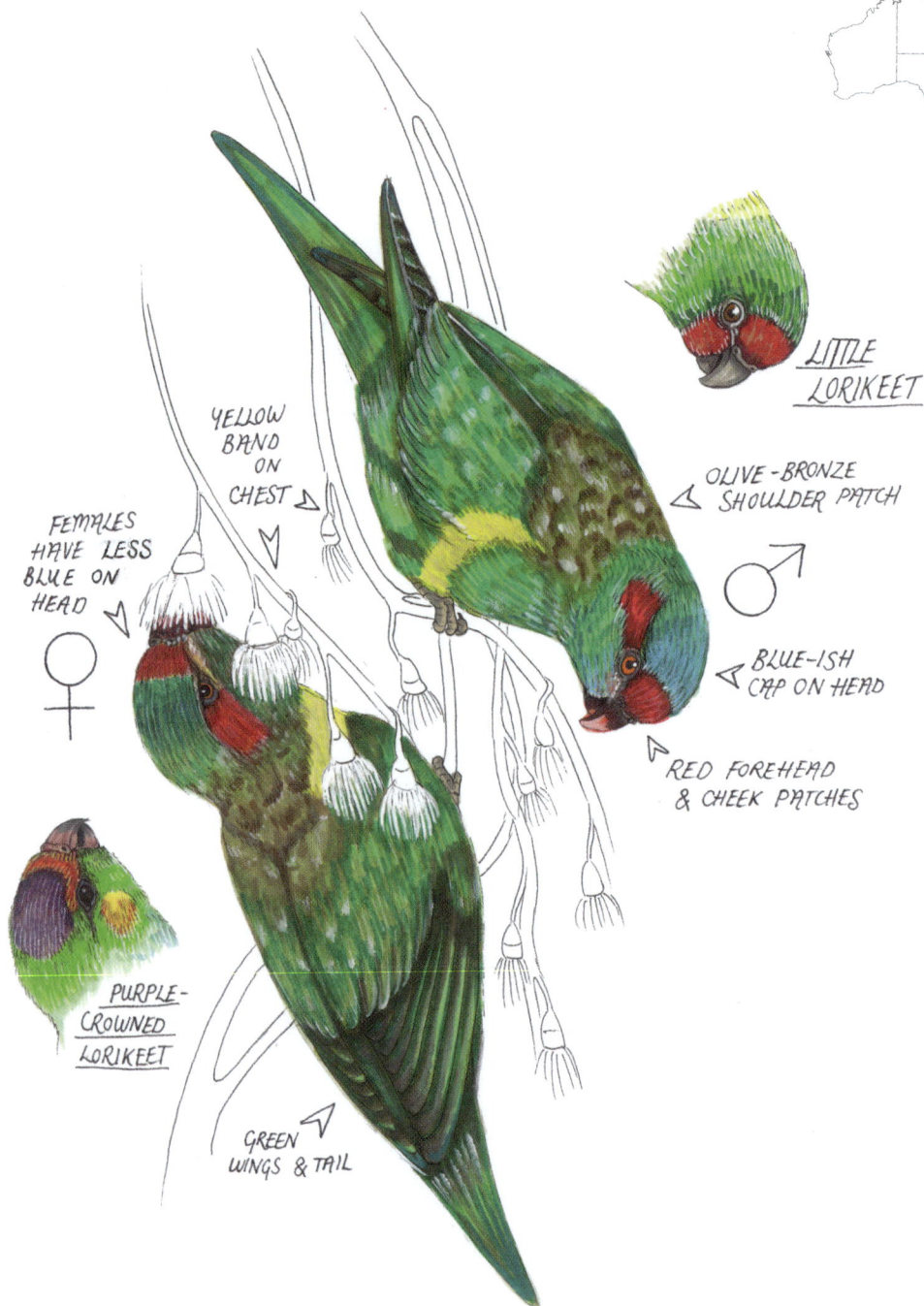

LITTLE LORIKEET

YELLOW BAND ON CHEST ↘

FEMALES HAVE LESS BLUE ON HEAD ↘
♀

OLIVE-BRONZE SHOULDER PATCH ◁

♂

BLUE-ISH CAP ON HEAD ◁

RED FOREHEAD & CHEEK PATCHES

PURPLE-CROWNED LORIKEET

GREEN WINGS & TAIL ↗

Musk lorikeet

Glossopsitta concinna

The musk lorikeet often feeds in flowering trees among other parrot and lorikeet species. It will lengthen and twist its neck this way and that to observe you from each eye, even while feeding directly from flowers. Like the rainbow lorikeet (*see* page 177), these birds are mini gymnasts in their pursuit of food, hanging upside down, twisting and clambering to graze systematically across a branchful of blossoms. Often a huge flock of musk lorikeets will occupy the same eucalyptus tree, so that it appears to 'seethe' with little green birds, all of them chattering happily about the feast they're having. The musk lorikeet, like the rainbow lorikeet, has a specialised 'brush' tongue that helps it lap up nectar.

WHAT TO LISTEN FOR	Musk lorikeets make a trilling call, interspersed with 'styrofoamy' squeaks. These birds chatter appreciatively while feeding, making similar calls to the rainbow lorikeet (*see* page 177), though slightly gentler and less 'velociraptory'.
WHAT TO LOOK FOR	The musk lorikeet is a small, vivid green parrot, often seen feeding in blossoming eucalyptus trees. The body is a verdant green, with yellowing at the shoulders. The top of the head is faintly blue. In <u>males</u>, the forehead above the beak is bright red and there is also a bright red 'panel' beneath the eye, extending across the cheek. <u>Females</u> have slightly less blue colouring to their heads. On both birds there is a patch of bronze colouring on the upper back between the wings. In flight, the underwing feathers are grey and the underside of the tail is yellowish. The beak is orange-red at the tip. You will notice that musk lorikeets are visibly smaller than rainbow lorikeets (*see* page 177).
IMMATURE BIRDS	Young musk lorikeets are similar to adults, but are more dull in colour. In particular, the patches on the cheek and head appear more orange than red.
WHERE TO START LOOKING	Musk lorikeets often congregate in large flocks in flowering eucalyptus trees. If you've noticed a local gum tree that is producing a lot of blossoms, this is the place to start looking. You could also try heading to inland bush with fruiting and flowering trees. In urban areas, you might see them in places where flowering trees have been planted on nature strips or in parking lots. I would often see musk lorikeets in the trees on the nearby university campus, where they fed alongside rainbow lorikeets, both of them making an absolute racket.
WHAT THEY EAT	Fruit, flowers and nectar.
SIMILAR BIRDS	Little lorikeet (pictured opposite; a very similar bird from afar, but note that it has a red 'mask' around the beak rather than panels on its cheeks, and there is no blue crown), purple-crowned lorikeet (pictured opposite; found across the southern and south-western coastline).

YELLOW
COLLAR

BLUE
HEAD

ORANGE
BEAK

GREEN
BACK

RED
ORANGE
NECK

RED-COLLARED
LORIKEET

(note orange
collar &
chest)

Rainbow lorikeet

Trichoglossus moluccanus/haematodus

After observing the antics of rainbow lorikeets, it's hard not to think of them as tiny velociraptors wearing bird costumes: they are so raspy and vocal, and are full of cheeky, reptilian character. When I hear the noise they make, I can't help but imagine they are using bird language that is as colourful as their plumage, swearing enthusiastically about how excellent the nectar on a river red gum is. They often fly in big flocks and do some serious damage to local fruit trees, though more often they feed in flowering eucalypts and other Australian natives. These birds are such nectar lovers, they actually have a specialised brush tongue which assists them in 'licking' up nectar from eucalyptus blooms (several other nectar-feeding species in Australia have specialised brush tongues for this same purpose). Rainbow lorikeets will crawl up, over, around, between and through tree foliage, hanging upside down to access nectar from blossoms, perpetually acrobatic in pursuit of food. Like most other parrot species, the rainbow lorikeet uses tree hollows for nesting.

WHAT TO LISTEN FOR	These birds are extremely loud and sociable, screeching *det-det* in a piercing call. They also chatter in raspy squawks and squeaky 'mutterings' while feeding.
WHAT TO LOOK FOR	The rainbow lorikeet is a brilliantly coloured, medium-sized bird, most often seen feeding in flowering eucalyptus trees (these lorikeets are only a little smaller than the crimson rosella, *see* page 169). The head is sapphire blue, with a pale yellow-green collar and a reddish-orange chest that stipples into blue on the lower belly. Finally, the belly blends from blue to green at the feet. These birds truly encompass a rainbow's worth of colours. The back and tail of the rainbow lorikeet are vibrant green, while the underwing is red along the leading edge, and lined with a yellow 'bar' towards the tip of the wing feathers.
IMMATURE BIRDS	Young rainbow lorikeets are less brightly coloured than adults; the immature colouring is more 'mottled' and dull, reminiscent of the melding of colours when your rainbow paddle-pop starts to melt in the sun.
WHAT THEY EAT	Nectar! They drink it like city-goers drink coffee. Rainbow lorikeets will also feed on fruits, lerp, insects or pollen if need be.
WHERE TO START LOOKING	Rainbow lorikeets are common birds, usually seen in any areas where there are flowering (and therefore nectar-bearing) trees. Try going to local parklands, open bush, heathlands and backyards (if you have blossoming trees). (These birds can also be spotted in Perth, where they escaped from captivity a few decades ago and have since established a small local population there in Western Australia.)
SIMILAR BIRDS	Red-collared lorikeet (pictured opposite; found in the north of the Northern Territory and Western Australia; note the vivid orange-yellow collar that extends higher onto the head than in the rainbow lorikeet), varied lorikeet (a parrot with a red head and green body, which is only seen in northern areas of Australia), musk lorikeet (*see* page 175) and little lorikeet (pictured on page 174).

♂

PINK RING
AROUND
EYE

LARGE STRONG
BEAK

YELLOW
PATCH ON
CHEEK

DARK RING
AROUND EYE

♀

GLOSSY
BLACK-COCKATOO (♀)

YELLOW
PANELS IN TAIL

Yellow-tailed black-cockatoo

Bilirr [bi-li-rr], **garadiil** [ga-ra-dii-l], **niyaran** [ni-ya-ra-n] (Wiradjuri); **ngurna** [ngurn-a ('ng' as in 'si<u>ng</u>')] (Taungurung)
Calyptorhynchus funereus

Unlike the more confident sulphur-crested cockatoos and galahs, yellow-tailed black cockatoos are quite shy and will gracefully 'lift off' if you approach a tree they are feeding in. The sound of yellow-tailed black cockatoos' gentle, creaking call is usually the first and best sign of their presence, as they otherwise blend into the canopy surprisingly well for such big birds. If you hear a gentle, high creaking noise from the skies, race outside to see if you can spot them as they go overhead. They are kite-like in their flight, holding their wings in a beautiful umbrella curve as they circle downwards to land on tree branches. Their wingspan is so large that their wingbeats seem slow; their tail is held out flat and straight in flight.

WHAT TO LISTEN FOR	The yellow-tailed black-cockatoo makes a squeaking, screechy call, like a thinner, much more gentle call of a galah (*see* page 167) and sulphur-crested cockatoo (*see* page 165). These big birds make a drawn out *cree-aaah*, which can sound a little like a seabird (I mostly seem to hear them calling like this when they are in flight). When perched and feeding, these cockatoos will also chat to one another in creaky, squeaky voices.
WHAT TO LOOK FOR	Yellow-tailed black cockatoos are large black cockatoos with yellow crescent-shaped panels on each cheek. When settled on a branch, you may be able to see the yellow panels in their tail (close to the body), though these are easier to observe in flight. They have long, widespread wings, similar to a bird of prey, though they don't seem to 'soar' as birds of prey do, instead moving onwards with steady, graceful wingbeats. The <u>females</u> have a grey ring around the eye, while the <u>males</u> have a pink ring.
WHERE TO START LOOKING	Yellow-tailed black cockatoos love seeds and pine cones – especially in pine plantations (usually Monterey pine, *Pinus radiata*). If there's a local pine plantation near you, it's worth heading there to scan the treetops for these black birds, which 'drape' over branches while feeding. They are also easily spotted when they fly overhead, calling. Other places to look for them include open wooded bushland, coastal heath and areas with lots of banksias (*Banksia* genus) or she-oaks (*Casuarina* genus). Any areas with native, seed-bearing trees are a great place to start. They tend not to venture into thick bushland, preferring to stay near the canopy where they can easily take off.
WHAT THEY EAT	These birds feed on seeds, as do most other cockatoos, but they also eat wood-boring grubs, using their strong beak to tear through bark and into trees themselves to get at them.
SIMILAR BIRDS	Glossy black-cockatoo (pictured opposite; this threatened species is smaller, with a more limited range, the glossy black-cockatoo has a large, stout beak and a red patch in the tail instead of yellow), red-tailed black-cockatoo (more northern and western ranges; has a red panel in the tail, yellow streaks on the chest and a big beak), Carnaby's black-cockatoo (a Western Australian cockatoo with a white crescent on the cheek, and white panels in the tail).

WINGTIPS
FLARED IN
FLIGHT

WEDGED
TAIL

HOOKED
BEAK

ANGULAR
BOXY
SHOULDERS

STRONG, LARGE
FEET

Wedge-tailed eagle

Maliyan [ma-li-ya-n], **bagadaa** [ba-ga-daa], **yibaay** [yi-b-aay], **yibay** [yi-bay] (Wiradjuri); **Bundjil** [Bun-djil ('dj' as in 'da<u>ng</u>er')] (Taungurung)
Aquila audax

Wedge-tailed eagles soar on thermals for long periods of the day, sometimes in pairs, sometimes solo. These powerful birds cross enormous distances with easy wingbeats, scanning the ground for prey. I have a big soft spot for wedge-tailed eagles, as they often spend their hunting time in pursuit of the destructive introduced animals in Australia, including rats, foxes and rabbits. I've also heard of 'wedgies' using team tactics to overcome larger prey, which is more advanced behaviour than some humans I know. Occasionally, wedge-tailed eagles are seen feeding on roadkill, which is an incredible sight – it's hard to register the true size of these birds until you see them on the ground. If you do see a wedge-tailed eagle on the road, slow down if you can. These birds are so huge, lift-off takes a little while – besides, you'll want to be able to soak in the sight of that incredible wingspan. Goosebumps!

WHAT TO LISTEN FOR	Wedge-tailed eagles are rarely heard calling, but when they do, they make a seabird-like keening, a piercing *dup-deww-dup-deww* call.
WHAT TO LOOK FOR	A big shadow in the sky! Wedge-tailed eagles are *huge*. They're the biggest predatory birds we have in Australia, with a wingspan that is often over 200 centimetres. Think about that: the wingspan of the wedge-tailed eagle is as long (or longer!) than a human is tall. They are a mottled dark brown, near to black, with muscular shoulders, making them look sort of 'boxy' when perched. In flight, the wingtips are outstretched and flared like fingers, and the tail-wedge can be seen (the wedge that gives these birds their name). When the wedge-tailed eagle is perched, you might be able to see that its feathered legs are long and muscular, which no doubt assists in grabbing prey. The clawed feet are yellowish-grey and ferocious looking. The beak is large and hooked, a similar yellowish-grey to the claws and almost the same length as the head of the bird, another feature that helps these birds take their quarry. The <u>females</u> are larger than the <u>males</u>.
IMMATURE BIRDS	Young wedge-tailed eagles are much lighter in colour than adults – closer to brown than black – with more mottled colours.
WHERE TO START LOOKING	You're most likely to see a wedge-tailed eagle while it's in flight. They usually hunt over areas of sparse bushland, rivers, lakes, farmland or open plains, where they can easily spot prey. That said, these birds are able to survive in a diverse range of ecosystems. Try exploring in open bushland and along waterways, over heath and coastlines, drier inland reaches of open ground, and agricultural pasture (keeping an eye on the sky for their distinctive wedge-tailed silhouette).
WHAT THEY EAT	These birds are carnivores, going in for mammals, other birds, reptiles and carrion. They have been reported to hunt emus (*see page 131*), which blows my mind.
SIMILAR BIRDS	Immature white-bellied sea-eagle (*see page 187*), little eagle (which, you guessed it, is littler than the wedge-tailed, has a pale underbelly and no 'wedge' to the tail).

SHORTER, FLUFFIER FEATHERS OVER HEAD

TWISTS TAIL LIKE RUDDER

BEAK HAS A YELLOW BASE

BROWN LAYERED FEATHERS OVER BODY

KITE TAILS FROM BELOW

BLACK KITE

SQUARE-TAILED KITE

WHISTLING KITE

YELLOW FEET

Black kite

Milvus migrans

The black kite is known as the 'forked-tailed kite', as their tail forms a cake-fork shape at perch or when folded. These birds of prey usually roost or hunt in groups of several birds, unlike most other raptors, which I more often see solo or in a mating pair. Black kites are seen scavenging together where food is plentiful and may cruise overhead in large flocks. They are skilful hunters and flyers, often eating their smaller catches in midair. These birds are also sometimes called the 'firehawk', a name that stems from their habit of flocking at a fire front. Instead of flying away from a fire, these birds choose to fly *towards* it. The silhouette of several black kites circling above the edges of a bushfire is a common sight. As the vegetation burns, many small critters race away from the fire front, making them easy prey for the waiting black kites. Though I respect the wiles of the black kite's strategy, I can't help but feel sad for the poor animals that were just pausing to wipe their brows after escaping a fire, only to be snatched away in the talons of a hungry bird.

WHAT TO LISTEN FOR	The black kite makes a descending, trilling call, which morphs into a cricket-like warbling.
WHAT TO LOOK FOR	The black kite is a medium-sized bird of prey, usually more of a dark brown than black. It has a lighter-brown head and underbelly, with darker wings and tail. This kite has a yellow base to its otherwise grey beak, and large dark eyes. In flight, these birds can be difficult to distinguish from other kite species. When you suspect a kite is flying overhead, try looking specifically at the tail, as this will help you distinguish them. The black kite has a tail with a concave tip (see kite tails opposite, and the birds of prey tail comparison in the appendix). They will often 'twist' their tail in flight, using it for steerage. When at perch, or when the tail is 'folded' compactly, it appears forked.
WHERE TO START LOOKING	Often black kites will feed on carrion and roadkill, so keep your eyes out for them on the verge of the road in country or inland areas. Otherwise they often hunt over open pasture or farmland, looking for smaller prey. Try heading out to agricultural areas, or along the banks of rivers or creeks, where these birds can get a clear view of a potential catch. Dry floodplains or irrigation channels may also prove worthwhile to check out.
WHAT THEY EAT	As birds of prey, black kites often take smaller animals such as rats, mice and rabbits. They also happily scavenge at landfill sites, scour for scraps at composting facilities, or snack on roadkill or other carrion; they will take food wherever they can get it.
SIMILAR BIRDS	Square-tailed kite and whistling kite (tails pictured opposite), swamp harriers (*see* page 189) and spotted harrier (pictured on page 188). Harriers may trip you up, though these birds usually cruise solo or in pairs, are a more chestnutty brown, and have lighter underwing feathers.

(FROM BELOW)

SLIGHTLY DARK WINGTIPS

NANKEEN KESTREL

BLACK TAIL TIP

DARKER WINGTIPS

WHITE TAIL TIP

BLACK SHOULDERED KITE

BROWN HEAD

STREAKED CHEST

GREY HEAD

BASE OF BEAK & EYE ARE YELLOW

COPPER BACK

DARK TAIL TIP

WHITE UNDERBELLY

YELLOW FEET

Nankeen kestrel

Falco cenchroides

The nankeen kestrel is actually part of the falcon family (Falconidae), though it is smaller than its fellow brown, black and peregrine falcons. While most falcons are renowned for their fast flying, the nankeen kestrel tends to use a different strategy for capturing prey. These birds hover over open ground using fast, fluttering wingbeats to hold their position, almost 'hanging' in the sky. As they hover, they manage to hold their heads *incredibly* still, using their wings to maintain their position, allowing them to scan the ground below them for potential food. Upon seeing prey, these birds speedily dive down to grab it.

I usually see nankeen kestrels when they are skilfully hovering above pasture, as they are visible from a distance, allowing me to see their darkened wingtips and russet-brown back (the real giveaway identifiers of this species). I have only seen one other small Australian bird regularly hovering at roadsides, and that's the black-shouldered kite, which has darker wingtips and a white back, so you should be able to distinguish it from the nankeen kestrel. Other names for the nankeen kestrel include 'mosquitohawk' and 'windhover', appropriate names for this small but skilled hunter.

WHAT TO LISTEN FOR	High-pitched, piercing *yeet-yeet-yeet*, which carries over long distances.
WHAT TO LOOK FOR	The nankeen kestrel is a small copper-brown raptor often seen hovering at roadsides or over farmland. The underside of the bird is white with faintly darkened wingtips. The tail fans widely, and across the tip of each tail feather is a thin, dark band. The feet are yellow. <u>Males</u> have a russet-brown back, with black wingtips and a grey tail. The head is slightly grey, with yellow at the base of the beak and the eye. Beneath the eye is a 'teardrop' of black feathers, running down towards the shoulder. The pale chest is patterned with faint vertical streaks. <u>Females</u> have a similarly russet brown back, but have more vivid streaking on their chest, and have a brown head where the male head is grey. The upper side of the female's tail is copper brown where the male's tail is grey.
IMMATURE BIRDS	Young nankeen kestrels look like the females, but with more intense striations over the breast, neck and face.
WHERE TO START LOOKING	If you're in the passenger seat while driving somewhere outside the city, it's a good idea to keep an eye out when driving past farmland, or any open grassy field, as these are places where birds of prey will glide while on the lookout for an easy catch. I've often seen nankeen kestrels when driving through agricultural areas. They tend to hover, facing into the wind at a fenceline, where mice or other small critters hide in the tall grasses. Keep an eye out for these birds in grasslands and other kinds of open ground, especially over pasture or at roadsides. I have also seen them cruising along heathland slopes of the Australian Alps during summer (above the tree line), where the hunting is made easier.
WHAT THEY EAT	These birds will snack on larger insects (e.g. grasshoppers) and will hunt smaller mammals, reptiles and birds.
SIMILAR BIRDS	Letter-winged kite (a rare species similar to the black-shouldered kite), black-shouldered kite (pictured opposite; especially juveniles, which are brown).

HALF COLOURS OF WING VISIBLE IN FLIGHT

TAIL IS SLIGHTLY WEDGED

IMMATURE

LARGE HOOKED BEAK

BODY IS MOTTLED BROWN

DARK NAVY WINGS & BACK

ADULT

WHITE BELLY

White-bellied sea-eagle

Ngangaarr [ngung-ahr ('ng' as in 'su<u>ng</u>')]
(Gumbaynggirr)
Haliaeetus leucogaster

I most often see white-belled sea-eagles (also known as the 'white-breasted sea-eagle') cruising down the Snowy River on Gunaikurnai Country (East Gippsland, Victoria). As they're territorial birds, they usually fly alone or in mating pairs. You're also likely to see a solo immature bird (different from the adults, see below) out exploring. The juveniles seem to cover larger areas than the more territorial adults, going on a kind of rumspringa before settling into more grounded adult life. When it comes time to raise young, the white-bellied sea-eagle builds a conglomerate of large branches, bark and other windfall, thrown into a hodgepodge structure, which is easily overlooked as debris in the fork of a tree. From below it can look more like a tangle of branches than a nest. However messy, these structures really are the thrones of the bush – these birds are so big, their nests are like castles, positioned high up in the canopy, usually with a commanding view over the surrounds. While seeing them at perch can be tricky, these birds are incredible to watch as they soar along the coast, huge and steady in their flight.

WHAT TO LISTEN FOR	A honking, repetitive goose-like call, *ekk-ekk-ekk-ekk-ekk*.
WHAT TO LOOK FOR	The white-bellied sea-eagle is a huge, majestic bird of prey, usually spotted gliding above rivers, estuaries or the seashore. Only a little smaller than the enormous wedge-tailed eagle, these birds have a gloriously large wingspan, making them a striking sight as they cruise above the shoreline. The underside of the body is mostly white, with dark navy wing feathers. The head is also white, with a large hooked beak. The back of the bird is grey. The white tail, when unfurled, is similar to that of the wedge-tailed eagle (*see* page 181), though less severe in its 'wedge'. The feet are yellow.
IMMATURE BIRDS	Just to complicate matters, the colouring of the young white-bellied sea-eagle is almost completely the opposite to that of the adult. They are a mottled brown over the body, a colour which darkens at the wingtips. Thus, young sea-eagles look very similar to the immature wedge-tailed eagle (*see* page 181). I find the best way to distinguish the young sea-eagle from other birds of prey is to look for their white, slightly wedged tail with black-tipped feathers.
WHERE TO START LOOKING	White-bellied sea-eagles are sometimes seen inland, but if you head to coastlines or bushy areas along brackish waterways, these are the best places to try spotting them. You are also much more likely to see them in flight than at perch, so keep an eye out for any large silhouettes in the sky. These birds are widespread, but as they are territorial and range over large areas of land, you won't find too many of them in any one area.
WHAT THEY EAT	White-bellied sea-eagles are carnivorous hunting birds, taking fish and mammals, and will sometimes take carrion (e.g. roadkill).
SIMILAR BIRDS	Wedge-tailed eagle (*see* page 181; as described above, this eagle is similar to the juvenile white-bellied sea-eagle), little eagle (found across the country, these are slightly smaller birds of prey with a white, square-shaped tail). The eastern osprey may initially look similar, but these birds are smaller and often have a visible 'collar' of brown feathers across the chest.

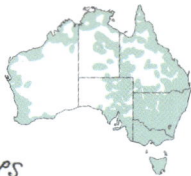

(NOTE ♀ LARGER THAN ♂)

SLIGHTLY BARRED WINGTIPS

DARKER UNDERWING

MORE BARRED TAIL

DARKER CHEST

NOTE YELLOW BASE OF BEAK & YELLOW EYE

ADULT

LESS VIVID TAIL BAND

IMMATURE (DARKER OVERALL)

STREAKY PALER BELLY

LIGHTER UNDERWING

ADULT IN FLIGHT (FROM ABOVE)

NOTE WHITE BAND

SPOTTED HARRIER

Swamp harrier

Circus approximans

Also known as the 'marsh harrier', the swamp harrier loves to frequent irrigated land or dairy flats where there is plenty of small prey to be taken. The scientific name '*Circus*' is shared with this bird's close relative, the spotted harrier (*Circus assimilis*), and I imagine it refers to the broad circles they make when looking over a pasture for prey. Harriers are real 'soarers', curving across the sky with their huge wings held steady between sparse wingbeats. They sometimes come down to perch on fenceposts, which is a good opportunity to get a better look at their beautiful streaky patterning.

WHAT TO LISTEN FOR	Short, barking *yap!*, high pitched and abrupt.
WHAT TO LOOK FOR	Swamp harriers are large copper-brown birds of prey that are most easily seen when in flight. The head and upper breast of the <u>male</u> are covered with brown vertical streaks. The wings are dark brown and the tail is white with horizontal stripes. These birds also have a vivid and characteristic 'bar' of white across the base of the tail (where it meets with the body, see picture opposite). The beak is pale yellow with a darkened tip. The <u>females</u> are larger than the males, and have a similar patterning, but are a darker chestnut brown, with stronger streaks on the breast. They also have a more vivid white tail-bar.
IMMATURE BIRDS	Young swamp harriers are much darker overall, almost solidly coloured a rich chestnut brown. The young birds have a less vivid tail-bar.
WHERE TO START LOOKING	The swamp harrier loves to hunt over wet, open ground, so try heading out to flat, swampy country – irrigated pasture, wetlands and floodplains. Old water treatment plants or dams are also good places to look, as they're often located alongside broad, flat farmland where these birds can easily hunt.
WHAT THEY EAT	Swamp harriers take live prey, hunting for rabbits, smaller birds (especially wading or paddling birds – ducklings are easy prey) and other small water-dwelling critters.
SIMILAR BIRDS	Spotted harrier (pictured opposite; found in drier, more inland areas and is less frequently seen than the swamp harrier), whistling kite, square-tailed kite (*see* Tails of birds of prey in the appendix, page 209), wedge-tailed eagle (*see* page 181, note its size, colour and tail shape). I recommend looking specifically for the white tail-bar on the bird, as this is a useful distinguishing feature between the swamp harrier and similar birds of prey.

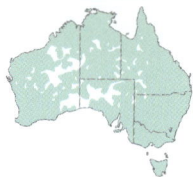

TASMANIAN
MOREPORK

SMALL
(BUT SHARP)
BEAK

(MAINLAND)
SOUTHERN
BOOBOOK

WHITE
EYE
RINGS
(GRANDFATHER
GLASSES)

CHEQUERED
PATTERNING
ON UNDERBELLY

DARKER
WINGS

STRONG
FEET & LEGS
FOR TAKING PREY

Southern boobook

Guunbuny [goo-booyn] (Gumbaynggirr); **ngugug** [ngu-gu-g], **bugbug** [bu-g-bu-g], **wangi** [wa-ngi], **mugii** [mu-gii], **gugug** [gu-gu-g] (Wiradjuri); **muk muk** [muk muk ('u' as in 'p<u>u</u>t')] (Taungurung)
Ninox boobook

If you're out around twilight, you're likely to spot a southern boobook in silhouette while they perch on a tree branch or powerline. If you do get to see one, you'll notice their distinctively wide, low head and rounded body, a shape which is very characteristic of predatory night birds. If you've ever startled a southern boobook and you've seen it fly away, you may have noticed how *silent* these birds are in flight. It's not just your hearing – these owls have special feathers that assist them in their hunting pursuits. While the feathers on the wings of the crested pigeon (*see* page 145) encourage noisy flight, the southern boobook has distinctive feathers on their wings that disrupt, or 'break up', the flow of air over the wing. By disrupting the air flow, the motion of the wings is prevented from making any 'flapping' or 'swooping' noises. Most nocturnal hunting birds have similarly modified feathers that (I think) make them all the more mysterious and awe-inspiring.

During the day, southern boobooks seem to roost in dense canopies, usually in quiet spots away from human activity. I have encountered one on a morning walk and felt very privileged to see their patterned plumage (and angry eyebrows) in full daylight.

WHAT TO LISTEN FOR	The southern boobook makes an insistent *brooh-broohk*, a melancholy call often repeated in the early hours of the evening. I love this sound – I find it very soothing as it echoes through the suburbs at night.
WHAT TO LOOK FOR	The southern boobook is a medium-sized, (adorably) angry-looking owl. They are generally a mottled dark brown colour with some paler brown tortoiseshell patterning on the underbelly. The two wide-set eyes are large, with pale irises, and are framed by pale, sweeping eyebrows that arch around the eye to meet up with the beak. The beak itself is small, sharp and pressed nearly flat against the face. The sweeping eyebrows have two primary visual effects: a) the owl looks like it is wearing silver-rimmed grandfather glasses, and b) they give the owl a profoundly disgruntled appearance.
WHERE TO START LOOKING	Southern boobook owls defy their name and can be seen across Australia, not just in the south. However, they prefer both wooded areas and places with an abundance of marsupial prey. The best places to start your search are areas where you've heard them calling at night. Try heading for bushland reserves and parks – during the day, the boobooks roost on high tree branches, so keep a look out for a fluffy, motionless figure huddled up in the canopy. They also venture into more suburban areas if there is adequate vegetation for roosting, although, again, they will be hidden among the trees, so it can take a bit of patience to find one. If you head out at night, please be sure to use red-filtered light so as to avoid disturbing the nocturnal wildlife unnecessarily (*see* How to use this book, page xxii, for more information).
WHAT THEY EAT	Southern boobooks generally feed on small reptiles and birds, mammals and insects..
SIMILAR BIRDS	The morepork of Tasmania (pictured opposite) has recently been separated as a distinct species. These birds are very similar to the southern boobook, but the Tasmanian morepork has yellow irises where the mainland southern boobook has pale cream to white irises. Other similar birds include the powerful owl (much larger) and the tawny frogmouth (*see* page 193).

LARGE
YELLOW
EYE

BEAK
PARTIALLY
HIDDEN UNDER
WHISKERY
FEATHERS

SOME PALER
FEATHERS ON
BACK

STREAKED,
LAYERED
FEATHERS OVER
WHOLE BODY

Tawny frogmouth

Jinijinu [gin-ee-gin-oo] (Gumbaynggirr);
dhurrgang [dhu-rr-ga-ng], **nguruwiya**
[ngu-ru-wi-ya] (Wiradjuri)
Podargus strigoides

Tawny frogmouths are common night-birds, often seen in silhouette when perched on powerlines or branches. They usually remain on a perch, waiting for an insect or small critter to creep within swooping reach. They pounce in short, silent flights, sometimes pausing on the ground to gulp down their catch. They are very well camouflaged against trees with their blocky, branch-like bodies and grey, streaked plumage. I think of these birds as the feathered version of Peeta Mellark from *The Hunger Games*: excellent at disguise, patient and quiet, but capable of striking out (to grab prey) when necessary. If you do manage to see a tawny frogmouth during the day, you'll notice these birds enhance the camouflaging effect of their plumage by remaining frozen for long periods of time.

WHAT TO LISTEN FOR	A deep, resonant, yet soft *whooom-whoom-whoom-whoom*. This is continued, insistently, like a low drumbeat. These birds usually call during twilight hours (early morning and just after the sun sets).
WHAT TO LOOK FOR	The tawny frogmouth is a night-bird that has a very low, wide head and a squat body. The large, wide-set eyes are yellow. The beak is broad and triangular when opened, reminiscent of a paper chatterbox. The breast is grey with dark vertical streaks, while the wings are a slightly darker colour with similar patterning to the breast. If you ever see these birds during daylight hours, you'll notice their feathers look almost hair-like and layered, similar to stringy bark. Note: There is much variation in the colouring of tawny frogmouths' feathers, so the peculiar shape of the body and beak is probably the most obvious and consistent identifier of these birds.
WHERE TO START LOOKING	Anywhere with trees and water where lizards, frogs and other small critters will hang out. Like the southern boobook (*see* page 191), tawny frogmouths are relatively common birds – I've seen them in parks in the middle of Melbourne, so they do well even in urban environments. I would recommend scanning the canopy in your local park or at a nearby creek or river, or going for a twilight walk with a buddy, keeping an eye out on powerlines and branches for a tawny frogmouth silhouette. As with all nocturnal wildlife, spotting for tawny frogmouths at night should be done with care using a red-filtered light to minimise unnecessary disturbance (*see* How to use this book, page xxii, for more information). You may have some luck seeing them roosting in the upper canopies of trees in parks or bushland during the day, however their distinctive plumage makes them very well camouflaged in the eucalyptus trees they so often frequent.
WHAT THEY EAT	Tawny frogmouths mostly go for large insects and small mammals, swooping quickly from perches to grab them. Sometimes you can see tawny frogmouths swooping intermittently around a streetlamp, chasing insects that have been drawn towards the light.
SIMILAR BIRDS	Southern boobook (*see* page 191), powerful owl (a very large, pale-coloured owl), Australian owlet-nightjar (a smaller bird that hangs out in tree hollows).

PHEASANT
COUCAL (♂)

♂
MALES
ARE
BLACK

RED EYE

NOTE STRIPE
DOWN CHEEK

♀

FEMALES
ARE
PATTERNED
BROWN

STRIPED
TAIL

Eastern ('common') koel

Bibimgirr [bib-im-girr] (Gumbaynggirr)
Eudynamys orientalis

Pronounced 'koll' (similar to 'coal'), the eastern koel is a large, secretive – but very vocal – bird. On the south-eastern coast of Australia, these birds are exotic vagrants, while in the warmer areas of the north, they are a constant neighbourhood menace, singing around the clock, but rarely emerging from the canopy where they hide so well. Other names for the koel are the 'stormbird' or 'rainbird' as it sings even during wet weather. On several such stormy afternoons, I have heard a koel calling from a nearby tree and raced outside to spot it. Usually the bird manages to remain out of sight among the foliage, leaving me to be pummelled by rain, as the koel's distinctive call taunts me.

The eastern koel is actually a cuckoo. Cuckoos are a group of birds that trick other birds into raising their young. These interspecies tactics are specific to cuckoos – termed 'brood parasitism', or more broadly 'kleptoparasitism', the thieving of resources. The parent cuckoos are like over-worked adults who send their kids off to boarding school for reprieve, only the boarding school is someone else's nest. As with other cuckoos, koel manoeuvres work like this: when ready to lay, a female koel will find the nest of another species. While the owners of the nest are away on other business, the female koel lays its egg amongst the other eggs already in the nest. The koel then heads off on its merry way.

The unsuspecting owners of the nest will return to care for the eggs, none the wiser. Ideally, when the koel egg hatches, it will be the first of the clutch of eggs in the nest. Next, in an impressive feat of evolution, the barely functional koel chick will follow its instincts and push all the other eggs out of the nest. (There are plenty of disturbing online videos of blind, naked cuckoo chicks pushing rival eggs out of nests with feeble, stumbling efforts.) Now, alone in the nest, the young koel will then have the full attention of its forcibly adopted parents. The parents will raise the koel as if it is their own, just occasionally stopping to wonder why their enormous child is entirely the wrong colour.

Having performed this switcharoo, the adult eastern koel can freely continue taunting birdwatchers in the middle of thunderstorms.

WHAT TO LISTEN FOR	The eastern koel makes a baby-like, melancholy call, composed of 3–4 notes that rise in pitch, like the sound of a glass being filled in three bursts, *weeeup-weeeup-weeeup*.
WHAT TO LOOK FOR	The eastern koel is a dark-coloured, medium-sized bird (a similar size to the pied currawong, *see page 11*). Male eastern koels are black with a striking red eye and grey beak. The metallic sheen on their feathers makes them well camouflaged and (infuriatingly) hard to spot when they are perched in the canopy. Instead of being black like the male, females have dark brown wings spotted with fine white polka dots. They have a dark head, a cream-coloured chest and a pale belly patterned with faint horizontal streaks. Their tail is long and is thickly barred with pale stripes.
IMMATURE BIRDS	Young eastern koels look much like the females, but their colouring is more dilute and they have less defined patterning. They also have a rust-coloured patch of feathers above the eye, where the adult birds have only dark feathers.

EASTERN KOEL (♀)

PHEASANT COUCAL (♀)

WHERE TO START LOOKING	The koel is a fruit-loving bird, so areas where there are fruiting trees are a good place to start. Try keeping an ear out for their strange call when you visit lush gardens in green suburbs, warmer rainforest, parklands or botanical gardens. The eastern koel migrates to and from tropical regions in the Pacific, breeding in Australia during the warmer seasons, so you may only hear their strange, melancholy call for certain periods of the year, depending on your location.
WHAT THEY EAT	Fruits.
SIMILAR BIRDS	Raven species (*see* page 7), white-winged chough (*see* page 9), pied currawong (*see* page 11), male satin bowerbird (*see* page 149). Another similar bird is the pheasant coucal, found along the northern half Australia's forested areas (pictured opposite; these are larger, browner birds with long tails).
DID YOU KNOW?	Kleptoparasitism specifically refers to the thieving of any resources from another organism. This term can be applied to any organism that habitually steals resources from another organism, and many animals other than cuckoos do this! Nest parasitism even occurs in some bee species (including the genus *Thyreus*, also known as 'cloak and dagger' cuckoo bees).
	By stealing resources from another animal, the kleptoparasite is saved the efforts that gathering, building or organising those supplies would have taken. Imagine it as someone stealing cookies from your cookie jar, rather than going to the effort of baking their own cookies.
	Other examples of kleptoparasitism include stealing of food (e.g. the magnificent frigatebird stealing food from the blue-footed booby), birds stealing nesting materials from other birds' nests, or, in the case of bowerbirds, male birds stealing bower-decorating materials from other bowerbirds (*see* page 149). Whilst stealing resources has advantages, it also comes with risks – if an animal catches you with your hand in their cookie jar, they're not going to be happy about it!

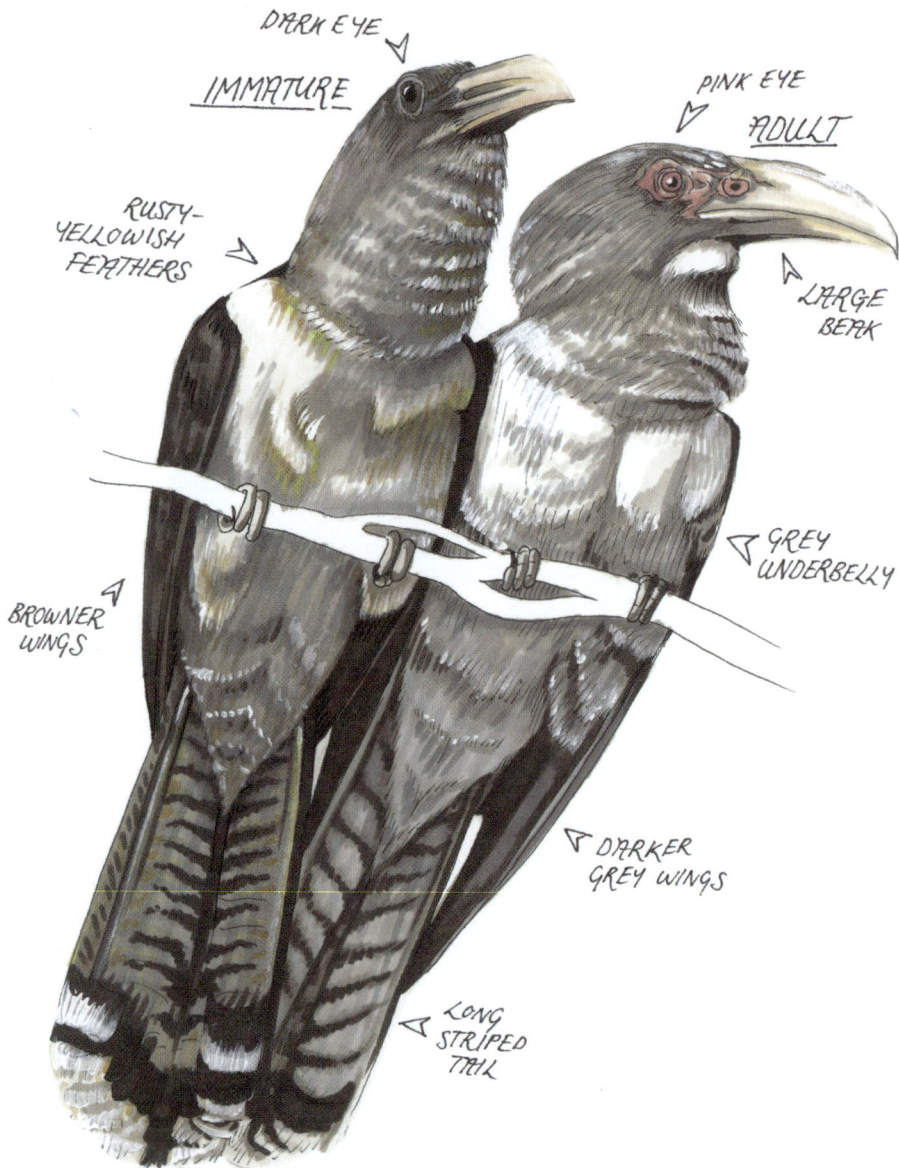

DARK EYE ▽

IMMATURE

PINK EYE
▽   ADULT

RUSTY-
YELLOWISH
FEATHERS   ▷

◁ LARGE
BEAK

BROWNER
WINGS ◥

◁ GREY
UNDERBELLY

◁ DARKER
GREY WINGS

◁ LONG
STRIPED
TAIL

Channel-billed cuckoo

Scythrops novaehollandiae

These large fruit-loving birds have developed fascinating strategies for raising their young. As one of the cuckoo species (*see* pages 195–203), this bird lays its eggs in the nest of another bird species. Thus, the other species is 'tricked' into raising one of the cuckoo chicks as its own, freeing the channel-billed cuckoo from the burden of parenting.

Whereas many other cuckoo species, such as Horsfield's bronze-cuckoo (*see* page 203), or the fan-tailed cuckoo (*see* page 201), have to sneak into a nest to do their dastardly work while the parents are away, the channel-billed can be much bolder. Given their enormous size, they can sometimes 'muscle' their way into their selected nest, even if the parents *are* there to protest. They are so large, they are able to disregard the attacks of the parents. These birds usually target the nests of a pied currawong or a raven, as they prefer to parasitise species that are similar to their own size.

As you can imagine, the sheer size of the channel-billed cuckoo means it demands hefty amounts of food, so parent birds are often run ragged in trying to meet the needs of their adoptee kid.

WHAT TO LISTEN FOR	A whingy, throaty screech, which rises in pitch, pulsing each time, *dew-dup, deeewww-dup, deeeeew-dup!* This is similar in 'structure' to that of the eastern ('common') koel (*see* page 195) but the channel-billed cuckoo song is more throaty, guttural and rasping. This call tends to rise into a cluster of shorter, more frenzied screeches.
WHAT TO LOOK FOR	The biggest of the parasitic cuckoos in Australia, the channel-billed cuckoo is a grey bird with a long tail and a huge beak, which makes it look kind of like an understated toucan. The head, belly and underside of the tail are pale grey and patterned with horizontal stripes, while the back of the bird is darker grey. The tail itself is large and paddle-like, with a black and white band towards its tip. The large beak is shaped in a banana curve and is pinkish-grey. The eye is pink-red, which makes these birds look a little eerie.
IMMATURE BIRDS	Young channel-billed cuckoos are generally more yellowish or rusty-looking than the adults and do not develop the pink-red eye until they fully mature.
WHERE TO START LOOKING	When seasonally migrating to Australia during the warm months, these birds prefer the tropical, fruit-rich regions of eastern and northern Australia (though they occasionally make it as far inland as Alice Springs). They otherwise stick to the warm, humid and well-treed reaches of Papua New Guinea and Indonesia. They are often seen in fruiting trees – especially fig trees – in people's gardens or locals parks.
WHAT THEY EAT	Channel-billed cuckoos go mainly for fruit, supplementing this with insects. They may also eat the eggs in the nests of other birds, thus 'making room' for their own young (shudder).
SIMILAR BIRDS	These are quite distinctive birds – not many other species have a beak like that!

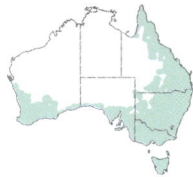

BRUSH CUCKOO
(note white eye ring)

GREY CHIN

SMALL HOOKED BEAK

PALE EYE RING

IMMATURE

BROWN BACK & HEAD

MOTTLED CHEST

YELLOW EYE RING

ADULT

PINK BELLY EXTENDS UP ONTO CHIN

TAIL PATTERNING (FROM ABOVE)

TAIL PATTERNING (FROM BELOW)

Fan-tailed cuckoo

Cacomantis flabelliformis

The fan-tailed cuckoo is another parasitic cuckoo, like the eastern ('common') koel (*see* page 195), channel-billed cuckoo (*see* page 199) and Horsfield's bronze-cuckoo (*see* page 203). These birds tend to lay their eggs in the nests of bird species with a similar size and habitat to them, so one likely 'target' species for the fan-tailed cuckoo is the superb fairywren (*see* page 67), as well as even tinier birds, like thornbills (*see* pages 41 and 51). When walking in the Blue Mountains in New South Wales, I saw a tiny brown thornbill feeding grubs to a young fan-tailed cuckoo. The poor thornbill was desperately racing around to get food for its young'un, which was double its size and incessantly 'crying' (ahem, whingeing) as it sat immobile on a branch. I find myself wanting to rage about the injustice, but the cuckoo is only doing what it's genetically programmed to do. In its mind, this little thornbill is its parent, as much as the thornbill believes the enormous cuckoo to be its child. A *Rosemary's Baby* kind of situation, if you will.

Adult fan-tailed cuckoos are quite shy, making it hard to get a close look at them. Usually you'll be alerted to their presence by their trilling call. They tend to perch inactively on high branches, staring out at their surrounds with a mopey look. I sometimes wonder if part of this 'inactivity' when at perch is due to their feet. The cuckoos actually have feet like cockatoos and parrots – that is, feet that have two toes forward and two toes back. Most other birds (e.g. perching birds, *see* pages 17–73) have three forward-facing toes and one that faces back. I never seem to see cuckoos hopping or moving around on branches as much as other bird species – perhaps the cuckoo toe arrangement is better suited to grabbing and climbing.

WHAT TO LISTEN FOR	Fan-tailed cuckoos give a very rapid, purring whistle that drops in pitch, *trewwwww*. Their spiralling, descending call sounds like a whistling firework before detonation.
WHAT TO LOOK FOR	The fan-tailed cuckoo is a medium-sized perching bird (about 25 cm long). The head, chin, back and wings are grey and the chest and belly are a blush-bronze colour. The underside of the tail is grey and white, in horizontal stripes. The upper side of the tail is dark grey, though you will be able to see a little 'overhang' of the striped underside, making the outer edges of these feathers look spotted. The eye is ringed with yellow and the beak is dark, small and curved in a slight hook. The feet are yellow.
IMMATURE BIRDS	Young fan-tailed cuckoos are brown, with a mottled chest and less distinct tail stripes. They also lack the yellow eye-ring of the adults.
WHERE TO START LOOKING	The fan-tailed cuckoo is fairly common in most kinds of bush across the southern and eastern coast. They are stealthy, flighty birds that will flee at the slightest approach, so it may take a little while to spot one. I would recommend heading to the nearest bushland reserve, park or botanical garden and walking among the taller trees in the area. If you have a section of creek or lake near you with decent native bushland along the bank, this may prove a worthwhile place to start.
WHAT THEY EAT	Mostly insects, grubs and larvae.
SIMILAR BIRDS	Brush cuckoo (pictured opposite; their underbellies are also blush coloured, but this emerges lower on the body, and it has a grey eye), pallid cuckoo (seen across the mainland; a slightly larger, greyer cuckoo).

APPROX 15 cm. LONG

HORIZONTAL BARRING

PARROT-LIKE FEET
(two toes forward, two toes back)

WHITE EYEBROW

IRIDESCENT GREENISH BACK

SHINING BRONZE CUCKOO
(NOTE LACK OF EYEBROW AND STRONG BARRING BELOW CHIN.)

Horsfield's bronze-cuckoo

Chrysococcyx basalis

Horsfield's bronze-cuckoos, just like the eastern ('common') koel (*see* page 195) and fan-tailed cuckoo (*see* page 201), must be devious to survive in the Australian bush. By laying their eggs in the nests of other birds, they avoid the effort of raising their young, off-loading that duty onto another species. Horsfield's bronze-cuckoos are stealthy egg layers – by which I mean that one of these little birds can swoop into a nest, lay an egg in a matter of seconds and swoop out of reach again, all before its morning coffee. These cuckoos seem mostly to roam solo, tucking themselves away in denser shrubs along riverbanks or in the tree canopy. They sometimes fluff themselves up at perch, which makes them look quite round and smug, though this is actually an effort to stay warm (by fluffing their feathers up, the finely interlinked fibres of their feathers trap air against the body and act as a buffer against the cold). I've found the Horsfield's bronze-cuckoo to be very shy and flighty, so getting a good look at them can prove difficult.

WHAT TO LISTEN FOR	A descending short whistle, repeated like a metronome, alternating with a more chirruping *chreeeww, chreeww, chreeww*.
WHAT TO LOOK FOR	The Horsfield's bronze-cuckoo is a small bird with green, mother-of-pearl wings. The chest is a creamy pale colour, patterned with horizontal brown bars that fade towards the middle of the chest. The head is grey, with a striking white eyebrow and chin. The eye is faintly red. The wings are a bronze-turquoise colour with a beautiful reflective sheen. When these birds are hiding among green foliage, these opalescent wing feathers camouflage them well from over-curious birders and predators both.
IMMATURE BIRDS	Young Horsfield's bronze-cuckoos have more dilute, browner colouring than the adults, and their wings are less iridescent.
WHERE TO START LOOKING	Try looking for these little birds in open woodland, along riversides, in trees on the edge of irrigated pasture or in beachside scrub. They are secretive, shy birds that blend in well with the bush and fly away quite readily if they hear you approaching. Just occasionally you may be fortunate enough to spot the movement of a little green bird in a nearby shrub or tree, and with some stealthy binocular work you might be able to see them in detail. Try keeping a close eye out in any denser areas of bushland, windbreaks in farmland or along watercourses.
WHAT THEY EAT	Insects, grubs and larvae.
SIMILAR BIRDS	Black-eared cuckoo (this cuckoo has no chest bars, no iridescent turquoise and is found sparsely through inland areas and north-western coastlines), shining bronze-cuckoo (pictured opposite; has a similar range to Horsfield's bronze-cuckoo; its chest barring continues up on to the face and it has no distinctive eyebrow), little bronze-cuckoo (confined to Queensland and northern coastal regions).

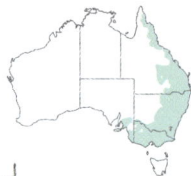

♂ JUVENILE HAS RED RUMP

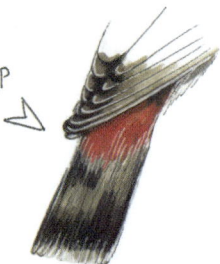

Note red 'cheek'

♀

♂

'creeps' up tree trunk grabbing grubs

VARIED SITTELLA (note upturned beak)

RED-BROWED TREECREEPER (red patch over face)

BROWN TREECREEPER (brown chin, white brow)

White-throated treecreeper

Niyin [nee-yin] (Gumbaynggirr)
Cormobates leucophaea

White-throated treecreepers are most often spotted while they climb vertically up tree trunks. They have large feet that help them to scale trees rapidly, working methodically upwards in a spiral as they climb. As they ascend the tree trunk, climbing like little Alex Honnolds going up El Capitan, they'll grab grubs and bugs from bark fissures. In local stringybark forest, I often see them methodically moving up one tree trunk, swooping to the next tree trunk, then to the next, relentless in their scan for food. These birds will often sing as they climb, which can help you 'triangulate' where to look (hopefully you'll soon see the movement of a little brown bird creeping up a tree nearby and be able to get a better look). I love watching these birds circumnavigate tree trunks, singing as they go. Some birdwatchers will call treecreepers 'woodpeckers' colloquially, though they do not drill into trees like their North American counterparts.

WHAT TO LISTEN FOR	A long series of repeated, abrupt whistles, *dee-dee-dee-dee-dee-deep-deep*. This rapid call carries through open bush, sometimes slowing in pace. The tone is similar to the call of the eastern spinebill (*see* page 37), though more 'determined' (slower and less panicked).
WHAT TO LOOK FOR	White-throated treecreepers are small grey-brown birds with a white throat patch. The wings and back are grey-brown. The black beak is sharp and slightly curved, which helps these birds to pick grubs out of the crevices in tree bark. The chin and upper chest are white, fading into a cream underbelly that is stippled with brown. The <u>females</u> have a small rust-red patch on their cheek.
IMMATURE BIRDS	Like the adults, the young male and female white-throated treecreepers also differ in appearance. The young <u>male</u> white-throated treecreeper looks similar to the adult male. The <u>female</u>, however, has both the red cheek patch and a red rump, which may be hidden under the folded wings.
WHERE TO START LOOKING	White-throated treecreepers tend to stick to bushland areas with a decent 'selection' of larger trees, so try heading to parks that have woodland areas, or to bush reserves along rivers and lakes (places where there are often remnant older trees, which these birds rely on for food). If you're able to, going to the nearest bushland reserve or state or national park will be a good place to start, as white-throated treecreepers occupy a large range of forest types (dry, open bushland through to dense, wetter rainforests). These birds particularly love to feed in bushland with rough-barked gum trees – basically eucalyptus trees that have thick bark with deep fissures, like stringy-bark, ironwood or some box-barked trees. White-throated treecreepers rarely venture into suburbs, unless they have large established stands of native trees in which to feed.
WHAT THEY EAT	Insects, grubs and larvae.
SIMILAR BIRDS	Red-browed treecreeper (pictured opposite; similar range), white-browed treecreeper (inland southern Australia; has a white brow above the eye), rufous treecreeper (found in south-west Western Australia; has rusty red colouring), brown treecreeper (pictured opposite; found across eastern states), varied sittella (pictured opposite; distributed across the mainland).

Bibliography, further reading & resources for birdwatchers

Field guides

Books

George Adams, *Complete Guide to Australian Birds*, Penguin Books, Australia, 2018.

Robin Hill, *Australian Birds*, Nelson, Australia, 1967.

Peter Menkhorst, Danny Rogers, Rohan Clarke, Jeff Davies, Peter Marsack & Kim Franklin, *The Australian Bird Guide (Revised Edition)*, CSIRO Publishing, Australia, 2019.

Michael Morcombe, *Field Guide to Australian Birds*, 2nd edition, Steve Parish Publishing, Australia, 2003.

Graham Pizzey & Frank Knight, *The Field Guide to the Birds of Australia*, 8th edition, HarperCollins Publishers, Australia, 2007.

Ken Simpson, Nicholas Day & Peter Trusler, *Field Guide to the Birds of Australia*, 8th edition, Viking, Australia, 2010.

Pat Slater, Peter Slater & Raoul Slater, *The Slater Field Guide to Australian Birds*, 2nd edition, Rigby, Australia, 2009.

Location-specific guides

Tim Dolby & Rohan Clarke, *Finding Australian Birds: A Field Guide to Birding Locations*, CSIRO Publishing, Australia, 2014.

Tim Dolby, Penny Johns & Sally Symonds, *Where to See Birds in Victoria*, Jacana, Australia, 2009.

Frank Knight, Graham Pizzey & Sarah Pizzey, *Regional Field Guide to Birds: South-east Coast and Ranges*, HarperCollins, Australia, 2013. Others in this series include: *Central East Coast and Ranges, Mallee to Limestone Coast* and *Red Centre to the Top End*.

Richard Thomas, Sarah Thomas, David Andrew & Alan McBride, *The Complete Guide to Finding the Birds of Australia*, 2nd edition, CSIRO Publishing, Australia, 2011.

Apps

Guy Gibbon, Graham Pizzey & Frank Knight, *Pizzey and Knight Birds of Australia: Digital Edition*, version 1.5, Gibbon Multimedia (Aus) and HarperCollins Publishers, Sydney, 2013.

Michael Morcombe, *Morcombe's Birds of Australia* (version 1.5.1), Steve Parish Publishing and MyDigitalEarth, Australia, 2016.

Resources

Websites and other online resources

Ausbird: ausbird.com

Australian Bird Identification (ABID) group on Facebook: facebook.com/groups/209677085864957

Backyard Buddies (FNPW): backyardbuddies.org.au

Birdata (associated with Birdlife Australia): birdata.birdlife.org.au

Birdlife Australia: birdlife.org.au

BirdsinBackyards (Birdlife): birdsinbackyards.net

eBird Australia: https://ebird.org/australia/homeebird.org/australia/home

Eremaea Birdlines – Interesting and Unusual Bird Observations: eremaea.com

IOC World Bird List, F Gill, D Donsker & P Rasmussen (eds), IOC World Bird List, version 10.1, 2020, doi: 10.14344/IOC.ML.10.1.

Parks Australia: parksaustralia.gov.au

Xeno-Canto: Sharing Bird Sounds from Around the World: xeno-canto.org

Apps

eBird by Cornell Lab

Merlin Bird ID by Cornell Lab

OzAtlas by Atlas of Living Australia

Other relevant reading & listening

Tim Low, *Where Song Began*, Penguin, Australia, 2014.

Sean Dooley, *The Big Twitch*, Allen & Unwin, Australia, 2005.

Don Watson, *The Bush: Travels in the Heart of Australia*, Penguin, Australia, 2014.

AIATSIS map of Indigenous Australia: aiatsis.gov.au/explore/articles/aiatsis-map-indigenous-australia (David R Horton, Aboriginal Studies Press, AIATSIS, and Auslig/Sinclair, Knight, Merz, 1996.)

Off Track with Ann Jones [ABC Radio National]

Appendix

BIRD FEET

OYSTERCATCHERS

PIGEONS & DOVES

EMU

PARROTS & CUCKOOS (TWO TOES FORWARD, TWO TOES BACK)

DUCKS (WEBBED)

TWO PARTIALLY WEBBED TOES

KING-FISHERS

MAGPIE GOOSE (SEMI-WEBBED)

SONGBIRDS (PERCHING BIRDS)

PELICANS (FULLY WEBBED)

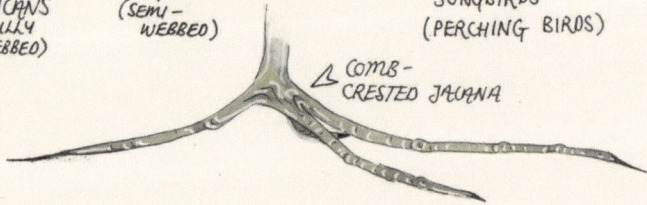
COMB-CRESTED JACANA

SOME INTRODUCED BIRDS:

COMMON (EURASIAN) BLACKBIRD

SPOTTED DOVE

HOUSE SPARROW

ROCK DOVE (FERAL PIGEON)

COMMON STARLING

COMMON MYNA

TAILS OF BIRDS OF PREY
(SEEN FROM BELOW)

WHITE - BELLIED
SEA - EAGLE

WHISTLING
KITE

SPOTTED & SWAMP
HARRIERS

FALCONS
(SLIGHTLY TAPERED)

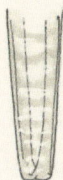

SPARROWHAWKS
& GOSHAWKS
(LONG & NARROW)

BLACK
KITE

EASTERN
OSPREY

LITTLE
EAGLE

BLACK-SHOULDERED
KITE
(FANS TAIL
IN FLIGHT)

WEDGE-TAILED
EAGLE

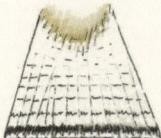

SQUARE-TAILED
KITE

NANKEEN KESTREL
(FANS TAIL
IN FLIGHT)

Index

About the author

Georgia Angus is an author, artist and bird nerd who lives on the lands of the Kulin nation in southeastern Australia. She splits her time between studying environmental science, writing and bushwalking.

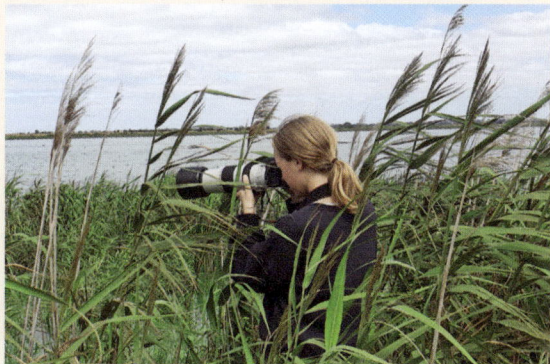

Acknowledgements

Foremost, my gratitude goes to the birdwatching community Australia-wide, whose collective efforts have built a rich body of knowledge and a culture of sharing information and experiences. Thank you for helping interested people of all levels of familiarity to get into the field and appreciate birds in context. Thank you to the team at eBird Australia, particularly Richard Fuller for his enthusiasm for this project and his generosity in providing the data that allowed us to create the maps in this volume. Thanks as well to Tim Flannery for his thoughtful foreword.

To Dallas Walker, Brother Steve Morelli and the language workers at Muurrbay Aboriginal Language and Culture Co-operative, thank you for tolerating my endless communications, for being the first to get involved in the project and giving me the encouragement I needed to pursue further translations, and for your generosity in sharing Gumbaynggirr culture with readers. To Sharon Briggs and the language workers at Taungurung Land and Waters, thank you for your translations and willingness to share some of your culture with readers. Thanks also to Wiradjuri Codoblin Corporation Language Program, and particularly Dr Stan Grant and Dr John Rudder for helping Wiradjuri language to be further shared. To Wayne Thorpe at Gunaikurnai Land and Waters Aboriginal Corporation, thank you for your time and for teaching me some social truths about the superb lyrebird.

To Alex Maisey, thank you for sharing your knowledge of the Dandenong Ranges, the life of superb lyrebirds and your broader wisdom about local ecology. Chris McRae and Susan Patterson, thank you for sending me maps and encouragement a long time ago when I was abroad and first learning to look up when I was bushwalking. Allison Shultz of the Natural History Museum of Los Angeles, thank you for allowing me to be so nerdy about bird feathers and for being generous with your time

and support. Thanks to Harry Saddler for answering my many questions and for sharing moments of grounding natural description during the pandemic. Simon Verdon, thank you for sharing some lesser known aspects of the malleefowl with me, and for sharing many experiences and your insightful knowledge of the environment. Jacob Dietrich, thank you for your lessons and for your information, especially about butcherbirds. Jason Caruso, thank you for your endless encouragement in all pursuits relating to birds and for your wise pointers with regards to making identifications. Also an enormous thank you for the crispy photographs you supplied to assist me in creating illustrations for this book (see natureimprintedphotography.com for more of Jason's beautiful work).

Thank you to the team at Hardie Grant, including Emily Maffei for her maps, Ngaio Parr for her book design and Cherry Cai for her social media wisdom. Enormous thanks to Melissa Kayser and Megan Cuthbert, who displayed saintly patience in the face of my endless emails and saw me through the tricky process of pulling together all the different threads of the book. Another huge thank you to Marg Bowman for her edits, for sharing her own experiences in observing nature, and helping me to provide a clearer vision of Australian birdlife than I could have produced on my own. An enormous thank you to Rosanna Dutson for the opportunity, her edits (and her friendship and humour).

Thanks to Sean, Vera and Yss, for kind words and support when I needed it. To my parents, thanks for your endless optimism, your grounding perspective and encouragement (Dad, thanks for chopping a piece of wood for me). To my sister, Kate, thank you for coming on the strange journey with me – poking moss, crossing creeks and agreeing to take a different road. Thanks finally to Orien Humennyj-Jameson, for his photographs, for his unfailing support, his grounding positivity and his shared enthusiasm for the world outside.